Fundamental Freedoms
and Jehovah's Witnesses

Fundamental Freedoms and Jehovah's Witnesses

by

Gary Botting

University of Calgary Press

University of Calgary Press
2500 University Drive N.W.
Calgary, Alberta, Canada T2N 1N4

Canadian Cataloguing in Publication Data

Botting, Gary, 1943–
    Fundamental freedoms and Jehovah's Witnesses

    Includes bibliographical references and index.
    ISBN 1-895176-06-9

    1. Civil rights—Canada. 2. Freedom of speech—Canada.
3. Jehovah's Witnesses—Civil rights—Canada. I. Title.

JC599.C2B68 1993   323'.0971   C93-091085-0

Cover design by Jon Paine
Printed in Canada by Kromar Printing Limited

⊚ This book is printed on acid-free paper.

Contents

Acknowledgments

This book has been published with the help of a grant from the Social Science Federation of Canada, using funds provided by the Social Sciences and Humanities Research Council of Canada.

We acknowledge the following publishers and authors for granting us permission to quote from their publications: Sandra Djwa; the University of Toronto Press for quotations from F.R. Scott, William Kaplan, and James Penton; *Saturday Night* for quotation from the poem "Destruction of Roncarelli"; McGill-Queen's University Press for quotations from Walter Tarnopolsky; Carswell, A Division of Thomson Canada, for quotations from Walter Tarnopolsky, Gerald-A. Beaudoin, and Peter Hogg; and Thomas R. Berger for quotations from the late Thomas Berger. Quotations from D.A. Schmeiser are reproduced by permission of Oxford University Press.

For Doris Windrim,
who made the improbable possible
and the impossible probable

Table of Cases

Preface

When my family immigrated to Canada from England in 1954, Jehovah's Witnesses in Canada were in the midst of a series of important court battles that were to change the legal landscape of Canada forever. At that time my world was small and as an active Jehovah's Witness my world view even smaller. There were not many Witnesses in Canada in the 1950s, and I came to meet most of the principals involved in the Supreme Court of Canada cases which now are touted as being of central importance to the establishment and preservation of civil liberties in Canada. I met and heard first hand the experiences of Frank Roncarelli, Laurier Saumur, Leo Greenlees, Louise Lamb, and Aime Boucher. Saumur and Greenlees stayed with us frequently during their visits as "district overseers" for Jehovah's Witnesses. W. Glen How, still the official legal counsel of Jehovah's Witnesses in Canada, and his wife Margaret became close family friends.

Although most officially condoned persecution of Jehovah's Witnesses was a thing of the past by the 1950s, it persisted unofficially in the streets. Rarely did a day pass when I was not tormented by classmates for being a devout Jehovah's Witness. Teachers and students alike were unsympathetic with my bid to avoid cadet training and my steadfast refusal to sing or even stand for *God Save the Queen*. The recital of the Lord's Prayer with persons of other faiths was frowned upon by my religion, for although rival faiths called themselves Christian, we were taught that they were really members of "Christendom"—part of "Babylon the Great," the symbolic scarlet harlot governed by Satan the Devil. Whenever a new blood transfusion case surfaced I could be sure to suffer a beating at the hands of my schoolmates, who did not respect the right to be different in matters as serious as religious belief. Intolerance was the order of the day.

Yet never far beneath the surface of my awareness of the world was the knowledge that Jehovah's Witnesses had had a hand in shaping the officially recognized civil liberties that gave me the right to express anomalous thoughts, the right to be different.

Perhaps more than anyone else, Glen How was a great inspiration to my family during our first decade in Canada. He kept us informed of each victory in the Supreme Court of Canada, often coming to the Kingdom Hall in Peterborough, Ontario to visit and to give special addresses with respect to developments in Ottawa. In 1959, shortly after the *Lamb* and *Roncarelli* cases had been settled finally in favour of Jehovah's Witnesses, I worked with Glen as a volunteer at a major Jehovah's Witness convention in Ottawa; we wrote and distributed news releases, and during that time I came to meet most of the main officers of the Watch Tower Bible and Tract Society, the legal corporation representing Jehovah's Witnesses. Glen and I hit it off so well, in fact, that in 1961 Glen invited me to travel to London, England for another convention, where again we formed a team in the public relations department. Subsequently I travelled first to Spain and then to Hong Kong as a pioneer missionary for Jehovah's Witnesses, doing a two-year stint overseas.

Upon my return to Canada in 1964, Glen wrote letters of reference on my behalf to Osgoode and University of Toronto Law Schools, and introduced me to the two deans and to law professors of his acquaintance. He suggested that, although university was generally inappropriate for Jehovah's Witnesses, nonetheless the organization needed lawyers. Should I finish law school, he said, there would be a place for me at his side. However, by the time of my graduation from Trent University, I had become so enamoured of English literature, particularly such Renaissance writers as Christopher Marlowe, that I decided to pursue graduate studies in literature rather than a law degree.

The Jehovah's Witnesses generally impugn university education as a threat to faith, and in this they are quite correct. I can vouch for the fact that there is no greater challenge to blind faith than a liberal education.

It was understandable that the governing body of Jehovah's Witnesses should frown when the dispensation I had received to go to university in order to effect a pragmatic training in the law was put to more personal and "esoteric" ends. After completing a masters degree in English language and literature at Memorial University of Newfoundland, I enrolled in the Ph.D. program in English at the University of Alberta; by 1972 I was teaching university level English, drama and creative writing in Alberta.

In 1982, my wife Heather completed her Ph.D. on the cultural anthropology of Jehovah's Witnesses. Her analysis of our former religion led both of us to do some soul-searching and together we researched and wrote *The Orwellian World of Jehovah's Witnesses*, published by University of Toronto Press in 1984. By then, Canadian civil liberties once again faced a crisis, not only by the passage of the *Canadian Charter of Rights and Freedoms* as part of the *Constitution Act, 1982,* but with the pressing of criminal charges against James Keegstra, an Alberta school teacher who used his Eckville classroom to teach vitriolic propaganda against the Jews, and Ernst Zundel, an Ontario graphic designer who published a Canadian edition of a revisionist tract questioning the traditional six million casualties of the Holocaust. Of course, I found their ideas untenable and distasteful. Yet, in my view, an important principle was being violated by their prosecution: the principle of freedom of expression, including academic freedom and freedom of the press. I therefore expressed support, not for their ideas, but for their right to express these ideas without fear of criminal prosecution.

In many respects, the Holocaust denial cases of the 1980s seemed a replay of the Jehovah's Witnesses cases of the 1950s—except that now the charges were "promoting hatred" or "spreading false news" rather than straight "sedition," and the target of the quasireligious vitriol was Jews rather than Roman Catholics. As Alan Borovoy has pointed out, many of the old issues raised by the Jehovah's Witness cases were once more resurrected in the *Keegstra* and *Zundel* cases. Distasteful as "Holocaust denial" may be, the issue involved the right of the individual to state his beliefs with respect to a rival religious and ethnic group.

Perhaps because of my Jehovah's Witness roots, I was dumbfounded that the average Canadian did not seem to realize that the principle of freedom of expression outweighed in importance the understandable rancor of a highly vocal Jewish minority. After all, without freedom of expression, the Jewish minority would not so much as have an opportunity to be vocal, as the earlier experience of Jehovah's Witnesses had borne out. In pressing criminal charges against Keegstra and Zundel, the Attorneys-General of Alberta and Ontario unleashed a whole new era of uncertainty as to the threshold of freedom of expression in Canada. Yet, as with Jehovah's Witnesses decades ago, few lawyers appeared prepared to represent these men. The reputation of any who did so would be tainted.

Douglas Christie was one of the brace of lawyers who steadfastly pursued the legal question before the courts, shuttling back and forth between British Columbia, Alberta, Ontario and New Brunswick to defend the right of his clients to express their genuinely-held beliefs. The broad geographical scope of his well-reported activities bears mute testimony to the fact that no other barristers in the land seemed prepared to represent the new pariahs of western democracy. It was largely for this reason that I decided in 1986 to return to law school—exactly 20 years after submitting my first applications in Ontario. Upon graduating from the University of Calgary Faculty of Law, I applied to article for Doug Christie at a time when the *Keegstra, Zundel, Finta, John Ross Taylor,* and

Malcolm Ross cases—all of them important constitutional cases, in my view—wended their way towards the Supreme Court of Canada, some for the second time, for final resolution.

Perhaps because of my association with Christie, I too was lambasted by a hostile press, despite the fact that from the beginning I was unambiguous of my disavowal of the validity of the ideas held by some of his clients. However, for me the principle of freedom of expression was at stake, a principle fought for long and haid by fellow Jehovah's Witnesses during my youth. Accordingly, after I was called to the bar in 1991, I adopted Voltaire's flamboyant statement as my credo: "I may not agree with what you say, but I'll fight to the death for your right to say it!"

For me the most inspiring law professor at the University of Calgary was Alastair Lucas, an expert on the Constitution who volunteered to supervise my independent research into the role of Jehovah's Witnesses in the formation of the *Canadian Bill of Rights* and the *Charter*. At last I was able to come to grips with the true legal significance of the cases I had heard so much about in my youth. That research formed the basis for this book on the relationship between my former faith and civil liberties.

Civil liberties or fundamental freedoms form the fragile warp of democracy—a warp which supports and sustains the colourful weft of Canadian multicultural society, including the principles of legal and equal rights. Both warp and weft are needed to sustain the complex fabric of a multicultural society, I realized, but most authorities concede that civil liberties are more "fundamental" than other rights. Indeed, even the *Canadian Charter of Rights and Freedoms* makes the distinction between "fundamental freedoms" and legal and egalitarian rights. Walter Tarnopolsky, addressing the Special Joint Committee on the Constitution in 1971, expressed the view that the two kinds of rights should be kept separate, and that "fundamental freedoms" were of a higher order than egalitarian rights. Civil liberties form a "condition precedent" to the existence of egalitarian rights that most Canadians hold dear. Unfortunately in later years Tarnopolsky moved away from this early unambiguous position.

In my view, it is myopic for governments and the courts to hack away at the warp of fundamental freedoms simply because a tiny minority in Canada has the temerity to spout distasteful slogans or pose questions that the majority believes to be nonsense anyway. In the broader context of the development of civil liberties, it is retrogressive in the extreme, taking us back to the era when Jehovah's Witnesses were persecuted for their vitriolic verbal attacks on Roman Catholics. How does a tract such as *The Watchtower* differ from a tract of similar length called, provocatively, *Did Six Million Really Die?* This newfound propensity to prosecute—and indeed to persecute—individuals for expressing their anomalous beliefs compels us to look once again at the parallel situation of Jehovah's Witnesses in the past.

I wish to thank the lawyers who have been a particular inspiration to me in the area of civil liberties, despite their both being indisputable "black sheep" of the legal profession in their time: W. Glen How and Douglas H. Christie. How, as I have said, was the first person to interest me in the law. Christie, an equally persuasive orator, helped revive that early interest. Both men were counsel, thirty years apart, in what I firmly believe to be among the central civil liberties cases of this century.

Gary Botting
Barrister & Solicitor
Victoria, 1 January 1993

1

The Sect that Roared

1. POWER AND PACIFISM

Jehovah's Witnesses have had a major impact on the development of fundamental freedoms throughout the world. In many ways the sect can be characterized as the mouse that roared; certainly its effect on governments has been disproportionate to its size. The fanaticism of sect members and their willingness to march in lock-step to the orders of the governing body of Jehovah's Witnesses in New York without ever questioning the motives or integrity of the leadership has led to direct conflict with the secular governments of many nations. The will of the governing body, as published through *The Watchtower* and other publications of the Watch Tower Bible and Tract Society of Pennsylvania, Inc. (the corporate voice of Jehovah's Witnesses), is regarded as synonymous with the will of "Jehovah God." Accordingly, Jehovah's Witnesses have never been a people who backed down from an ideological position without a legal battle. Confident in the knowledge that they occupy the moral high ground, they remain tenacious in their zeal, which is in part the product of righteous indignation that "Jehovah's will" should ever be impugned by secular authorities.

"Caesar's things to Caesar and God's things to God" has become something of a battle-cry for Jehovah's Witnesses: as long as the power of secular authorities is exercised within the proper sphere of constitutional government, Jehovah's Witnesses have no complaint. But those authorities who trench upon the domain of God-given civil liberties or who pointedly violate the specific fundamental freedom to worship do so at their own peril. Fortunately, most of the moral imperatives of Jehovah's Witnesses are ones which the Judeo-Christian value system purports to uphold, and so a philosophy of live and let live has been adopted by most contemporary democracies. It is fair to say that these days, Jehovah's Witnesses are persecuted only where dictatorships prevail and freedom is curtailed.

Yet the very threat of opposition or persecution has always been a boundary mechanism for the growing sect that has given it definition in times of tribulation. Jehovah's Witnesses delight in exchanging tales of how they coped with opposition from within their own secular families, from persons of rival faiths, or from bureaucrats bent on thwarting the publication of their sometimes vitriolic messages. Although today Jehovah's Witnesses are usually accepted at the door and on the street corner with a sigh of resignation, acts of violence directed against them were at one time commonplace, particularly in times of war when pacifist Witnesses preach loudly that the war effort is inherently evil.

Those whose loved ones are off at the battlefield and, more specifically, the politicians and bureaucrats who sent them there may understandably be outraged by pacifist remarks that they all too eagerly characterize as "sedition." Similarly, committed Roman Catholics can be expected to react with a measure of impatience when their religious values are attacked frontally by an upstart sect that claims to have all the answers. Such confrontationism has led Jehovah's Witnesses to stand at the forefront of controversy throughout much of the twentieth century. Especially in the first half of the century, the sect leadership went out of its way to provoke the establishment, yet was the first to cry "foul" when governments attempted to muzzle and control the Witnesses.

Under the sect's first president, Charles Taze Russell, most of the focus had been on the development of doctrine and the interpretation of Bible prophecy. Born to a strict Presbyterian family in 1852, Russell dabbled in Adventism before striking out on his own with the publication of *Zion's Watch Tower* (later *The Watchtower*) in 1879. Subsequently he wrote a series of books called *Studies in the Scriptures* which became the mainstay of Witness doctrine for years to come. Russell's followers were known as "Bible Students" or, disparagingly, "Russellites." His infrequent forays into Canada were usually met with hostility, partly because he was a declared pacifist.

Russell had believed that Christ must return by 1914, and it was he who declared in that year that Jesus Christ, who was synonymous with Michael the Archangel, had returned invisibly: the First World War could be viewed as the beginning of the Time of the End which would culminate in Armageddon. Jehovah's Witnesses have not deviated materially from this doctrinal stance ever since.[1]

---

1 See "The Historical Development of Jehovah's Witnesses," in Heather and Gary Botting, *The Orwellian World of Jehovah's Witnesses* (Toronto: University of Toronto Press, 1984) at 34–39; M. James Penton, *Apocalypse Delayed: The Story of Jehovah's Witnesses* (Toronto: University of Toronto Press, 1985) at 13–46; *Jehovah's Witnesses in the Divine Purpose* (New York: Watch Tower Bible and Tract Society, 1959) at 16–27.

Russell died in October 1916 while on a preaching tour of the United States. In his will, published in *The Watchtower* shortly after his death, he appointed a committee of five men to run the Watch Tower Society, with five alternate members, one of whom was Joseph Franklin Rutherford. Interestingly, the vitriolic stance subsequently adopted by the sect can be traced to his influence.

Initially a "second string" administrator of the leaderless Society, Rutherford proved to be a ruthless opportunist, using his training as a lawyer and prestige as occasional substitute judge to manipulate corporate power.[2] In January 1917, he took over the presidency of the Watch Tower Society by fiat, then purged the Board of Directors, replacing them with his own hand-picked officers.[3] He then consolidated his position by commissioning and then publishing the final volume of *Studies in the Scriptures*, called *The Finished Mystery*, which attacked the clergy for supporting the war effort.

Militarism was also the target of *The Bible Students Monthly*, which like *The Finished Mystery* invited the wrath of governments and clergy throughout the English-speaking world. The Canadian government took the lead in banning these and other Watch Tower publications early in 1918, at the behest of Canada's chief press censor, Colonel Ernest Chambers, who claimed that the publications had a direct negative effect upon recruiting.[4] Arrests of Watch Tower Society supporters followed, first in Canada and then across North America, culminating in the arrest of Rutherford himself.

2. ARREST OF THE LEADERSHIP

The U.S. Attorney-General had attempted to draft legislation intended specifically to enable the prosecution of the Society, as is clear from the U.S. *Congressional Record*.[5] However, such extraordinary measures proved unnecessary, for on 15 June 1917 the U.S. government had enacted the *Espionage Act*, America's answer to the *War Measures Act*, which gave broad powers to the government during wartime. Rutherford, along with seven other directors of the Watch Tower Society, were arrested under the *Espionage Act* on 21 June 1918, an event that is accorded mythic

---

2 Penton, *supra*, note 1 at 47–55.

3 *Ibid.* at 50–53; Barbara Grizzuti Harrison, *Visions of Glory: A History and a Memory of Jehovah's Witnesses* (New York: Simon and Schuster, 1978) at 118–20.

4 *Canada Gazette*, February , 1918, 9–16. For an insightful discussion of Chambers' role in the banning, see M. James Penton, *Jehovah's Witnesses in Canada* (Toronto: Macmillan of Canada, 1976) at 50–54.

5 *Congressional Record* (Vol. 56, Part 6), Senate, 24 April 1918, p. 5542; 4 May 1918, pp. 6051, 6052.

dimensions by Jehovah's Witnesses to this day. The specific charges alleged that they

> unlawfully and feloniously did conspire, combine, confederate and agree together, and with divers other persons to the said Grand Jurors unknown, to commit a certain offense of unlawfully, feloniously and wilfully causing insubordination, disloyalty and refusal of duty in the military and naval forces of the United States of America when the United States was at war . . . by personal solicitations, letters, public speeches, distributing and publicly circulating throughout the United States of America a certain book called "Volume VII. Bible Studies. The Finished Mystery," and distributing and publicly circulating through the United States certain articles printed in pamphlets called "Bible Students Monthly," "Watch Tower," "Kingdom News" and other pamphlets not named.[6]

After a 15-day trial marked by serious procedural irregularities, Rutherford and six other Watch Tower Society directors received 10-year sentences; the eighth director received a 2-year sentence.

That due process was not followed became clear from the way various witnesses at the trial were treated. For example, William Hudgings, the Watch Tower secretary, was found by the trial judge, Judge H.B. Howe, to be in contempt simply because he testified that he could not remember seeing two of the defendants engaged in the act of writing. Incarcerated for an indefinite term, Hudgings spent six months in jail before being released through a writ of *habeas corpus* obtained from Chief Justice White of the U.S. Supreme Court.[7]

Rutherford and the other Watch Tower directors were held in custody for nine months until their appeal for bail was heard by Justice Louis Brandeis of the U.S. Supreme Court, who in March 1919 ordered them released on bail, which was set at $10,000.00 each. The following month, Justice Ward of the Federal Second Court of Appeal ruled, in something of an understatement:

> The defendants in this case did not have the temperate and impartial trial to which they were entitled, and for that reason the judgment is reversed.[8]

A year later, all charges were dropped.[9]

---

6 *Rutherford* v. *United States*, 258 F. 655 (14 May 1919), Transcript of Record, Vol. 1, p. 12.

7 *Jehovah's Witnesses in the Divine Purpose, supra*, note 1 at 81.

8 *Rutherford, supra*, note 6 at 863.

9 A.H. Macmillan, *Faith on the March* (Englewood Cliffs, N.J.: Prentice Hall, 1957) at 105–113.

The initial arrest of the Watch Tower officials seemed justification enough for the authorities throughout North America to increase the pressure on the membership. Several reports surfaced of Jehovah's Witnesses (or "Bible Students," as they were known then) being tarred and feathered and beaten and dunked in icy creeks in towns and cities from Oregon to Oklahoma and from Arkansas to Arizona. Often this type of activity was performed with the sanction of municipal authorities, who sometimes simply handed over the Bible Students to waiting mobs. The courts contributed their share to the suspension of civil liberties, however: possession of a copy of *The Finished Mystery* typically garnered a sentence of three years in prison.[10]

By the time Rutherford and the other directors had been released, World War I was over and the ban on Watch Tower literature, including *The Finished Mystery*, had been lifted. Rutherford directed the distribution of thousands of copies of the controversial book that had been hidden from the authorities for the duration of his incarceration. He also introduced a new magazine, *The Golden Age*, later to be known as *Awake!*.[11]

Conventions were held to rally the embattled Bible Students, the first held at Cedar Point, Ohio in 1919. The conventions were always theatrical events, and culminated in the release of publications that carried through with the convention theme. Over the following two decades, Rutherford published 20 books and 76 booklets on doctrinal topics as diverse as "Talking with the Dead" (1920) to "End of Nazism" (1940). The sect grew steadily through the early 1920s, but growth levelled out at about 90,000 from 1925 through 1927 and plummeted in 1928. Ironically, the onset of the Depression led many of the fiscally disillusioned into the fold, and growth resumed, if slowly, during the 1930s.

3. "JEHOVAH'S WITNESSES" AND THE FLAG

The Bible Students first adopted the name "Jehovah's Witnesses" by a resolution drafted by Rutherford and read to a convention at Columbus, Ohio on 26 July 1931.[12] The following year, Jehovah's Witnesses were banned in Italy, the first of what were to become the "Axis" powers to attempt to control the sect. Germany and Japan banned distribution of Watch Tower literature in 1933. The Witnesses responded with a global protest, including a campaign of letter and telegram writing from the membership. This action only intensified the persecution, however. As

---

10 "The Case of the International Bible Students Association," cited at length in *Jehovah's Witnesses in the Divine Purpose, supra*, note 1 at 81–82.

11 *Jehovah's Witnesses in the Divine Purpose, ibid.* at 88–90.

12 Penton, *Apocalypse Delayed, supra*, note 1 at 62.

Karl R.A. Wittig, a plenipotentiary of General Ludendorff, deposed in an affidavit sworn 13 November 1945:

> On October 7, 1934, having been previously summoned, I visited Dr. Wilhelm Frick, at that time Minister of the Interior of the Reich and Prussia, in his home office of the Reich. . . . During my discussion with Dr. Frick, Hitler suddenly appeared and began taking part in the conversation. . . . Dr. Frick showed Hitler a number of telegrams protesting against the Third Reich's persecution of the Bible Students, saying: "If the Bible Students do not immediately get in line we will act against them using the strongest means." After which Hitler jumped to his feet and with clenched fists hysterically screamed: "This brood will be exterminated in Germany!" Four years after this discussion I was able, by my own observations, to convince myself, during my seven years in protective custody in the hell of the Nazi concentration-camps at Sachsenhausen, Flossenburg and Mauthausen—I was in prison until released by the Allies—that Hitler's outburst of anger was not just an idle threat. No other group of prisoners of the named concentration-camps was exposed to the sadism of the SS-soldiery in such a fashion as the Bible Students were. It was a sadism marked by an unending chain of physical and mental tortures, the likes of which no language in the world can express.[13]

Part of the reason for Hitler's ire was the fact that Jehovah's Witnesses steadfastly refused to salute the German flag or the swastika on the grounds that allegiance was owed only to God.

Jehovah's Witnesses saw the insistence of the Nazis that all German citizens pay homage to the symbols of state, including the swastika and the graven image of an eagle, as unambiguously trenching upon the Second Commandment at Exodus 20:4–5:

> Thou shalt not make unto thee any graven image, or any likeness of anything that is in heaven above, or that is in the earth beneath, or that is in the water under the earth: Thou shalt not bow down thyself to them, nor serve them: for I the Lord thy God am a jealous God, visiting the iniquity of the fathers upon the children unto the third and fourth generation of them that hate me.

After coming to power in 1933, the Nazis responded to Jehovah's Witnesses' reluctance to commit idolatry by locking them away in concentration camps.[14]

---

13 *Jehovah's Witnesses in the Divine Purpose, supra,* note 1 at 142.

14 J.S. Conway, *The Nazi Persecution of the Churches 1933–1945* (New York: Basic Books Inc., 1968) at 195–97.

The plight of their German brothers led Jehovah's Witnesses elsewhere to adopt the same position at a time when nationalism was on the rise, and when schools across the United States were instituting the flag-salute ceremony as an object-lesson in loyalty to one's country.[15] On 3 June 1935, Rutherford announced at a convention at Washington, D.C. that Jehovah's Witnesses should refuse to salute the flag.

Witnesses across America instituted the policy faithfully, educating their children to the fact that they must not salute the flag at school. On 20 September 1935, Carleton Nicholls, a Grade 3 student in Lynn, Massachusetts, refused to salute the flag, resulting in litigation against his father.[16]

In response to the Massachusetts litigation, on 6 October 1935 Rutherford broadcast the new policy publicly from coast to coast and released a new booklet outlining the objections of Jehovah's Witnesses to saluting the flag. The 32-page booklet, *Loyalty*, was distributed in the millions. Witness children across North America were encouraged to follow Rutherford's edict. On 6 November 1935 in Minersville, Pennsylvania, the Gobitis children were expelled from grammar school for refusing to salute the flag, and their father was acquitted by the Federal District Court.[17] Minersville School District appealed to the Circuit Court of Appeals, only to lose there as well.[18] The School District's second appeal to the U.S. Supreme Court, however, came at a time when war hysteria was mounting. In an 8–1 decision written by Justice Felix Frankfurter, the Supreme Court reversed the Court of Appeals decision, stating that flag-saluting fostered national unity and therefore national security, "an interest inferior to none in the hierarchy of legal values."[19]

Many saw the Supreme Court decision in *Gobitis* v. *Minersville School District* as an invitation to renew hostilities against Jehovah's Witnesses. Since Rutherford's announcement in 1933 there had been a movement afoot at the municipal level to restrict the activities of Jehovah's Witnesses by the passage of by-laws governing soliciting, peddling without a license, trespassing, breach of the peace, sedition, group libel, and other regulations that Jehovah's Witnesses steadfastly appealed through the courts. In 1933 there were 269 arrests throughout the United States. In 1936, 1,149 Witnesses were arrested for allegedly breaching municipal

---

15 David R. Manwaring, *Render Unto Caesar* (Chicago: University of Chicago Press, 1962) at 1–33.

16 *The Golden Age*, Vol. XVI, 17 July 1935, pp. 653–54; *1936 Yearbook of Jehovah's Witnesses* (New York: Watch Tower Bible and Tract Society, 1936) at 22–38.

17 *Gobitis* v. *Minersville School District*, 24 F. Supp. 271 (18 June 1938).

18 108 F. 2d 683 (10 November 1939).

19 310 U.S. 586, 60 S. Ct. 1010, 87 L. Ed. 1375 (1940).

ordinances of various kinds.[20] All of these cases were contested, and many appealed, several all the way to the U.S. Supreme Court. In *Lovell* v. *City of Griffin*,[21] the ordinance in question forbade the distribution of literature "without first obtaining written permission from the city Manager of the city of Griffin." Lovell and other Jehovah's Witnesses went about their distribution work, but refused to apply for a permit. The U.S. Supreme Court held, "We think that the ordinance is invalid on its face. Whatever the motive which induced its adoption, its character is such that it strikes at the very foundation of the freedom of the press by subjecting it to license and censorship."[22] The following year, the U.S. Supreme Court took a similar view in *Schneider* v. *New Jersey*:[23]

> This court has characterized the freedom of speech and that of the press as fundamental personal rights and liberties. The phrase is not an empty one and was not lightly used. It reflects the belief of the framers of the Constitution that exercise of its rights lies at the foundation of free government by free men. It stresses, as do may opinions of this court, the importance of preventing the restriction of enjoyment of these liberties.[24]

Adopting its earlier observations from *Lovell*, the court concluded, "To require a censorship through license which makes impossible the free and unhampered distribution of pamphlets strikes at the very heart of the constitutional guarantees."[25]

A similar position was taken by the U.S. Supreme Court in 1940 in *Cantwell* v. *Connecticut*,[26] where a state law attempted to prohibit soliciting funds for a religious purpose. Here, for the first time, the Supreme Court held that the statute in question violated the Fourteenth Amendment, since the legislatures of the states cannot enact a law which deprives members of a religious group from the free exercise of their religion. To enact such a restriction "is to lay a forbidden burden upon the exercise of liberty protected by the constitution."[27]

---

20 *Jehovah's Witnesses in the Divine Purpose, supra,* note 1 at 175.

21 303 U.S. 444, 58 S. Ct. 666, 82 L. Ed. 949 (1938) [hereinafter *Lovell* cited to U.S.].

22 *Lovell, ibid.* at 451–52.

23 308 U.S. 147, 60 S. Ct. 146, 84 L. Ed. 155 (1939) [hereinafter *Schneider* cited to U.S.].

24 *Schneider, ibid.* at 161.

25 *Schneider, ibid.* at 164.

26 310 U.S. 296, 60 S. Ct. 900, 84 L. Ed. 1213 (1940) [hereinafter *Cantwell* cited to U.S.].

27 *Cantwell, ibid.* at 306–307.

The *Gobitis* decision, however, negated the effect of these small triumphs. Described as "a backwash in the stream of liberal decisions,"[28] it gave the discretionary right to school boards to expel children who refused to salute the flag.

The Gobitis decision itself was relatively innocuous; but throughout the United States mobs began to put a different construction on the decision. As the American Civil Liberties Union reported in January, 1941,

> Documents filed with the Department of Justice by attorneys for Jehovah's Witnesses and the American Civil Liberties Union showed over three hundred thirty-five instances of mob violence in forty-four states during 1940, involving one thousand four hundred eighty-eight men, women and children. . . .
>
> Jehovah's Witnesses were the object of immediate and widespread attack, chiefly because of their position on flag-saluting, well advertised by their widespread distribution of the May 29, 1940, issue of the magazine *Consolation* giving details of the hearing before the U.S. Supreme Court of the Gobitis flag salute case. Following the decision of June 3, 1940, in which school boards were upheld in their right to expel children of this sect who refused to salute the flag, this propaganda was taken as being seditious.[29]

Even the intervention of the U.S. Solicitor General, Francis Biddle, did not quell the mob action. On 16 June 1940 less than two weeks after the *Gobitis* decision, he broadcast an appeal on NBC coast to coast, stating in part:

> Jehovah's Witness have been repeatedly set upon and beaten. They had committed no crime; but the mob adjudged they had, and meted out mob punishment. The Attorney General has ordered an immediate investigation of these outrages.
>
> The people must be alert and watchful, and above all cool and sane. Since mob violence will make the government's task infinitely more difficult, it will not be tolerated. We shall not defeat the Nazi evil by emulating its methods.[30]

Yet official action against Jehovah's Witnesses by municipalities bent on controlling their activities continued to mount, with close to 10,000 arrests over the three-year period from 1940–1942. Only occasionally were Jeho-

---

28 (1944), 28 Minn. L. Rev. 209 at 227.

29 American Civil Liberties Union, *The Persecution of Jehovah's Witnesses*, brief published by ACLU in January 1941, p. 3.

30 *Jehovah's Witnesses in the Divine Purpose, supra*, note 1 at 181–82, citing the Appellees' Brief, *West Virginia State Board of Education* v. *Barnette*, p. 74.

vah's Witnesses able to prosecute their tormentors successfully through the courts.[31]

4. SUPREME COURT REVERSALS

On 8 June 1942, the U.S. Supreme Court handed down another decision that seemed on its face to go against Jehovah's Witnesses, yet which contained the seeds which were to lead to reform of the law in America. *Jones* v. *City of Opelika*[32] held in a 5–4 decision that Jehovah's Witnesses in Opelikea, Alabama, as well as two other cities in Arkansas and Arizona, were legitimately required to pay a licence tax to sell their religious books. This seemed on its face to be a reversal of the *Lovell, Schneider* and *Cantwell* cases that had ruled such licencing unconstitutional. Interestingly, all four of the dissenting judges had sat on the *Gobitis* case. One, Chief Justice Stone, had dissented in that opinion also. The other three, Justices Murphy, Black and Douglas, had gone along with Mr. Justice Frankfurter in the earlier decision, and now, in a rare confession of error, expressed their regret at having done so:

> The opinion of the Court sanctions a device which in our opinion suppresses or tends to suppress the free exercise of a religion practiced by a minority group. *Minersville School District* v. *Gobitis* . . . took against the same religious minority and is a logical extension of the principles upon which that decision rested. Since we joined in the opinion in the Gobitis case, we think this is an appropriate occasion to state that we now believe that it was also wrongly decided. Certainly our democratic form of government functioning under the historic Bill of Rights has a high responsibility to accommodate itself to the religious views of minorities however unpopular and unorthodox those views may be. The First Amendment does not put the right freely to exercise religion in a subordinate position. We fear, however, that the opinions in these and in the Gobitis case do exactly that.[33]

Within a year, more than a dozen U.S. Supreme Court decisions seemed to reaffirm the principle expressed in *Lovell, Schneider* and *Cantwell*, flying in the case of the *Jones* case. *Jamison* v. *Texas*[34] held that an ordinance forbidding distribution of handbills by Jehovah's Witnesses abridged the First Amendment right to freedom of the press. In *Largent*

---

31 See, for example, *Catlette* v. *United States*, 132 F. 2d 902 (1943).

32 316 U.S. 584, 62 S. Ct. 1231, 86 L. Ed. 1691 (1942).

33 316 U.S. 584 at 623–24; 62 S. Ct. 1231 at 1251–52 (1942).

34 318 U.S. 413, 63 S. Ct. 669, 87 L. Ed. 869 (1943).

v. *Texas*,[35] the Supreme Court set aside a conviction under an ordinance requiring Jehovah's Witnesses to obtain a permit before they canvassed a residential area, on the grounds that the ordinance was tantamount to press censorship. Similarly, in *Martin v. City of Struthers*[36] the Court held that a local ordinance prohibiting doorbell ringing by Jehovah's Witnesses engaged in distributing leaflets constituted an abridgement to freedom of the press. Although Jehovah's Witnesses appeared to lose ground in *Douglas v. City of Jeannette*,[37] which held that they did not have the right to enjoin enforcement of a licence tax law by reliance upon injunctions through the federal courts, that decision was at most a temporary setback, since the Court also held that the ordinace in question was unconstitutional in the first place and therefore Jehovah's Witnesses were adequately protected.

By far the most important decision in the series of judgments released by the U.S. Supreme Court on 3 May 1943, however, was *Murdock v. Commonwealth of Pennsylvania*,[38] in which *Jones v. Opelika* was specifically and irrevocably reversed by the Supreme Court:

> The judgment in *Jones* v. *Opelika* has this day been vacated. Freed from that controlling precedent, we can restore to their high, constitutional position the liberties of itinerant evangelists who disseminate their religious beliefs and the tenets of their faith through distribution of literature. . . .
>
> Plainly a community may not suppress, or the state tax, the dissemination of views because they are unpopular, annoying or distasteful. If that device were ever sanctioned, there would have been forged a ready instrument for the suppression of the faith which any minority cherishes but which does not happen to be in favor. That would be a complete repudiation of the philosophy of the Bill of Rights.[39]

Two more U.S. Supreme Court decisions were required before Jehovah's Witnesses were on an equal footing with other Americans, however. Jehovah's Witnesses had already been convicted in the lower courts for sedition, defined as advocating or inciting subversive action against the state. In *Taylor v. Mississippi*,[40] the Supreme Court ruled:

---

35 318 U.S. 105, 63 S. Ct. 677, 87 L. Ed. 873 (1943).

36 319 U.S. 141, 63 S. Ct. 862, 87 L. Ed. 1313 (1943).

37 319 U.S. 157, 63 S. Ct. 877, 87 L. Ed. 1324 (1943).

38 319 U.S. 105, 63 S. Ct. 870, 87 L. Ed. 1292 (1943) [hereinafter *Murdock* cited to U.S.].

39 *Murdock, ibid.* at 117, 116.

40 319 U.S. 583, 63 S. Ct. 1200, 87 L. Ed. 1600 (1943) [hereinafter *Taylor* cited to U.S.].

> The statute as construed in these cases makes it a criminal offense to communicate to others views and opinions rejecting governmental policies, and prophecies concerning the future of our own and other nations. As applied to the appellants it punishes them although what they communicated is not claimed or shown to have been done with any evil or sinister purpose, to have advocated or incited subversive action against the nation or state, or to have threatened any clear and present danger to our institutions or our government. What these appellants communicated were their beliefs and opinions concerning domestic measures and trends in national and world affairs.
>
> Under our decisions criminal sanction cannot be imposed for such communication.[41]

The central principle enunciated in the *Taylor* and *Barnette* cases would bear repetition in cases in other jurisdictions around the world, including Canada, the United Kingdom and Australia.

Jehovah's Witnesses were vocal in their opposition to Fascism and Nazism and therefore after the war began faced a total ban and indescribable persecution by the Axis powers. Curiously, however, their clear stand on this issue did not seem to have much impact in North America, where members of the sect were persecuted by the Allied authorities as well as by mobs intent on applying their own version of the law. Virtually every nation regarded the Watch Tower Society's opposition to militarism as a threat to the war effort, and accordingly Watch Tower literature and the publishing activity of Jehovah's Witnesses were widely banned.

5. GROWTH OF THE "THEOCRACY"

By the time Rutherford died at age 72 in 1942, he had set up what he called a "Theocracy" through which, he believed, Jehovah God had a voice on earth that could not fail to be heard.[42] That year, the distribution of books and booklets reached an incredible 39,030,595 copies, despite—and perhaps because of—massive persecution. The new president, Nathan H. Knorr, was able to parlay the backlash against the persecution of the Witnesses into fantastic growth during the 35 years of his tenure, so that they came to be numbered in the millions. Another factor in the sect's fantastic growth after the war was the unique ability of the organization to capitalize on the grief of those widowed and orphaned by the war effort and to offer them a new and strange kind of hope: the physical resurrection of their loved ones. In 1945, there were 140,000 Witnesses worldwide. Ten years later, there were 643,000 Witnesses, and

---

41 *Taylor, ibid.* at 589–90. See also *Barnette, supra,* note 30.

42 Penton, *Apocalypse Delayed, supra,* note 1 at 74–76.

by 1964, their numbers had topped a million.[43] By 1974, the number of Witnesses worldwide was in excess of two million, and by 1992 there were four million active Jehovah's Witnesses preaching around the world, with millions more sitting in the wings.

Especially in their formative years, Jehovah's Witnesses helped shape the constitutional law of the United States of America, as Mulder and Comisky remarked as early as 1942:

> Seldom, if ever, in the past has one individual or group been able to shape the course, over a period of time, of any phase of our vast body of constitutional law. But it *can* happen, and it *has* happened, here. The group is Jehovah's Witnesses. Through almost constant litigation this organization has made possible an ever increasing list of precedents concerning the application of the Fourteenth Amendment to freedom of speech and religion. . . . To this development Jehovah's Witnesses have contributed the most, both in quantity and significance.[44]

Judge Edward F. Waite remarked in an article in the *Minnesota Law Review* in 1944:

> Jehovah's Witnesses . . . have performed a signal service to democracy by their fight to preserve their civil rights, for in their struggle they have done much to secure those rights for every minority group in America. When the civil rights of one group are invaded, the rights of no other group are safe. They have therefore made a definite contribution to the preservation of some of the most precious things in our democracy.[45]

It is not generally recognized that exactly the same remark could be made with equal accuracy in respect to Jehovah's Witnesses in Canada, where for 40 years they suffered almost unrelenting persecution. Sad to say, Canadian legislators and the Canadian judiciary were slow to apply the principles of freedom of speech and religion established in the American cases. In fact they seemed to think it necessary to reinvent the wheel.

Subsequent chapters of this book will trace the tortuous path pursued by Jehovah's Witnesses in Canada in attempting to establish what they considered to be their God-given right to freedom of expression, freedom of the press, freedom of religion—in short, all the fundamental freedoms that are now enshrined in the *Canadian Charter of Rights and Freedoms*. The book constitutes a legal history of this specific denomination, especially

---

43 Botting and Botting, *The Orwellian World, ibid.,* note 1 at 47.

44 John E. Mulder and Marvin Comisky, "Jehovah's Witnesses and Constitutional Law," (1942), 2 Bill of Rights Rev. 262.

45 (1944), 28 Minn. L. Rev. 209 at 226.

focusing upon the influence Jehovah's Witnesses have had upon the courts, upon Parliament, and most importantly upon public opinion. Clearly some of the activities and experiences of Jehovah's Witnesses mirror what happened south of the border during the critical years of the sect's development; but more often than not the cases to be examined have a distinctly Canadian flavour—especially those emanating from Quebec. Suffice to say that the fundamental freedoms now so taken for granted by most Canadians were not so easily won.

2

The Rules of War in English Canada

I. THE "RUSSELLITES" AND MILITARY EXEMPTION

The sect that was to become known as Jehovah's Witnesses first gained a foothold in Canada about a century ago.[1] The founding president of the Watch Tower Bible and Tract Society and the International Bible Students Association, Pastor Charles Taze Russell, first visited Canada in 1891 to give a public address to some 700 persons.[2] In 1916, the Bible Students or "Russellites" (as they were then known) came to the attention of federal authorities as being conscientious objectors who believed that warfare was in conflict with the teachings of Christ. The sect's official magazine, the *Watchtower*,[3] published exerpts from the *Canadian Militia Act*,[4] ss 11 and 12 of which dealt with exemption from military service:

11. The following persons only shall be exempt from liability to service in the Militia:–
   . . .
   Persons who, from the doctrines of their religion, are averse to bearing arms or rendering personal military service, under such conditions as are prescribed.

12. No person shall be entitled to exemption unless he has, at least one month before he claims such exemption, filed with the commanding officer within the limits whereof he resides, his affidavit, made before some justice of the peace, of the facts of which he rests his claim.

---

1 W. Glen How, Leo W. Greenlees and Percy Chapman, *History of Jehovah's Witnesses in Canada*. (Report to the Watch Tower Society, 1958). This report was later incorporated into the special report on Canada in the *1979 Yearbook of Jehovah's Witnesses* (New York: Watch Tower Bible and Tract Society, 1978) at 79–80 [hereinafter *1979 Yearbook*].

2 *1979 Yearbook* at 80.

3 15 November 1915.

4 R.S.C. 1906, c. 41, ss. 11–12.

These sections clearly implied that conscientious objectors could claim exemption from military service on religious grounds simply by filing an affidavit with the local commanding officer of the militia. In the wake of the *Watchtower* article, hundreds of affidavits were dutifully submitted by Bible Students.[5]

The press was outraged. On 7 March 1916, The *Ottawa Free Press* published a news story under the heading, "Pastor Russell's People Try to Hurt Recruiting," and on 18 March, *Victoria Week* stated: "Now that we know that [Russell's] organization is simply a cover for a pro-German anti-recruiting propaganda, it is time for someone to act."[6] Militia officers and justices of the peace registered their complaints with the Minister of Defence and Militia, suggesting that s. 11 of the *Militia Act* should be expunged and the applicants court-martialled on charges of "disloyalty" or even treason.[7]

The Adjutant-General of the Militia, Major-General W. E. Hodgkins, stood firm, stating that the Bible Students "have not been transgressing any law."[8] Immigration authorities were not as conciliatory, however. When Russell attempted to travel to Winnipeg to address a scheduled Bible Students convention, he was removed from the train at the border and forced to return to the United States.[9] The decision to prevent Russell from entering the country seems to have been planned well ahead of time. It was a decision made, not at the border by an immigration officer acting upon a whim, but at the national level by the Superintendent of Immigration, W.D. Scott, himself. Scott gave his rationale for refusing Russell admission to Canada in a letter to the Chief Press Censor of Canada, Ernest Chambers, in which he stated, "We had enough of Pastor Russell's kind already in the country without importing more trouble and opposition."[10] His cavalier attitude became fairly common as individuals with power came up against Jehovah's Witnesses. Neither was it uncommon for officialdom to wink at the civil liberties of

---

5 Public Archives of Canada Ref. R.G. 24A, Vol. 2199, M.D. (Militia/Defence) H.Q. 54-21-10-21 [hereinafter R.G.24A].

6 Cited in M. James Penton, *Jehovah's Witnesses in Canada: Champions of Freedom of Speech and Worship* (Toronto: Macmillan, 1976) at 49.

7 See, for example, the letter dated 7 March 1916 from W. H. Chittick, J.P. of London, Ontario to the Minister of Defence and Militia, and the correspondence dated 24 March 1916 between Lieutenant-General S.C. Mewburn and Lieutenant-Colonel C.S. MacInness. R.G. 24A, Vol. 2199.

8 Letter dated 3 April 1916 to District Officer Commanding, Winnipeg. R.G. 24A, Vol. 2199.

9 *Winnipeg Free Press*, 8 July 1916.

10 21 August 1916, in Public Archives of Canada Ref. R.G. 6 E-I, Vol. 67, file CPC (Chief Press Censor) 206-W-I [hereinafter R.G. 6].

Jehovah's Witnesses in the process. As early as 1916, a pattern was becoming established that was to lead forty years later to *Roncarelli* v. *Duplessis*,[11] a case that was to challenge the right of officials to act arbitrarily against the rule of law.

II. WARTIME CENSORSHIP OF THE BIBLE STUDENTS

i. Censorship of Moving Pictures

Many of the objections voiced against the Bible Students were, like Scott's letter, directed specifically against Russell himself, and therefore when Russell died in October 1916, much of the ammunition with which the Chief Press Censor and others had been arming themselves was effectively neutralized. Nonetheless, the charisma of Russell outlasted him, for he appeared in film in the popular *Photo-Drama of Creation* to audiences that were not used to seeing motion pictures:

> The quality of the Photo-Drama photography and sound was so good that some viewers thought C.T. Russell was present in person when he appeared on the screen in the opening scene to introduce the presentation.[12]

The mixed media production, released initially in 1914, was one of the most prescient and effective preaching techniques used by the Bible Students at the time—an eight-hour event combining cinematography, slides and cartoons, in colour, with a parallel sound-track incorporating music and narration on separate phonograph records.[13]

The *Photo-Drama* was shown from coast to coast, from Halifax to Victoria. In Hamilton, it was presented for three weeks to full houses at the Grand Opera House. Thousands of Canadians saw it. Yet at the local level, there were rumblings of discontent that the Bible Students could show moving pictures on a Sunday. The clergy in particular complained that the Bible Students, by showing the *Photo-Drama* on Sundays, often drew curious parishioners away from their regular church services. The Guelph Town Council passed a by-law specifically aimed at the *Photo-Drama* which stated that "no moving pictures be allowed to be shown on Sunday, except for war purposes." But the theatre manager had a

---

11 (1956), [1956] Que. Q.B. 447, rev'd (1959), [1959] S.C.R. 121, 16 D.L.R. (2d) 689 [hereinafter *Roncarelli* cited to S.C.R.].

12 *1979 Yearbook* at 99.

13 *Ibid.* at 98–99. See also *Ottawa Evening Journal*, 10 April 1917.

provincial licence that allowed him to show films on Sunday, and the mayor and Town Council were forced to back down.[14]

Russell had been replaced as president of the Watch Tower Society by an equally dynamic leader, J.F. Rutherford, who in April 1917 gave a stirring speech in the Royal Alexandra Theatre in Toronto urging Christians not to take up arms. In response, the Provincial Treasurer of Ontario, T.W. McGarry, cancelled the organization's moving-picture licence, thereby curtailing the Bible Student presentations of the *Photo-Drama* in Ontario. It was the first example of provincial censorship of movies to be experienced in Canada.

ii. Censorship of the Printed Word

On 17 July 1917, Rutherford released the book *The Finished Mystery*, representing it as the posthumous publication of the seventh and final volume of Russell's popular *Studies in the Scriptures* series. It attacked organized religion, politics and business and provided a complex calculation by which the faithful could predict the end of the world. Most controversial of all, from the standpoint of Canadian officialdom, was the statement that "the most virulent and devastating disease of humanity now raging on earth is militarism." War was antithetical to Christianity, the book maintained; one could not be a Christian and a soldier at the same time. Naturally the book raised the ire of any committed soldier or veteran who read it. On 25 August 1917, the Kingston Veterans' Association wrote to Ernest Chambers with reference to the publication, alleging treason. Other complaints came from the clergy, the press, and immigration officials including W.D. Scott. On October 23, Chambers requested the Secretary of State, Martin Burrell, to suppress *The Finished Mystery* because it and other Watch Tower publications were "objectionable and dangerous, doubly so on account of the insidious attacks on the military system."[15]

On 30 January 1918, *The Finished Mystery* and the newsletter *Bible Students Monthly* were banned by order-in-council.[16] Possession of either publication could garner a maximum fine of $5,000, a maximum jail term of five years, or both.[17] In April, three more Watch Tower publications were added to the list of banned books,[18] and in June, a comparatively

---

14 *Ibid.* at 100–101.

15 Letter from Chambers to Burrell dated 27 August 1917, in Public Archives of Canada Ref. R.G. 6 F-1, CPC 206-B-6.

16 *Canada Gazette*, 9 February 1918 at 2701–2702.

17 *Canada Gazette*, 16 February 1918 at 2767.

18 *Canada Gazette*, 13 April 1918 at 3569; 27 April 1918 at 2824; 25 May 1918 at 4133.

bland tract, the *Morning Messenger*, was banned after protests had been received from the establishment clergy, even though a Winnipeg press censor had approved it prior to publication. J.F.B. Livesay, press censor for Western Canada, stated in a letter to Chambers that he could find nothing objectionable in the tract:

> I read the thing very carefully—as I thought—and as it had no bearing to all seeming on the prosecution of the war, I could not see that it could be prohibited on the ground that it was an attack on religion that not being, to my idea, the business of Press Censorship.

Livesay even offered to resign over the controversy.[19]

Finally, on 20 July 1918, all Watch Tower literature was banned. Subsequently, raids were conducted across the nation and Watch Tower literature was seized by the wagon-load. Dozens of Bible Students were charged with possession of banned literature, receiving fines of up to $1,000 and jail terms of up to two years.[20]

III. *RE COOKE* AND ITS AFTERMATH

The penalties for possession of banned literature were not nearly as severe as penalties for refusing to serve in the military, however. On 6 July 1917, the *Military Service Act*[21] came into effect, imposing a draft with exemptions similar to those outlined in s. 11 of the *Militia Act*. Section 11(1)(*f*) of the *Military Service Act* specified the grounds for exemption:

> That he conscientiously objects to the undertaking of combatant service and is prohibited from so doing by the tenets and articles of faith, in effect on the sixth day of July, 1917, of any organized religious denomination existing and well recognized in Canada at such date, and to which he in good faith belongs.[22]

Unhappily for the Bible Students, the courts quickly decided that the International Bible Students Association was merely a company, not a religious denomination. In *Re Cooke*,[23] the applicant, David Cooke, a

---

19 R.G. 6 F-I. Cited in Penton, *supra*, note 6 at 329.

20 Penton, *supra*, note 6 at 75.

21 S.C. 1917, c. 19, s. 11(1)(*f*). See also s. 11(2)(*a*) and Schedule Exemption 6.

22 Compare s. 11 of the *Militia Act*, cited *supra*, note 4.

23 *Re Cooke* (unreported) 14 January 1918 (Serial No. 548250 JC) per Duff J. (Central Appeal Court). Cited in full in Penton, *supra*, note 6 at 259–62 (Appendix B) [hereinafter *Cooke*, cited to Penton].

Winnipeg member of the International Bible Students Association, sought to overturn the decision of a military tribunal that had refused exemption under s. 11(1)(f) of the *Military Service Act*. In his judgment, Mr. Justice Lyman Duff, in his capacity as Central Appeal Judge (he was later to become the Chief Justice of Canada) pointed out that the International Bible Students Association was an unlimited company incorporated under the Companies Acts of 1908 and 1913 (United Kingdom). He read into the record the objects of the company as stated in the memorandum of association, and concluded:

> The Company as appears from the evidence, issues publications, in which certain views are advocated touching the interpretation of the Bible, and certain religious beliefs advanced and supported; and of the subscribers to these publications, who accept the doctrine so expounded, there are in various countries, including Canada, groups who meet for the study of the Bible and the discussion of questions of theology and ethics. . . .
>
> The evidence before me does not justify the conclusion that these groups or associations so-called, either individually or collectively come within the description—"organized religious denomination existing and well recognized in Canada" within the contemplation of the Military Service Act.[24]

Mr. Justice Duff found that the local groups were only loosely associated by adherence to and advocacy of the set of beliefs advocated by the company, and the writings were not entirely consistent as to whether a Bible Student might conscientiously engage in military service. Furthermore, he expressed doubt whether the individual local groups "have for the primary object a common worship, which is, I think, an essential characteristic of a 'religious denomination' within the meaning of Section 11":

> The Statute plainly implies as a characteristic of religious denominations, falling within its scope, that there should be conditions of membership, compliance or non-compliance with which can be ascertained by reference to some practical criterion, and of such conditions there is, although I pressed for it on hearing, no evidence, and there are no indicia to serve as reliable guides for the Tribunals.[25]

Mr. Justice Duff's decision dealt the Bible Students a terrible blow, one that was to remain with them for decades, through two world wars. As a direct result of the decision, virtually any Bible Student who had previously filed an affidavit for exemption under the *Militia Act* was now

---

24 *Ibid.* at 261.

25 *Ibid.* at 262.

deemed to be draftable. Once Bible Students were drafted, they were found to be insubordinate when they refused to put on a uniform or bear arms, even for training. Accordingly, they were court-martialled time and time again. George Naish received a 10-year sentence upon his third court-martial linked to his conscription. When Naish's younger brother, Ralph, and two other Manitoba Bible Students refused to comply with orders to don uniforms, they were beaten, choked, kicked and whipped, were confined in stiflingly hot closets, and then, stripped naked, were forced to take prolonged cold showers to the point where they displayed the symptoms of hypothermia and lost consciousness. News of this treatment reached the press, and both the *Winnipeg Tribune*[26] and the *Winnipeg Free Press*[27] gave the story front page play.

At least seven of the conscientious objectors, including Ralph Naish, were sent overseas to England despite their objections; in England, the men were treated even more harshly than in Canada, and were repeatedly beaten, threatened with execution, shot at, kicked, goaded with a stick, knocked unconscious with gun-butts, and forced at bayonet-point to hear the religious services of rival church groups.[28]

IV. POST-WAR RADIO CENSORSHIP

In 1920, long after the end of the First World War, the ban on Watch Tower Literature was lifted, and the International Bible Students Association began to experience unprecedented growth in English Canada, from about 1,900 in 1922 to 3,000 in 1925. Always at the forefront of innovation, the International Bible Students Association in 1921 applied for a licence to operate radio stations in Toronto and on the prairies. Although they were not immediately successful, by 1927 individual congregations (or "companies" as they were then called) owned and operated two radio stations in Toronto and others in Saskatoon, Edmonton and Vancouver, and in 1927 the central branch office in Toronto successfully applied to renew the licences of all of the stations. But in 1926, at least one of the radio stations had sold air time to the Ku Klux Klan, and some of the programming was controlled by the Klan. On 7 January 1927, the radio director of the Department of Marine and Fisheries informed the Deputy Minister that the Royal Canadian Mounted Police had reported to his department about Klan programming on CHUC in Saskatoon, one of the stations owned by the International Bible Students Association.[29] That

---

26 24 January 1918 at 1: "Treatment of Drafted Men Under Probe" (headline).

27 25 January 1918 at 1. "Conscientious Objectors Said To Have Been Roughly Treated."

28 Penton, *supra*, note 6 at 56–62.

29 *Ibid.* at 96.

winter, the Ku Klux Klan used CHUC for its major organizing campaign of 1927–28, a period when some 1,000 persons joined or openly expressed support for the Klan in Saskatchewan alone.[30]

The Klan and the Bible Students shared the ideological position of anti-Roman Catholicism. As protest mounted against this strange alliance, the question of the appropriateness of the content of the IBSA radio programming was aired in editorial form by *Saturday Night* in a rare front-page editorial ascribed to the editor, Hector Charlesworth. Attacking "Judge" Rutherford, whose public address was called "Millions Now Living May Never Die," the editorial declared:

> The reason this loquacious "Judge" has received so much attention of late is that he managed to bulldoze his way into control of the air during the progress of the Russellite convention of Toronto. He gave credit for this, not to himself, but to "Jehovah, the only true God," who, he said had "graciously used the National Broadcasting Company for his divine purposes." The tribal god of the Russellites certainly gained no popularity with users of radio thereby; their deliberations were a nightly nuisance on the air. On the night of July 21st reputable fathers of families anxious to listen in on the progress of the Dempsey-Sharkey prize fight were kept out by the high power oratory at the Toronto Coliseum. On Sunday, July 24th, the religiously inclined were prevented from hearing their favorite message because the leather-lunged Rutherford had the air. Millions now living would rather die than be compelled to listen very often to his discourses.[31]

Responsibility for radio licencing fell to the Minister of Marine and Fisheries, Arthur Cardin, a staunch Roman Catholic, who, succumbing to pressure from the clergy, business interests and the press, revoked the International Bible Students Association radio licences, and resigned himself to defending his actions in the House.[32] The Bible Students and the Ku Klux Klan responded with a petition that garnered a total of 458,026 signatures.[33] At the height of the controversy, J.J. Maloney, the leader of the K.K.K., had the temerity to cable Prime Minister Mackenzie King with the following message:

CHUC BROADCASTING STATION INFORMS ME THAT THE DEPUTY MINISTER OF MARINES HAS DENIED THEM RENEWAL OF THEIR LICENCE BECAUSE OF PRO-

---

30 Public Archives of Canada Ref. R.G. 42, Vol. 493, M & F (Marine and Fisheries)-IBSA [hereinafter R.G. 42].

31 *Saturday Night*, 6 August 1927 at 1.

32 *Debates of the House of Commons of Canada*, 1928, Vol. 2 at 1951. See also Vol. 3 at 3618–25, 3644–51, and 3654–72. [Hereinafter *Debates*].

33 *Debates*, 1928, Vol. 3 at 3644.

TESTANT LECTURES GOING OVER THEIR STATION STOP PETITIONS WITH TWO
HUNDRED THOUSAND NAMES BEING CIRCULATED IN THIS PROVINCE WHICH
IS 80 PERCENT PROTESTANT STOP I AM CALLING YOUR ATTENTION ON THE
ADVICE OF THE PRESIDENT OF THE LIBERAL EXECUTIVE[34]

Maloney obtained 1,000 signatures at a single K.K.K. rally.[35] Despite the
public outcry in the Bible Students' favour, Cardin refused to renew the
radio licences, defending instead the notion of a national broadcasting
system that was eventually to become the Canadian Broadcasting Corporation.[36]

Rutherford resigned himself to buying time on other radio stations,
but soon this right too was challenged. The chairman of the Canadian
Radio Commission by this time was none other than Rutherford's
avowed enemy, Hector Charlesworth, the former editor of *Saturday Night*.
On 18 January 1933, Charlesworth sent a telegram to radio stations across
the country, signed by himself, stating:

> Speeches of one Judge Rutherford, foreign anti-social agitator, must not
> be broadcast on Canadian stations until the continuity or records of
> same are submitted to Canadian radio broadcasting for approval. Hector
> Charlesworth, Chairman.[37]

Journalists across the country were quick to point out that Charlesworth
was not exactly unbiased. On 28 January 1933, the *Winnipeg Free Press*
criticized the ideas of those "in high places" such as the Canadian Radio
Commission, and urged the Commission to "make up its mind that it is
dealing with a free people." *Hush* magazine was even more pointed,
referring to Charlesworth as "that old Saturday Night Big Interest
sweetheart."[38] The debate was taken up in the House of Commons by
J.L. Brown, Liberal-Progressive M.P. for Lisgar, Saskatchewan. Armed
with the 1927 *Saturday Night* editorial, he set out to demonstrate that
Charlesworth was biased, reading segments of the editorial to the
House.[39] He concluded:

---

34 R.G. 42, telegram dated 15 March 1928.

35 *Ibid.*, letter dated 2 April 1928. See also William Calderwood, "The Rise and Fall of the
    Ku Klux Klan in Saskatchewan" (M.A. thesis, University of Saskatchewan, Saskatoon,
    1968), chapter 9; and Penton *supra*, note 6, chapter 5.

36 Frank W. Peers, *The Politics of Canadian Broadcasting—1921–1951* (Toronto: University of
    Toronto Press, 1969) at 29–34.

37 *Debates*, 1932–33, Vol. 3 at 2619.

38 4 February 1933.

39 *Debates*, 1932–33, Vol. 4 at 4149.

The action of the radio commission is not in harmony with my views in regard to the rights of a man to promulgate whatever doctrine he wishes.[40]

By this time the Bible Students had adopted the name Jehovah's Witnesses.[41] They themselves were far from silent on the radio ban issue; rather, the Watch Tower Society attacked Charlesworth indirectly in a tract called *Important Notice* which had a circulation of 1,250,000, and directly and personally in the *Golden Age*, the precursor to *Awake!*.[42] This distribution campaign did not go unnoticed in the House of Commons; in fact the ensuing debate on 21 April 1933 filled eight columns in *Hansard*. Referring to his earlier statement in the House, J.L. Brown remarked,

It will be recalled that a short time ago the minister, in reply to a question of mine, made a statement to the house with reference to the banning of Judge Rutherford's lectures from the radio. . . . I had received a good many communications protesting against the banning. . . . To forbid men interpreting the scriptures and teaching whatever doctrines they see fit, so long as it is done without transcending the bounds of decency and without needless offence, does not agree with my views regarding religious liberty.[43]

Other members of Parliament expressed similar concerns with what they saw as "an infringement on the right of free speech."[44] The Minister of Marine and Fisheries, Duranleau, stated that the *Important Notice* "was left at every door, according to my information; I know I received a copy at my office here and also at my house in Montreal."[45]

In the year that followed, Jehovah's Witnesses launched a new petition, obtaining 406,270 signatures before submitting it to Parliament.[46] Jehovah's Witnesses used more conventional lobbying tactics as well. According to the Watch Tower Society, two of its representatives arranged a meeting with Prime Minister R.B. Bennett, who "promised to

---

40 *Ibid.*

41 As of 1931.

42 The tract was reprinted in its entirety in *Golden Age*, 1 March 1933.

43 *Debates*, 1932–33, Vol. 4 at 4149.

44 *Ibid.* at 4152.

45 *Ibid.* at 4153.

46 *Debates*, 1932–33, Vol. V, p. 4672.

have the radio commission appear before him and look thoroughly into the matter with a view to taking proper action."[47]

Despite an apology from Rutherford for the vitriolic words attacking Charlesworth that had been published without Rutherford's permission in the *Golden Age*, Charlesworth refused to back down from his position of insistence upon prior censorship of Rutherford's radio programs and addresses. The Witnesses refused to submit material to the censor, and resigned themselves to the fact that their broadcasting days in Canada were finished. From then on, Jehovah's Witnesses put their energies into distributing the printed word, and their future course seemed to be set: to this day, the Watch Tower Society relies primarily on the written word to get their message across, now printing 13,000,000 copies of each issue of *The Watchtower* and *Awake!* every week.[48]

V. THE WARTIME BAN ON JEHOVAH'S WITNESSES

On 4 July 1940, a notice appeared in the *Canada Gazette* that, by order-in-council, declared Jehovah's Witnesses an illegal organization.[49] The *Defence of Canada Regulations*[50] to which the notice referred specified how "illegal organizations" and their members should be treated:

2. Every person who is an officer or member of an illegal organization, or professes to be such, or who advocates or defends the acts, principles or policies of such illegal organization shall be guilty of an offence against this Regulation.

3. In any prosecution under the Regulation for the offence of being a member of an illegal organization, if it be proved that the person charged has—

   (a) attended meetings of an illegal organization;

   (b) spoken publicly in advocacy of an illegal organization; or

   (c) distributed literature of an illegal organization by circulation through the Post Office mails of Canada, or otherwise it shall be presumed, in the absence of proof to the contrary, that he is a member of such illegal organization.[51]

---

47 *1934 Yearbook of Jehovah's Witnesses* (New York: Watch Tower Bible and Tract Society, 1933) at 84–86.

48 Current circulation figures are contained on p. 2 of each issue.

49 Vol. 74 (July–September 1940) at 87. Compare (January–March 1941), at 2681, 2682, 2846 and 2847, in which the Watch Tower Society and the International Bible Students Association were banned.

50 Consolidation, 1941.

51 *Ibid.* at 54.

Under the regulations, all property, rights and interests belonging to any illegal organization became vested in the Custodian, in compliance with the *Regulations respecting Trading with the Enemy*,[52] "to the same extent as if such property, rights and interests belonged to an enemy."[53] Even after the termination of the war, according to the regulations, the property, rights and interests vested in and subject to the management and control of the Custodian, and any proceeds arising from the seizure, would be dealt with "in such a manner as the Governor in Council may direct."[54]

The government action of banning Jehovah's Witnesses was defended in the House of Commons by Prime Minister Mackenzie King himself, reading a statement prepared by the Minister of Justice, Ernest Lapointe:

> The literature of Jehovah's Witnesses discloses, in effect, that man-made authority or law should not be recognized if it conflicts with the Jehovah's Witnesses' interpretation of the Bible; that they refuse to salute the flag of any nation or to hail any man; and, that they oppose war.
>
> The general effect of this literature is, amongst other things, to undermine the ordinary responsibility of citizens, particularly in time of war.[55]

In the wake of the order-in-council that proclaimed Jehovah's Witnesses illegal, government officials within a week made their first arrest and seized large quantities of Watch Tower literature.[56] Raids were conducted on the homes of known Jehovah's Witnesses, and literally tons of literature were seized. Twenty-nine Witnesses were charged with being members of an illegal organization in 1940 alone, and sentenced initially to a total of 300 months in prison.[57] Government officials also impounded about $100,000 worth of real property, according to the Watch Tower Society.[58]

Jehovah's Witnesses went underground. In November 1940, they conducted a nation-wide "blitz" similar to the one experienced by Quebec City in 1933. Of the 7,000 Witnesses who participated, fewer than ten

---

52 *Ibid.*, s. 4(*a*).

53 *Ibid.*, s. 4(*b*).

54 *Ibid.*, s. 4(*c*).

55 *Debates*, 1940, Vol. 2 at 1646 (16 July 1940).

56 Gordon Cripps was arrested on 9 July 1940 under the *Defence of Canada Regulations*. See Penton, *supra*, note 6 at 137.

57 Penton, *supra*, note 6 at 137, citing 1942 memo from Charles Morrell (private secretary to Duff C.J.C.) to Percy Chapman, Branch Servant of the Watch Tower Bible and Tract Society.

58 Letter from Charles Morrell (private secretary to Duff C.J.C.) to Sir Ellsworth Flavelle dated 29 March 1943, cited in Penton, *supra*, note 6 at 345.

were arrested.[59] In fact, few Jehovah's Witnesses were apprehended in the course of proselytizing. Most of the litigation against them in the war years arose from the refusal of individual Witnesses to salute the flag, to stand for the national anthem, and to serve in the armed forces.[60] These acts of omission were deemed to be "seditious."

In *R. v. Leeson*,[61] the police raided the Leeson home searching for Watch Tower literature. Two of their children were expelled from school when they refused to stand for "God Save the King" or salute the flag. Subsequently, the Leesons were arrested and jailed and all four Leeson children were made temporary wards of the Children's Aid Society. The parents, after being held incommunicado for 11 days, were charged with "advocating the principles of Jehovah's Witnesses contrary to Section 39C of the Defence of Canada Regulations and of having made statements intended or likely to cause disaffection to the King in violation of Section 39A of the same regulations."[62] Each was sentenced to four months in jail and fined $100 plus $500 costs. Pending an appeal to the Supreme Court of Ontario, they were released on $2,000 bail each. The superior court postponed their hearing indefinitely.[63] In another Ontario case, *Donald v. Hamilton Board of Education*,[64] two Jehovah's Witness boys were suspended from school in September 1940 for refusing to sing the national anthem or salute the flag; one of the boys was later expelled. Donald, who could not initiate his suit until after the ban on Jehovah's Witnesses was lifted, lost at trial. But on appeal, Mr. Justice Gillanders of the appeal division of the Supreme Court of Ontario ruled that the "personal views" of judges should not enter into the picture when deliberating on the question of refusing to salute the flag "on religious or other grounds." The Supreme Court of Canada refused to hear the appeal of the Hamilton

---

59 *1942 Yearbook of Jehovah's Witnesses* (New York: Watch Tower Bible and Tract Society, 1941) at 157.

60 Penton states that the files of the Watch Tower Society in Toronto indicate that some 30 Witnesses were "sentenced to prison for refusing military or alternative service prior to 1943." *Supra*, note 6 at 354.

61 (Unreported) County Police Court for the County of Middlesex, Ontario, 6 November 1940 (Magistrate C.W. Hawkshaw presiding), as reviewed in Penton, *supra*, note 6 at 140–41.

62 *Ibid.* at 141.

63 *Ibid.*

64 (1944), [1944] O.R. 475, [1944] 4 D.L.R. 227, [1944] O.W.N. 559 (H.C.), rev'd (1945), [1945] O.R. 518, [1945] 3 D.L.R. 424, [1945] O.W.N. 526 (C.A.).

Board of Education from the Ontario Court of Appeal decision. Similar cases arose in Saskatchewan,[65] Manitoba,[66] Alberta,[67] and Quebec.[68]

Jehovah's Witnesses and other groups that had been declared illegal were defended in the House of Commons by members of the minority parties, especially United Progressive Party MP Dorise Nielsen and Co-operative Commonwealth Federation MP T.C. Douglas, who cited violations of civil liberties again and again in the Commons.[69] On 27 February 1941, Prime Minister King responded to this political pressure by establishing an all-party select committee to suggest revisions to the Defence of Canada Regulations; but the verbal attacks in the House continued. Douglas in particular demanded that the regulations be changed so as to give an opportunity to Jehovah's Witnesses and others "of appearing before some judicial or quasi-judicial body, so that they may state their case and have a hearing. That is the very least we can give to any organization or individual."[70]

On 25 June 1942, the select committee heard representations from spokesmen of Jehovah's Witnesses that the ban should be lifted, and a month later, the committee's unanimous recommendation that the ban be removed was tabled in the House.[71] However, Parliament chose not to act on the recommendation; indeed, one of the Witness spokesmen, Charles Morrell, ironically personal secretary to Sir Lyman Duff, former Chief Justice of Canada, was investigated and his home raided.[72] True, on 15 February 1943 the ban was modified slightly with the decree that "No person shall be guilty of an offence against this regulation by reason only of his attending a meeting the sole purpose of which is religious worship or instruction,"[73] but only after sustained pressure from both

---

65 *R. v. Woodward* (unreported). Press report in *Edmonton Journal*, 28 November 1940; see also *R. v. Naish* (1950), [1950] 1 W.W.R. 987, 10 C.R. 65, 97 C.C.C. 19.

66 *R. v. Clark* (1941), [1941] 3 W.W.R. 229 (Man. Police Ct.), rev'd (1941), [1941] 3 W.W.R. 567, [1941] 4 D.L.R. 299 (Man. C.A.).

67 *Ruman* v. *Lethbridge School Board Trustees* (1943), [1943] 3 W.W.R. 340, [1944], D.L.R. 360 (Alta. T.D.). In *Ruman*, the Supreme Court of Alberta held that the school board acted within its powers under the *School Act* in insisting that school children salute the flag.

68 *Chabot* v. *School Commissioners of Lamorandière* (1957), [1957] Que. Q.B. 707, 12 D.L.R. (2d) 796 (C.A.); and *Perron* v. *Rouyen School Trustees* (1955), [1955] Que. Q.B. 841, 1 D.L.R. (2d) 414 (C.A.).

69 See *Debates*, 1940, Vol. 1 at 752–53; Vol. 2 at 1068–71, 1078–79, 1206–07, 1215; 1941, Vol. 2 at 1068–70, 1089, 1188–201, 1203–17, 1251–52.

70 *Debates* 1941, Vol. 2 at 1067–1070, 1188–201, 1203–17, 1251, 1252; citing 1189–90.

71 *Votes and Proceedings of the House of Commons of Canada*, 23 July 1942 at 59.

72 Penton, *supra*, note 6 at 148.

73 Order-in-Council PC 1266 (15 February 1943).

the opposition[74] and the press did the Minister of Justice, Louis St. Laurent, on 14 October 1943, finally sign an order in council deleting "Jehovah's Witnesses" from the official list of subversive organizations.[75]

By then, as John Diefenbaker remarked in the House, there had been "some five hundred prosecutions of Jehovah's Witnesses, none of which had to do with subversive activities, the entire offence being that of belonging to an organization banned under the defence of Canada regulations." It is important to realize, however, that the International Bible Students Association of Canada remained under ban, for a further six months, until 13 June 1944,[76] and the ban on the Watch Tower Society was not lifted until 28 May 1945.[77]

VI. CONSCRIPTION AND ALTERNATIVE SERVICE

As long as the ban on Jehovah's Witnesses continued, members of the sect, including full-time ministers, could not defend themselves against conscription. Once the ban was lifted, however, those who had been charged for failing to report for military duty tried to use the exemption clauses of the new *National Selective Service Mobilization Regulations*[78] adopted under the *War Measures Act*.

Subsequent to the lift of the ban, many additional Witnesses became vulnerable to conscription for home defence purposes. The most common argument used by the Witnesses was that each and every Witness, by virtue of his commitment to preach, was an ordained minister. Justice Minister St. Laurent explained this line of reasoning in the House of Commons, when he said that the Witnesses had been banned in the first place partly because of "the propaganda to the effect that one could be an ordained minister of Jehovah's Witnesses by making an individual compact with the Almighty, that by doing so one became an ordained minister not subject to mobilization regulations."[79]

St. Laurent regarded this argument of the Witnesses as being "contrary to the policy which this state has to maintain in war time," and

---

74 See *Debates*, 1943, Vol. 1 at 606–32; Vol. 5 at 4853, 4861–62, 5197–210, 5214–15.

75 *Ibid.* at 615. "Order in Council amending the Defence of Canada Regulations (Consolidation) 1942," P.C. 8022 (14 October 1943), in *Canadian War Orders and Regulations*, 1943, Vol. 4, No. 3 (25 October 1943) at 127.

76 "Order-in-Council Amending Defence of Canada Regulations re International Bible Students Association," P.C. 4476 (13 June 1944), in *Canadian War Orders and Regulations* (26 June 1944) at 615–16.

77 "Order-in-Council Amending the Defence of Canada Regulations (Consolidation) 1942," P.C. 3635, *Canadian War Orders and Regulations* (28 May 1945) at 402.

78 Order-in-Council P.C. 10924 (1 December 1942).

79 *Debates*, 1944, Vol. 3 at 2917.

perhaps as a result of his position in this regard, no Jehovah's Witnesses, not even the overseers of large congregations, were acknowledged to be ordained ministers.[80] Most Witness men eligible for conscription were confined in alternative-service camps, but reports of beatings, severe bread-and-water rationing and inadequate clothing, as well as the "cold shower treatment" familiar from the First World War, surfaced in the House of Commons.[81]

The argument that at least those Jehovah's Witnesses in positions of authority were ministers was made time and time again before the courts, to little avail. In *R. v. Stewart,*[82] the British Columbia Court of Appeal ruled, in effect, that not even full time ministers of Jehovah's Witnesses could be regarded as "ministers of a religious denomination" for the purpose of applying the *National Selective Service Mobilization Regulations* exemption. Section 3(2)(*c*) of Part I of the Regulations specified:

> (2) Notwithstanding subsection one, these regulations shall not apply to the following:
>
> . . .
>
> (*c*) a regular clergyman or a minister of a religious denomination.

Earl Stewart was a district overseer who had been charged before the ban on the Witnesses was lifted with failing to report for military training pursuant to an order given to him under the Regulations. At trial, he produced a letter from the Canadian Branch of the Watch Tower Bible and Tract Society, dated in 1939, which stated that he was "a Minister of the Gospel" as well as "a fully recognized minister of the International Bible Students' Association of Canada, and of its parent organization The Watchtower Bible and Tract Society, Brooklyn, N.Y. He is sent forth by the Society for the purpose of furthering its work in promulgating Christian knowledge."[83] Judge Lennox of the County Court found that neither the Watch Tower Society nor the International Bible Students Association were religious denominations, but rather constituted "a commercial undertaking."[84] Since Stewart had been appointed by these societies and not by Jehovah's Witnesses, Stewart could not claim clerical status.

The Court of Appeal accepted the findings of fact of the trial judge with respect to the relationship adhering among the Watch Tower

---

80 Percy Chapman, writing in *1945 Yearbook of Jehovah's Witnesses* (New York: Watch Tower Bible and Tract Society, 1944) at 118.

81 *Debates,* 1944, Vol. 3 at 2905–09.

82 (1944), [1944] 2 W.W.R. 86, [1944] 3 D.L.R. 331 at 338 (B.C.C.A.), aff'g (1944), [1944] 1 W.W.R. 469, [1944] 3 D.L.R. 331 (B.C. Co. Ct.).

83 [1944] 1 W.W.R. 469 at 472.

84 *Ibid.* at 475.

Society, the International Bible Students Association and Jehovah's Witnesses.[85] Appeal Court Justice Sidney Smith, speaking for the court, concluded:

> I do not consider it necessary to make any finding as to whether or not the organization known as Jehovah's Witnesses is a religious denomination; but, assuming that it is, I am of opinion that the learned trial Judge was right in holding that the appellant was never duly appointed a regular minister thereof; and I am further of opinion that at no time was he a minister thereof in any sense in which that word can reasonably be used.[86]

He pointed out that although the ban on Jehovah's Witnesses had been removed on 14 October 1943, "the two parent bodies were declared illegal organizations in Canada in January 1941, and still continue under that disability." Regarding Stewart's letter from the Watch Tower Society, he remarked:

> It will be observed that this letter does not appoint him a Minister of Jehovah's Witnesses but of the other two organizations, which, as has been stated, were later declared illegal. He gave evidence that Jehovah's Witnesses were quite separate from both of them. But I think that he meant by such testimony no more than this, that collaboration of the three had been discontinued by compulsion of law while the two parent bodies remained under the illegal ban.[87]

Stewart found himself in a Catch–22, no-win situation.

Unlike *Stewart*, where the defendant did not report for induction into military training when scheduled, in *Greenlees* v. *A.G. Canada*[88] Leo Greenlees went on the offensive, requesting declaratory relief from the Ontario High Court to prevent his conscription. He prayed for a four-prong declaration:

> (1) a declaration that he is a minister of a religious denomination within the meaning of the aforesaid Regulations; (2) a declaration that the Regulations, save as to the said s. 3(2)(c), do not apply to the plaintiff; (3) a declaration that the notices received by the plaintiff to report for medical examination, and for military training, are *ultra vires* and not binding

---

85 [1944] 2 W.W.R. 86 at 87.

86 *Ibid.* at 88.

87 *Ibid.* at 88–89.

88 (1945), [1945] O.R. 411, [1945] 2 D.L.R. 641 (H.C.); aff'd (1946), [1946] O.R. 90, [1946] 1 D.L.R. 550 (C.A.); leave to appeal to S.C.C. refused (1946), [1946] S.C.R. 462 (S.C.C. claims no jurisdiction to hear) [hereinafter *Greenlees*].

upon the plaintiff; and (4) a declaration that any order, direction or proceeding affecting the plaintiff, and purporting to be made under the authority of the said Regulations, is illegal and *ultra vires*.[89]

At trial, Mr. Justice Hogg stated that although Jehovah's Witnesses as a group had no organizational structure of their own but rather were controlled by the Watch Tower Bible and Tract Society, and although they claimed not to be a religious denomination ("religion" being regarded as antithetical to "Christian" in their view),

> nevertheless I think the evidence shows that they are a group which, inasmuch as they appear to have a particular system of faith or belief, might be said to come within the ordinary and general conception of the term, "religious denomination."

This finding was not considered particularly relevant, however, because Justice Hogg went on to decide that Greenlees was not a "minister" as that term was used in the regulations. Had Hogg examined the function of Greenlees as a presiding overseer, he would have discovered that the position was very similar to that of "minister" as commonly used in other churches. But although Hogg was prepared to disregard the Witnesses' unorthodox definition of "religious," he was not prepared to make a similar concession in considering their unorthodox definition of "minister." Since Jehovah's Witnesses regarded "minister" to be synonymous with "member," he said, the term "does not denote a special status, such as is held by a minister of a religious denomination. It is this status which, in my view, constitutes a regular minister as contemplated by the Regulations."[90] Thus, although at trial *Greenlees* held to the proposition advanced in *Stewart* that Jehovah's Witnesses could not, by application of their own definition, be ministers, the Ontario Court of Appeal, in a judgment reminiscent of *Re Cooke*,[91] ruled that Jehovah's Witnesses did not so much as constitute a religion, and therefore the question of the ministerial status of Jehovah's Witnesses was irrelevant.

Greenlees appealed to the Supreme Court of Canada,[92] in the first of several Jehovah's Witness appeals to that court in the years after the war. The Supreme Court of Canada decided that it had no jurisdiction to grant leave to appeal, on the dubious grounds that economic rights were not directly in controversy.[93] Glen How, Greenlees' lawyer, subsequently

---

89 [1945] 2 D.L.R. 641 at 643.

90 *Ibid.* at 652.

91 *Supra*, note 23.

92 [1946] S.C.R. 462.

93 *Ibid.* at 463–66.

argued in an article in the *Canadian Bar Review* for increased power for the Supreme Court of Canada.[94]

In direct response to the *Greenlees* judgment, the *Fortnightly Law Journal* published an article, "Anomalies of Appeal to the Supreme Court," that was highly critical of Mr. Justice Kerwin's argument that the Supreme Court could hear questions of pecuniary interest amounting to $25 in one case and $33.80 in another, but could not hear a case such as *Greenlees* which, although it had no pecuniary component, was clearly important with regard to civil liberties:

> When the Supreme Court begins to reject admittedly important questions of law because they do not involve twenty-five or thirty-three dollars in damages, absurdity reaches completion.
>
> The recent discussion in the House of Commons over the proposed Bill of Rights brings sharply in issue the inadequacy of our law with respect to civil rights. . . . No law is stronger than the means of enforcing it. Basic constitutional rights are peculiarly matters for the Supreme Court of this or any other country. If, in fact, our Supreme Court has no jurisdiction over important questions of civil liberty it is high time some amendment was made to the Supreme Court Act to give it jurisdiction.[95]

In his article "The Too Limited Jurisdiction of the Supreme Court,"[96] How proposed several amendments to the *Supreme Court Act* "in order to make our Supreme Court a tribunal which would be of general value to the Canadian people," that would enlarge its jurisdiction, including the following:

1. It should be possible to appeal to the Supreme Court from courts other than the provincial court of appeal. Provided appeal has been taken to the final court in the province to which recourse may be had, there is no reason why the Supreme Court or a judge thereof should not have power to grant leave to appeal a case raising sufficiently important questions of law.

2. The appeals under the *Criminal Code* should be broadened to give the Court power to grant leave in cases of general importance irrespective of the decisions of the provincial courts.

3. The exclusion of "criminal causes" (which includes quasi-criminal and "provincial" criminal law) from the jurisdiction of the Supreme Court

---

94 "The Too Limited Jurisdiction of the Supreme Court of Canada" (1947), 25 Can. Bar Rev. 573.

95 (1946), 16 Fortnightly Law J. 38.

96 *Supra*, note 93.

pursuant to section 36 should be ended and such cases given a right or review with leave granted as suggested for the *Criminal Code*.

4. Appeals should be permitted on prerogative writs even when they do arise out of what are construed to be "criminal charges."

5. The Supreme Court should be allowed under section 41 unlimited powers to grant leave to appeal the same as the provincial courts already have.[97]

Interestingly, when the *Supreme Court Act* was revised two years later, many of these suggestions were incorporated into the Act.[98]

From the perspective of Jehovah's Witnesses, the pattern was set: from now on, wherever possible, they would take the initiative, becoming the plaintiffs in litigation rather than the defendants. If the Witnesses in English-speaking Canada had learned anything from the war years, it was that the best defence was a good offence. After the war, this strategy was to prove equally effective in Quebec.

---

97 *Ibid*. at 585–86.

98 *Ibid*. at 584–85.

3

The Rule of Law in French Canada

I. EARLY PERSECUTION IN QUEBEC

Even before the Second World War, Jehovah's Witnesses in Quebec were charged with unusual frequency with selling books in violation of municipal licencing laws. Sometimes, however, the charges were of a more serious, criminal nature. In *R. v. Kinler*,[1] Myra Kinler and Janet McCoy were charged on 18 May 1925 with "blasphemous libel" for distributing anti-Roman Catholic literature. They were acquitted when the magistrate held that such a form of libel must attack God as well as the clergy. Similar cases, usually connected with alleged licencing or *Lord's Day Act* infractions, were commonplace among Jehovah's Witnesses (or Bible Students as they were known until 1931) in Quebec in the 1920s and 1930s.

Witnesses received sentences as long as 30 days in jail for the distribution of literature "subversive of peace, order and good government," as in *R. v. Noreworthy*,[2] and were liable for much longer sentences for seditious conspiracy, as in *Brodie v. R.*[3]

In *Noreworthy*, the *Important Notice* tract, which was criticial of the alleged manipulation of radio licencing by officials in the Federal Government and elsewhere, was described by Recorder Semple of Montreal as "an invective against the Canadian radio commission for its

---

1 (1925), 63 Que. S.C. 483.

2 (Unreported). Heard before Recorder G. H. Semple in Montreal, and alluded to in *Debates*, 1932-33, Vol. IV at 4151. Described in *Montreal Daily Herald*, 14 April 1933. See also James Penton, *Jehovah's Witnesses in Canada: Champions of Freedom of Speech and Worship* (Toronto: Macmillan, 1976) at 107, where he refers to the same case as "Noseworthy." [Hereinafter *Noreworthy*, cited to *Debates*].

3 (1936), [1936] S.C.R. 188, 65 C.C.C. 289, [1936] 3 D.L.R. 81 [hereinafter *Brodie* cited to S.C.R.].

ruling against J.F. Rutherford, ex-judge from Brooklyn and president of the association of uncensored radio speeches." The tract was therefore deemed to be subversive:

> The circular itself is but a protest—thinly veiled and replete with quotation from the prophets—against authority as constituted by the Radio Broadcasting Act. That is its preconceived, determined and sole purpose; and in that respect it is subversive of peace, order and good government.[4]

In the House of Commons, Semple was criticized by one member as being "irresponsible."[5] Another M.P. protested,

> If we grant powers to a commission, and if when anyone chooses to protest against the decision of the commissioner his action is declared to be illegal, it seems to me that we have reached an intolerable situation. I cannot understand how there is any legal basis for this decision. . . . When we have a man awaiting sentence for having published a tract which has been held to be illegal simply because it criticizes the radio commission we have a serious situation.[6]

Even more serious than *Noreworthy* was the situation involving George H. Brodie of Toronto and G.C. Barrett of Belleville, Ontario, who were among 29 persons arrested during a Jehovah's Witness literature "blitz" of Quebec City on 3 October 1933, when some 158 Witnesses, mostly from Ontario, drove to the Quebec capital to distribute newly-translated French tracts. Of the 29 arrested, almost all of whom were unilingually anglophone, only six were subsequently identified by police; the rest were let go.[7]

At trial, Brodie and Barrett were found guilty of seditious conspiracy, and their conviction was unanimously upheld by the Appeal Division of the Court of King's Bench. On appeal to the Supreme Court of Canada, however, the decision was reversed on technical grounds: the court held that the indictment should have specified the seditious nature of the alleged conspiracy, including details of the alleged crime the accused were conspiring to commit.[8] In his judgment for the court, Mr. Justice Rinfret remarked:

---

4 *Debates*, 1932–33, Vol. IV at 4151.

5 *Ibid.*

6 *Ibid.*

7 *Brodie, supra*, note 3 at 190. The other four named in the indictment were W.F. Greenwood, W.G. Brown, Mrs. Charles Alton, and Mrs. A.M. Rose. See also Penton, *supra*, note 2 at 113-14.

8 *Ibid.* at 193.

It is not sufficient in a court to charge an indictable offence in the abstract. Concrete facts of a nature to identify the particular act which is charged and to give the accused notice of it are necessary ingredients of the indictment. . . . The appellants could not be charged merely with having been "parties to a seditious conspiracy," or having "committed the crime of seditious conspiracy." The particular agreement between each of them . . . into which they are alleged to have entered and into which the Attorney-General gave the appellation of "seditious conspiracy" ought to have been specified in the charge . . . in such a way as to show on its face that "the matter charged . . ." was an indictable offence.[9]

Since no overt criminal act was specified in the indictment, the indictment was illegal and therefore of no force or effect.[10]

The Supreme Court of Canada decision in *Brodie* merely led the Quebec courts to proceed with a little more caution when convicting Jehovah's Witnesses for seditious conspiracy. Later in 1936, several Witnesses were convicted of this charge at the provincial court level, this time with indictments that carefully specified the nature of the seditious conspiracy. On appeal to the Court of King's Bench Appeal Division in *Duval* v. *R.*,[11] the court upheld the convictions, stating that the pamphlets that the Witnesses had been distributing constituted "an appeal to all to condemn and have a supreme contempt for all forms of organized authority, whether civil or ecclesiastical." In any case, the Appeal Court had been supplied with the essential elements missing in *Brodie,* which the court insisted on applying on its merits.[12] The pleadings themselves obviated any anticipated objection from the Supreme Court of Canada, given that the arguments and issues were entirely procedural. Accordingly, Duval chose not to appeal to the Supreme Court of Canada.[13]

Brodie and *Duval* represented the first stirrings of discontent prior to the ban of Jehovah's Witnesses for alleged sedition a few years later. Penton points out that subsequent to the "blitz" in which Brodie was initially arrested, Quebec City Council passed By-law 184, which set a $100 fine for anyone distributing literature in the city without prior police approval. This by-law was to be challenged all the way to the Supreme

---

9 *Ibid.* at 194-95.

10 *Ibid.* at 198-99.

11 (1938), 64 Que. K.B. 270, leave to appeal to S.C.C. refused (1938), [1938] S.C.R. 390, [1938] 4 D.L.R. 747 [hereinafter *Duval* cited to Que. K.B.].

12 *Ibid.* at 280.

13 *Ibid.* at 271.

Court of Canada in the well-known civil liberties challenge, *Saumur* v. *City of Quebec*.[14]

In August 1936, Maurice Duplessis and the Union Nationale Party were elected in Quebec with a resounding majority. A year later, Duplessis pushed through the Quebec *Communistic Propaganda Act*,[15] otherwise known as the Padlock Act because of its provision whereby anyone found using his property to promulgate the ideology of communism or bolshevism could have his property padlocked shut for a year in reprisal. The law was potentially so all-encompassing that it drew criticism from the popular press, including *Maclean's* magazine, where J.E. Keith wrote:

> While ostensibly anti-communist, the law can also be used against anti-clericals, who are growing stronger every day in the province. It is significant that the only sedition charges laid in the Quebec courts in the past five years have not been against Communists, who attack the economic system but against Jehovah's Witnesses who attack the priesthood.[16]

Section 12 of the new law in particular left Jehovah's Witnesses open to attack:

> It shall be unlawful to print, to publish in any manner whatsoever or to distribute in the Province any newspaper, periodical, pamphlet, circular, document or writing whatsoever propagating or tending to propagate communism or bolshevism.

As M. James Penton has remarked, "While the new act was not specifically directed against Jehovah's Witnesses, almost any unpopular publication, including theirs, could be labelled as 'tending to propagate communism.'"[17]

Although few charges were laid against Jehovah's Witnesses under the "Padlock Act," the police used it as a pretext for search and seizure, especially in Montreal where they confiscated Jehovah's Witnesses' literature, phonograph records and private papers.[18] Furthermore, the number of charges against members of the sect in Quebec steadily climbed each year. The Canadian Branch Servant, Percy Chapman, repor-

---

14　(1953), [1953] 2 S.C.R. 299, [1953] 4 D.L.R. 641, 106 C.C.C. 289 [hereinafter *Saumur* cited to S.C.R.].

15　S.Q. 1937, c. 11.

16　1 August 1937.

17　Penton, *supra*, note 2 at 122.

18　*Ibid.*

ted in the *1939 Yearbook of Jehovah's Witnesses* that charges against Witnesses in Quebec included selling without a licence, soliciting without a licence, blasphemous libel, defamatory libel, distributing seditious literature, seditious conspiracy, and even indecent assault.[19] The following year, he reported that 115 Witnesses had been charged with various offences, almost all of them in Quebec.[20]

Ironically, Jehovah's Witnesses in Quebec experienced a measure of reprieve during the Second World War compared to their fellow Witnesses in English-speaking Canada. Up to the beginning of the War, the number of Witnesses in Quebec was comparatively small. Those who lived there had had an opportunity to become "street smart" in the days of persecution during Duplessis' first term. Duplessis' Union Nationale Party had suffered a serious setback in the 1939 election that left both the Party and the Premier in disarray. Conrad Black, Duplessis' biographer, observed,

> He blundered disastrously in Sept 1939 by calling a snap election on the issue of participation in the war effort. The Quebec federal ministers, including Ernest Lapointe, Arthur Cardin and C.G. Power, threatened to resign, leaving Quebec defenceless against a conscriptionist English Canada if Duplessis was re-elected, and pledged that they would prevent conscription if Duplessis was defeated.[21]

Duplessis himself suffered from failing health, including diabetes exacerbated by a drinking problem.[22] Jehovah's Witnesses thus found themselves "on-side" with the majority of Quebeckers on the conscription issue, and for the time being were not unduly persecuted by Premier J.-A. Godbout's Liberal government in Quebec.

With the return to power of Duplessis and the Union Nationale Party in 1944, however, the situation radically changed. Duplessis personally took up the battle with Jehovah's Witnesses once again. It was a battle that was to last 15 years, to be ended once and for all by the Supreme

---

19 *1939 Yearbook of Jehovah's Witnesses* (New York: Watch Tower Bible and Tract Society, 1938) at 126, 130.

20 *1940 Yearbook of Jehovah's Witnesses* (New York: Watch Tower Bible and Tract Society, 1938) at 126, 130.

21 Conrad Black, "Duplessis, Maurice Le Noblet," in *The Canadian Encyclopedia*, Vol. 1 at 636.

22 *Ibid.* at 636–37.

Court of Canada decisions in *Roncarelli* v. *Duplessis*[23] and *Lamb* v. *Benoit*.[24]

II. THE POST-WAR STRUGGLE FOR CIVIL LIBERTIES IN QUEBEC

Nearly a year after the end of the Second World War, the civil liberties of English Canadians who happened to be Jehovah's Witnesses were fully restored with the tabling of an order-in-council[25] that terminated the interning of Witnesses in, as John Diefenbaker put it, "concentration camps."[26] But the struggle for civil liberties for Jehovah's Witnesses in Quebec was only just beginning. In Chateauguay, after 15 Witnesses had been arrested for distributing literature without a licence, the outdoor meeting that they had been advertising was disrupted by a mob of more than 1,000 men, women and children, about ten of whom participated in beating and kicking an individual Witness.[27] In Lachine, five Witnesses were mobbed by young hoodlums, who ripped up their placards and literature, and the public meeting the Witnesses had been advertising had to relocate. Eventually the meeting was conducted under police guard.[28] Most of the time, however, the police were by no means protective of the rights of Jehovah's Witnesses, and by September 1946, some 800 charges had been laid against them, despite the fact that there were only 300 Witnesses in the entire province. About $100,000 had been levied in bail bonds,[29] most of the security being supplied by Montreal restaurateur Frank Roncarelli, himself a Jehovah's Witness.

Maurice Duplessis consolidated his power through the 1940s and '50s to almost dictatorial levels where Jehovah's Witnesses were concerned, as Professor Penton observed:

> Although the federal government in Ottawa was no longer able to do much to inhibit the activities of Jehovah's Witnesses—much as certain members of it might have liked to do so—in Quebec neither the Roman Catholic Church nor civil authorities had any intention of ending their anti-Witness campaign. Catholic clergymen, including Cardinal

---

23 (1959), [1959] S.C.R. 121, 16 D.L.R. (2d) 689 [hereinafter *Roncarelli* cited to S.C.R.].

24 (1959), [1959] S.C.R. 321, 123 C.C.C. 193, 17 D.L.R. (2d) 369 [hereinafter *Lamb* cited to S.C.R.].

25 Order-in-Council P.C. 3030 (15 August 1946).

26 *Debates*, 1946, Vol. 3 at 3308.

27 Penton, *supra*, note 2 at 184, citing the Montreal *Gazette* and the *Montreal Star*.

28 *Ibid.* at 183.

29 *Ibid.* at 185, 281-302. See also *1945 Yearbook of Jehovah's Witnesses* (New York: Watch Tower Bible and Tract Society, 1944) at 92, 93.

Villeneuve, continued to inveigh against them. Priests preached bitter sermons about "these apostles of heresy" and sometimes suggested the use of a broom, stove poker, or kettle of hot water on them when they called at Catholic homes. Catholic writers argued that they were the tools of communism, and now, once again, policemen, public officials and, above all, Premier Maurice Duplessis decided to suppress them through the most sweeping series of arrests ever carried out against any religious movement in Canadian history.[30]

This phenomenon was described by Mr. Justice Ivan Rand in the Supreme Court decision in *Roncarelli* v. *Duplessis*:[31]

In 1945 the provincial authorities began to take steps to bring an end to what was considered insulting and offensive to the religious beliefs and feelings of the Roman Catholic population. Large scale arrests were made of young men and women, by whom the publications mentioned were being held out for sale, under local by-laws requiring a licence for peddling any kind of wares. Altogether almost one thousand of such charges were laid. The penalty involved in Montreal, where most of the arrests took place, was a fine of $40, and as the Witnesses disputed liability, bail was in all cases resorted to.

The attempts of Duplessis to control the activities of the Witnesses continued to be thwarted by the fact that as quickly as they were arrested, the Witnesses were released on bail, thanks to the intervention of Frank Roncarelli. As Justice Rand explained, Roncarelli, "being a person of some means, was accepted by the Recorder's Court as bail without question, and up to 12 November 1946, he had gone security in about 380 cases, some of the accused being involved in repeated offences."[32] Rand elaborated:

. . . The security of the appellant [Roncarelli] was taken as so satisfactory that at times, to avoid delay when he was absent from the city, recognizances were signed by him in blank and kept ready for completion by the Court officials. The reason for the accumulation of charges was the doubt that they could be sustained in law. Apparently the legal officers of Montreal, acting in concert with those of the Province, had come to an agreement with the attorney for the Witnesses to have a test case proceeded with. Pending that, however, there was no stoppage of the sale of the tracts and this became the annoying circumstance that produced the volume of proceedings.[33]

---

30 Penton, *supra*, note 2 at 184-85.

31 *Supra*, note 23 at 131.

32 *Ibid.* at 131.

33 *Ibid.* at 131–32.

When on 12 November 1946 the province resorted to cash bail instead of security bonds, Roncarelli's role in providing security effectively ended.

In the wake of this persecution by both the authorities and the general public, the Witnesses circulated, beginning on 25 November 1946, more than a million copies of the exposé *Quebec's Burning Hate for God and Christ and Freedom Is the Shame of All Canada*,[34] a tract in which the Witnesses roundly condemned the Roman Catholic Church for allegedly supporting the mob action in Chateauguay and Lachine, and attacked the police and the judiciary for allegedly being under the thumb of the clergy. Later, the tract was described in detail by Justice Rand in his Supreme Court of Canada judgment in *Boucher v. R.*:[35]

> The document was headed "Quebec's Burning Hate for God and Christ and Freedom Is the Shame of All Canada": it consisted first of an invocation to calmness and reason in appraising the matters to be dealt with in support of the heading; then of general references to vindictive persecution accorded in Quebec to the Witnesses as brethren in Christ; a detailed narrative of specific incidents of persecution; and a concluding appeal to the people of the province, in protest against mob rule and gestapo tactics, that through the study of God's Word and obedience to its commands, there might be brought about a "bounteous crop of the good fruits of love for Him and Christ and human freedom."

Mr. Justice Rand went on to provide concise details:

> The incidents, as described, are of peaceable Canadians who seem not to be lacking in meekness, but who, for distributing, apparently without permits, bibles and tracts on Christian doctrine; for conducting religious services in private homes or on private lands in Christian fellowship; for holding public lecture meetings to teach religious truth as they believe it of the Christian religion; who, for this exercise of what has been taken for granted to be the unchallengeable rights of Canadians, have been assaulted and beaten and their bibles and publications torn up and destroyed, by individuals and by mobs; who have had their homes invaded and their property taken; and in hundreds have been charged with public offences and held to exorbitant bail. The police are declared to have exhibited an attitude of animosity toward them and to have treated them as the criminals in provoking by their action of Christian profession and teaching, the violence to which they have been subjected; and public officials and members of the Roman Catholic Clergy are said not only to have witnessed these outrages but to have been privy to

---

34 Toronto: Watch Tower Bible and Tract Society, 1946. Reprinted in *Awake!*, 8 January 1947. The tract is reproduced in its entirety in Penton, *supra*, note 2 at 281–302.

35 (1950), [1951] S.C.R. 265 at 284 [1950] 1 D.L.R. 657, 9 C.R. 127, 96 C.C.C. 48, rev'g (1949), [1949] Q.R. (K.B.) 238, 8 C.R. 97, 95 C.C.C. 119 [hereinafter *Boucher* cited to S.C.R.].

some of the prosecutions. The document charged that the Roman Catholic Church in Quebec was in some objectionable relation to the administration of justice and that the force behind the prosecutions was that of the priests of that Church.[36]

Duplessis declared that the tract *Quebec's Burning Hate* was "intolerable and seditious." As Attorney-General, he ordered a clamp-down. Within a month, according to Duplessis' estimate, 400 Witnesses were before the courts, facing more than 1,000 charges. Individual Witnesses had as many as 100 separate charges against them, and bail bonds were set as high as $500 cash.[37] In addition to the arrests, Duplessis ordered the cancellation of Frank Roncarelli's liquor licence to punish the restaurateur's temerity in declaring himself a Jehovah's Witness and providing bail for many of his fellow believers.

Although Roncarelli was neither arrested nor charged, his restaurant liquor licence was revoked on 4 December 1946, causing him so much economic hardship in the months to follow that he was forced to sell his business. Three of his fellow Witnesses arrested that week were, like Roncarelli, to argue their cases all the way up to the Supreme Court of Canada: Louise Lamb, a young lady who on 7 December was arrested without warrant and charged with publishing a seditious libel for distributing comparatively bland Watch Tower literature on a street corner in Verdun; Aime Boucher, a farmer who on December 11 was charged with publishing a seditious libel after distributing copies of *Quebec's Burning Hate* to several persons at St. Joseph in the District of Beauce, Quebec; and Laurier Saumur, "who, with over one hundred charges against him, was perhaps the most frequently arrested man in Canadian history."[38]

III. *RONCARELLI* V. *DUPLESSIS*

Frank Roncarelli had posted perhaps $90,000 in bail for fellow Witnesses by the time the bail system was changed to a cash basis on 12 November 1946; at that time, his role in providing bail ended, and in any case "all of the charges in relation to which he had become surety were dismissed."[39] By 21 November, when Duplessis discovered who had been providing bail, Roncarelli was no longer a surety for the Witnesses. Nonetheless, Duplessis acted with characteristic authoritarianism to revoke

---

36 *Ibid.* at 285.

37 Penton, *supra*, note 2 at 188-89, 211.

38 *Ibid.* at 211.

39 *Roncarelli, supra*, note 23 at 132.

Roncarelli's liquor licence. Duplessis himself announced his action to the press on the very day of the revocation, as reported in the *Montreal Gazette* of 5 December:

> In statement to the press yesterday, the Premier recalled that: "Two weeks ago, I pointed out that the Provincial Government had the firm intention to take the most rigorous and efficient measures possible to get rid of those who under the names of Witnesses of Jehovah, distribute circulars which in my opinion, are not only injurious for Quebec and its population, but which are of a very libellous and seditious character. The propaganda of the Witnesses of Jehovah cannot be tolerated and there are more than 400 of them now before the courts in Montreal, Quebec, Three Rivers and other centres.
>
> "A certain Mr. Roncarelli has supplied bail for hundreds of witnesses of Jehovah. The sympathy which this man has shown for the Witnesses, in such an evident, repeated and audacious manner, is a provocation to public order, to the administration of justice and is definitely contrary to the aims of justice."[40]

Roncarelli first learned of the revocation of his liquor licence and the seizure of his stock of liquor from the press reports.[41]

Prior to the cancellation of the licence, on 25 November, the police had raided a Kingdom Hall in Sherbrooke, Quebec and seized copies of *Quebec's Burning Hate*. Investigation revealed that the building which housed the Kingdom Hall was owned by Roncarelli. At about that time, the senior Crown Prosecutor in Montreal, Oscar Gagnon, "formed the opinion that the circular was a seditious libel and that its distribution should be prevented."[42] Erroneously concluding that Roncarelli had something to do with the distribution of the tract, Gagnon contacted Edouard Archambault, the manager and sole member of the Quebec Liquor Commission, to convey this information and to report that Roncarelli had also "acted as bailsman for a great number of Witnesses of Jehovah":

> On receiving this information from M. Gagnon, M. Archambault read the circular, "Quebec's burning hate" and had a conversation with M. Paquette, the Recorder-in-Chief at Montreal, who confirmed the statements as to the appellant furnishing bail.
>
> At this point M. Archambault formed the opinion that he should cancel the permit held by the appellant, but before taking any action he

---

40 *Ibid.* at 137 per Rand J.

41 *Ibid.* at 183 per Abbott J.

42 *Ibid.* at 162 per Cartwright J.

telephoned [Duplessis] at Quebec, told him what information he had received and that he proposed cancelling the permit.[43]

Archambault assigned an agent to ascertain if Roncarelli the restaurateur was also Roncarelli the bondsman. When he ascertained to his satisfaction that this was the case, he telephoned Duplessis again on 30 November, ". . . Et, la le Premier Ministre m'a autorise, il m'a donne son consentement, son approbation, sa permission, et son order de proceder."[44] Mr. Justice Cartwright found that what was said by Duplessis in this telephone conversation "was so far a determining factor in the cancellation of the permit as to render him liable for the damages caused thereby to the appellant."[45]

Roncarelli was given no prior notice and no opportunity to show cause why his licence ought not to be cancelled. After attempting to run his business for six months without a liquor licence, he found he could not operate it at a profit, and so was forced to sell.[46]

Roncarelli's whole loss flowed from the cancellation of the permit, Cartwright decided, but nevertheless he concluded that the act of the commission was "authorized by law" and "not an actionable wrong," and therefore Duplessis could not be answerable in damages for directing or approving the cancellation.[47] After all, the Commission had total discretion to "to grant, refuse, or cancel permits for the sale of alcoholic liquor" under s. 9(e) of the *Alcoholic Liquor Act*.[48] Had the Legislature intended to limit this discretion, it would have specified that in the Act. Hence, said Cartwright, "I am forced to conclude that the Legislature intended the commission 'to be a law unto itself'."[49]

Justices Taschereau and Fauteux both dissented on the basis of a technicality. Article 88 of the *Code of Civil Procedure* required a plaintiff in an action against a public officer to give notice of any action pending against him. This notice was in effect a condition precedent, and failure to fulfil the condition was a total bar to the claim. As Attorney-General, Duplessis was a public officer, not acting in a private capacity. He was also legal adviser to the Commission. Even if he committed an error, it would be a fallacy to conclude that he did not act in an official capacity

---

43 *Ibid.* at 163.

44 *Ibid.*

45 *Ibid.* at 164.

46 *Ibid.* at 147 per Martland J.

47 *Ibid.* at 169–70.

48 R.S.Q. 1941, c. 255.

49 *Roncarelli, supra,* note 23 at 168.

outside the scope of his duties.[50] Fauteux J. maintained that Duplessis acted in good faith, and even though he committed an illegality, that did not amount to a delict under the *Civil Code* or an offence known to penal law. The illegality in any case was made in the course of his function as Attorney-General. Article 88 of the *Civil Code* therefore applied.[51]

Mr. Justice Martland tackled the question of the propriety of Duplessis becoming involved in a matter that was clearly the domain of the Liquor Commission by asking four succinct questions:

1. Was there a relationship of cause and effect as between the respondent's acts and the cancellation of the appellant's permit?
2. If there was such a relationship, were the acts of the respondent justifiable on the ground that he acted in good faith in the exercise of his official functions as Attorney-General and Prime Minister of the Province of Quebec?
3. Was the cancellation of the appellant's permit a lawful act of the Commission, acting within the scope of its powers as defined in the *Alcoholic Liquor Act*?
4. Was the respondent entitled to the protection provided by art. 88 of the *Code of Civil Procedure*?[52]

He answered these questions as follows:

1. Yes;
2. No;
3. No; and
4. No.

Martland elaborated by saying that there was "ample evidence" to show that the cancellation of Roncarelli's permit was "the result of instructions given by the respondent to the manager of the Commission,"[53] but Duplessis was not acting in the exercise of any official capacity he possessed when he gave those instructions.[54] The Commission cannot abdicate its own discretionary functions and powers to act upon the direction of a third party, no matter who that party may be.[55] Martland concluded:

---

50 *Ibid.* at 129–30.

51 *Ibid.* at 178–181.

52 *Ibid.* at 150–51.

53 *Ibid.* at 151.

54 *Ibid.* at 155.

55 *Ibid.* at 157.

I do not think that it was a function either of the Prime Minister or of the Attorney-General to interfere with the administration of the Commission by causing the cancellation of a liquor permit. That was something entirely outside his legal functions. It involved the exercise of powers which, in law, he did not possess at all. . . . In my view, when he deliberately elected to use means which were entirely outside his powers and were unlawful, he did not act in the exercise of his functions as a public official.[56]

Chief Justice Kerwin and Justice Locke concurred with Martland. Justices Abbott and Rand, in separate judgments, were also in fundamental agreement with Martland, but framed the central question in *Roncarelli* in terms of the Rule of Law, for which the case has since been regarded as an important authority. Abbott said simply that he did not find it necessary to cite "the wealth of authority" supporting the notion that a public officer is responsible for acts peformed by him without legal justification. He cited Dicey's "Law of the Constitution":

. . . Every official, from the Prime Minister down to a constable or a collector of taxes, is under the same responsibility for every act done without legal justification as any other citizen. The Reports abound with cases in which officials have been brought before the courts, and made, in their personal capacity, liable to punishment, or to the payment of damages, for acts done in their official character but in excess of their lawful authority.[57]

It followed that Duplessis was acting without any legal authority whatsoever when he purported to authorize and instruct Archambault to cancel Roncarelli's licence.[58]

Perhaps the most scathing and memorable judgment came from Ivan Rand, who likened the decision to cancel Roncarelli's licence to an act of "fraud and corruption":[59]

What could be more malicious than to punish this licensee for having done what he had an absolute right to do in a matter utterly irrelevant to the *Liquor Act*? Malice in the proper sense is simply acting for a reason and purpose knowingly foreign to the administration, to which was added here the element of intentional punishment by what was virtually vocation outlawry.

---

56 *Ibid.* at 158.

57 9th ed. at 193.

58 *Roncarelli, supra,* note 23 at 185.

59 *Ibid.* at 140–41.

Duplessis' act "was a gross abuse of legal power" expressly intended to punish Roncarelli for an act wholly irrelevant to the *Liquor Act*. The arbitrary punishment intentionally inflicted on Roncarelli by Duplessis led to "the destruction of his economic life as a restaurant keeper within the province." Rand continued:[60]

> . . . Action dictated by and according to the arbitrary likes, dislikes and irrelevant purposes of public officers acting beyond their duty, would signalize the beginning of disintegration of the rule of law as a fundamental postulate of our constitutional structure.

This principle enunciated by Mr. Justice Rand makes *Roncarelli* one of the most important constitutional cases in Canada.

IV. *Lamb v. Benoit*

The case of Louise Lamb[61], like *Roncarelli*, took a dozen years to wend its way through the courts before being heard by the full Supreme Court of Canada in the same 1958-59 session as *Roncarelli*. Although not as well known as *Roncarelli*, it stands for almost the same proposition: that civil authorities who deliberately violate the rule of law cannot hide behind the mantle of office, or benefit from statutory protections designed to protect individuals in authority who are acting within the proper sphere of public duty.

On 7 December 1946, Louise Lamb stood on a street corner in downtown Verdun, Quebec, distributing Watch Tower literature along with three female companions, each of whom occupied a different corner of the intersection. A police constable approached Miss Lamb and told her that someone in a car nearby wished to question her. She was aware that the other three women had been recipients of a similar request and had complied, and so she complied as well.[62] She got into the car and immediately was interrogated by Paul Benoit, a special officer of the Quebec Provincial Police. He searched her hand bag, which contained copies of *The Watchtower* and *Awake!* magazines, but which did not contain any copies of *Quebec's Burning Hate* or any copies of the 8 January

---

60 *Ibid.* at 142.

61 *Lamb, supra*, note 24.

62 *Ibid.* at 345 per Locke J.

1947 issue of *Awake!*, in which the entire text of the tract had been reprinted.[63]

After examining the magazines in Miss Lamb's purse, Benoit remarked, "There is nothing here." He said they would let her go, but as she was getting out of the car he changed his mind, looked through her purse again, extracted and read a letter addressed to Miss Lamb from the Watch Tower Society, and decided to detain her after all. All four women were then driven to provincial police headquarters in Montreal, where they were told by Benoit that they would remain in custody over the weekend.[64] Although Benoit signed a detention order, no information was laid against any of the women, and no warrant had been issued for their arrest. They were not permitted to telephone a lawyer or anyone else. They were fingerprinted and photographed.[65]

On the following Monday, Lamb expected to go to Court, but instead was escorted by Benoit to his office in police headquarters. He told her he had "made arrangements to have her released," but there were "certain formalities" to be complied with first. He asked her to sign statements to the effect that she would take no action against the provincial police for having detained her. When Lamb refused to sign these disclaimers, Benoit told her that if she refused she would be charged with sedition and "it would cost her a lot of money to get out of gaol."[66] When Lamb persisted in her refusal, she was charged along with the other women with "publishing a seditious libel entitled 'Quebec's Burning Hate for God and Christ and Freedom'"

> by exhibiting it in public, by delivering it from door to door with the view to its being read, the said writing being likely to raise discontent and disaffection among His Majesty's subjects and being likely to provoke feelings of ill will and hostility between different classes of subjects of His Majesty in Canada.[67]

The women were also charged with conspiracy to publish a seditious libel.

---

63 Locke J. in his statement of facts incorrectly states that the booklet had been published in the 8 December 1946 issue of *The Watchtower*. (*Ibid.* at 344.) The *Watchtower* has always been published on the first and fifteenth of each month, the *Awake!* on the eighth and twenty-second. They are issued more than a month ahead of time to Witnesses for distribution, and so it would not be unusual for Witnesses to be distributing January issues of the *Awake!* in early December. Miss Lamb, apparently, was distributing December 1946 issues of the magazines.

64 *Ibid.* at 345.

65 *Ibid.* at 346.

66 *Ibid.*

67 *Ibid.*

As Mr. Justice Locke remarked, Lamb "had done nothing other than to stand offering the unobjectionable publications above mentioned"—and this had been the conclusion of the judge of the Sessions of the Peace, before whom Lamb appeared on 10 January 1947.[68] Through her solicitors, Lamb gave notice that she would bring an action against Benoit and three other policemen for false arrest and damages, and on 10 July 1947 an action was commenced in which Lamb asserted that the arrest had been unlawful, and that the charges had been laid and the prosecution conducted without reasonable or probable cause, maliciously and in bad faith.[69]

Benoit and the other officers countered in their defense that they had acted in good faith in discharging their duties as police officers, and that the action against them was statute-barred because it had not been brought within six months, as required by the *Magistrate's Privilege Act*[70] and the *Provincial Police Force Act*.[71] In order for these statutes to apply, however, the act complained of must have been "done by him in the performance of his public duty."[72] Although most of the officers had been performing their public duty by obeying the orders of Benoit, who was their superior officer, Benoit himself was in a different situation, as Mr. Justice Locke observed:

> He does not say that he was ordered to take the appellant or the others into custody and there were no circumstances entitling him to arrest the appellant without a warrant, and his conduct was from the outset unlawful. The appellant was not committing any offence at the time she was taken in charge and when, at police headquarters, she asked with what offence she was charged the information was refused to her.
>
> As no warrant had been issued either for the arrest or detention of the appellant, the person in charge of the cells apparently required some written authority to detain her and this appears to have been given by Benoit. . . . The evidence does not disclose that he believed that she had committed any offence justifying this detention. Indeed, as his conduct showed, the fact that he offered to release the appellant if she would sign the document, which presumably released him as well as the others concerned from any claim for damages, appears to me to show that he was well aware that the arrest and detention had been unlawful.[73]

---

68 *Ibid.* at 347.

69 *Ibid.* at 347–48.

70 R.S.Q. 1941, c. 18.

71 R.S.Q. 1941, c. 47.

72 *Lamb, supra,* note 24 at 348.

73 *Ibid.* at 354–56.

Since Benoit's actions were unlawful, and since (as the Quebec Court of Appeal had found) they were conducted in bad faith, he could not benefit from statutory protection that was designed to protect officials acting within the scope of their "public duty." Locke cited Halsbury on actions against public authorities and public officers, in a statement which seemed on all fours with the circumstances in *Lamb*: "In every case the defendant must have acted in good faith, and therefore actions for deceit or malicious prosecution may be commenced after the expiration of the six months' limit."[74] Locke concluded:

> As to Benoit, without any lawful justification, he caused the arrest and imprisonment of the appellant and was responsible for the laying of the information and the prosecution which followed. The appellant was subjected to the ignominy of arrest and prosecution for the offence of distributing a seditious libel, of which offence Benoit knew from the outset she was innocent.[75]

Mr. Justice Rand was even more explicit with respect to the six month statute of limitations not applying to Benoit:

> To Benoit it was patent that the appellant was not distributing the issue of the paper containing the alleged libel, nor was there a scrap of evidence on which he could have acted to connect her with the acts of the other three distributors. All this is concluded by what took place at the police station when, in what is said to be the routine practice, Miss Lamb was offered her liberty in exchange for a release of claims, a proposal which she spurned. There was lacking that state of mind necessary to the benefit of the limitation under either s. 7 [of the *Magistrate's Privilege Act*] or s. 24 [of the *Provincial Police Act*] and his defence must be rejected.[76]

Chief Justice Kerwin and Justices Cartwright and Judson concurred with Rand and were fundamentally in agreement with Locke and Martland. But still the court remained divided, Justices Taschereau, Fauteux and Abbott being of the opinion that Benoit should be protected by the provision of the *Provincial Police Act*, with its six-month limitation period. The court awarded Lamb $2,500 in damages, with costs in all courts, in her action against Benoit, but dismissed the action against the other three policemen involved.

---

74 *Ibid.* at 357.

75 *Ibid.* at 361.

76 *Ibid.* at 343 per Rand J.

V. *BOUCHER V. R.*

In a situation in which many members of a minority religious group had been charged under the *Criminal Code* with seditious libel and seditious conspiracy, the definition of "sedition" naturally became of paramount importance. A definition had been adopted by the legislature in the 1892 *Criminal Code*, but it was modified several times thereafter. By 1946, s. 133 of the *Code* read as follows:

133. Seditious words are words expressive of a seditious intention. . . .
   2. A seditious libel is a libel expressive of a seditious intention.
   3. A seditious conspiracy is an agreement between two or more persons to carry into execution a seditious intention.
   4. Without limiting the generality of the meaning of the expression "seditious intention" everyone shall be presumed to have a seditious intention who publishes or circulates any writing, printing or document in which it is advocated, or who teaches or advocates, the use, without the authority of law, of force, as a means of accomplishing any governmental change within Canada.[77]

Several defenses to a charge of sedition were contained in a separate, supplementary section, s. 133A, which had been enacted in 1930:

133A.   No one shall be deemed to have a seditious intention only because he intends in good faith,—
   (a)   to show that His Majesty has been misled or mistaken in his measures; or
   (b)   to point out errors or defects in the government or constitution of the United Kingdom, or of any part of it, or of Canada or of any province thereof, or in either House of Parliament of the United Kingdom or of Canada, or in any legislature, or in the administration of justice; or to excite His Majesty's subjects to attempt to procure, by lawful means, the alteration of any matter in the state; or,
   (c)   to point out, in order to their removal, matters which are producing or have a tendency to produce feelings of hatred and ill-will between different classes of His Majesty's subjects.[78]

It fell to the Supreme Court of Canada to determine whether the lower courts, which had convicted Boucher,[79] had applied these sections of the

---

77 *Criminal Code*, R.S.C. 1927. c. 36, s. 133, as am. S.C. 1936, c. 29, s. 4.

78 *Criminal Code*, R.S.C. 1927, c. 36, s. 133A, as en. S.C. 1930, c. 11, s. 2.

79 *R. v. Boucher* (1949), [1949] Q.R. (K.B.) 238, 8 C.R. 97, 95 C.C.C. 119.

Criminal Code fairly.

The Quebec Court of Appeal had been divided on the issue of whether the trial judge, Justice Savard, had misdirected the jury when he stated that all that had to be demonstrated was that the booklet *Quebec's Burning Hate* "might raise up illwill or hostility between different classes" of Canadians. In a 3-2 decision, Letourneau C.J. and Galipeault J.A. dissenting, the Appeal Division affirmed the conviction. An automatic right to appeal was thus established, and the appeal was heard by five justices of the Supreme Court of Canada in May and June of 1949. Here too, the court was divided, Chief Justice Rinfret and Justices Kerwin and Taschereau moving for a new trial and Justices Rand and Estey calling for the conviction to be quashed.

Thereafter, in June 1950, additional arguments were heard by the full court. Rinfret and Taschereau maintained their position, and were joined by Cartwright and Fauteax. They were of the opinion that the question of whether the tract was seditious was one of fact to be determined by a jury, and therefore was outside the domain of the Supreme Court of Canada, which should be concerned only with matters of law. On the other hand, Rand and Estey also stood fast, and were joined by Locke and Kellock. They applied s. 33A(*c*) of the *Code*, stating that the intention of the tract was not to stir up hatred to the point of violence, but "to point out, in order for their removal, matters which are producing or have a tendency to produce feelings of hatred and ill-will between different classes of His Majesty's subjects." As Justice Estey remarked, the facts set out in the pamphlet may be "objectionable, even repugnant to some and provoke ill-will and hatred. That, however, is not sufficient. It still remains to be proved as a fact that the accused acted with a seditious intention."[80] The onus of such proof rested on the Crown, but the Crown had not proved beyond a reasonable doubt that Boucher acted with such an intention. Furthermore, said Estey, "the intention to incite violence or public disorder or unlawful conduct against His Majesty or an institution of the State is essential" to all cases of sedition:

> This pamphlet, particularly when considered with due regard to the provisions of sections 133A, as I previously stated, does not disclose any evidence that would properly support a verdict that the accused possessed a seditious intention.[81]

Kerwin adopted his judgment from the first hearing, and it looked as if the case would go back for re-trial:

---

80 *Boucher, supra,* note 35 at 314.

81 *Ibid.* at 315.

There was evidence in the document itself, taken, as it must be, with all the other circumstances, upon which a jury after a proper charge as outlined above, could find the accused guilty, and the conviction should, therefore, be set aside and a new trial directed.

But then, at the eleventh hour, Kerwin had a change of heart. Immediately following this written judgment, he added:

> Since the distribution of my reasons in this appeal, there has been a reargument as a result of which I have been persuaded that the order suggested by me is not the proper one to make. With the exception of the last paragraph, what I have already said may stand, with the following additions. The intention on the part of the accused which is necessary to constitute seditious libel must be to incite the people to violence against constituted authority or to create a public disturbance or disorder against such authority. . . .
>
> Whatever else might be said of the contents of the pamphlet, there is not in it, read in the light of all the surrounding circumstances, any evidence upon which a jury, properly instructed, could find the appellant guilty of the crime with which he was charged. The conviction should be set aside and a judgment and verdict of acquittal entered.[82]

Thus one of the Supreme Court of Canada cliff-hangers of the century—rivalled only by *Saumur* v. *City of Quebec,* as we shall see—was resolved in favour of Aime Boucher and hundreds of other Jehovah's Witnesses charged with sedition. This did not deter prosecutors in Quebec from laying new charges against some Jehovah's Witnesses—this time for "spreading false news" rather than sedition.[83]

VI. *SAUMUR* V. *CITY OF QUEBEC*

Laurier Saumur was kept busy during the late 1940s defending himself from more than 100 charges of seditious libel, seditious conspiracy, and peddling religious literature without a licence. He received fines of $40 for some of the charges and served sentences of up to three months in jail for others. He also mounted litigation in his own right, even suing the courts themselves, although without much success: the Supreme Court of Canada in *Saumur* v. *Recorder's Court of Quebec*[84] quashed his appeal

---

82 *Ibid.* at 282-83.

83 *R.* v. *Carrier* (1951), 104 C.C.C. 75, 16 C.R. 18.

84 Quebec Superior Court No. 51647 (unreported); judgment on the merits in the Court of King's Bench (Appeal Side) also unreported. The judgment of the Court of King's Bench granting leave to appeal to the Supreme Court of Canada is reported under the name *Barry* v. *Recorder's Court (Quebec)* at [1947] Que. K.B. 308. A motion to quash the appeal

after ruling that a *habeas corpus* appeal arising out of a conviction under a municipal by-law arose out of a criminal charge, and therefore was outside the jurisdiction of the Supreme Court by virtue of s. 36 of the *Supreme Court Act*.

Saumur had already launched a separate action against the City of Quebec in which he asked that By-law 184, passed in 1933, be declared to be "ultra vires, unconstitutional, illegal, null and void and be quashed and set aside for all legal purposes."[85] A parallel action had been initiated by Damase Daviau in *Daviau* v. *City of Quebec*.[86] When Daviau decided not to pursue his case beyond the Court of Appeal level, Saumur was accepted as a substitute plaintiff in the appeal to the Supreme Court of Canada.[87] Both the Superior Court and the Court of Queen's Bench (appeal side) had dismissed the *Daviau* action, but Justice Bertrand had dissented, allowing the appeal to the Supreme Court.[88]

Saumur sought to quash By-law 184 by having it ruled *ultra vires* the City of Quebec and indeed *ultra vires* the Province of Quebec. Clause 1 of the by-law stated:

1. It is by the present by-law forbidden to distribute in the streets of the City of Quebec, any book, pamphlet, booklet, circular, or tract whatever without having previously obtained for so doing the written permission of the Chief of Police.

The by-law begged several questions. What was its "pith and substance"? Was it *intra vires* the provincial legislature? If so, was it within the power of the municipality to pass laws that seemed to encroach on freedom of the press and freedom of religion? Each of the justices considered these questions in turn, and came up with different answers.

Mr. Justice Rand pointed out that it was difficult to establish the pith and substance of a particular piece of legislation without first examining the practice or procedure followed in granting a licence.

The practice under it is undisputed and as stated to us by counsel is this: when a license is sought, a copy of the document or writing proposed to be distributed is brought to the police department and there the chief officer, acting with or without the city solicitor or others, or in his

---

was allowed by the Supreme Court of Canada, [1947] S.C.R. 492.

85 *Saumur* v. *City of Quebec* (1953), [1953] 2 S.C.R. 299, [1953] 4 D.L.R. 641, 106 C.C.C. 289, [hereinafter *Saumur* cited to S.C.R.].

86 (1951), [1951] Que. P.R. 140.

87 Penton, *supra*, note 2 at 210–11.

88 *Saumur*, *supra*, note 85 at 320.

absence, an official representing him, peruses the writing; if there is nothing in it considered from any standpoint to be objectionable, the license issues; if there is, suggestions are made that the offending matter be removed, but if that is not done the license is refused.[89]

This practice, said Rand, "comprehends the power of censorship," and is "not remotely connected with street regulation."[90] It therefore is parallel to the questions decided in the *Alberta Press Reference*,[91] where Sir Lyman Duff stated that free public discussion of public affairs is the "breath of life" for parliamentary institutions:

Any attempt to abrogate this right of public debate or to suppress the traditional forms of the exercise of the right (in public meeting and through the press), would, in our opinion, be incompetent to the legislatures of the provinces, or to the legislature of any one of the provinces, as repugnant to the provisions of The British North America Act.

Rand identified freedom of speech, religion and the inviolability of the person as "original freedoms" which were not only the "necessary attributes and modes of self-expression" of humanity, but also the "primary conditions of their community life within a legal order." Sanctions on civil rights lie within the exclusive jurisdiction of the nation, not of the province. This is especially so where religion is concerned:

That legislation "in relation" to religion and its profession is not a local or private matter would seem to me to be self-evident: the dimensions of this interest are nationwide; it is even today embodied in the highest level of the constitutionalism of Great Britain; it appertains to a boundless field of ideas, beliefs and faiths with the deepest roots and loyalties; a religious incident reverberates from one end of this country to the other, and there is nothing to which the "body politic of the Dominion" is more sensitive.[92]

Justices Rand, Kellock and Estey reviewed the legislative history of the principle of freedom of religion in Europe and America, including the *Quebec Act* of 1774, showing that religion "stands in the first rank of social, political and juristic importance." Only in despotisms, Rand remarked, does authority view "with fear and wrath the uncensored

---

89 *Ibid.* at 326.

90 *Ibid.* at 326, 332.

91 *Reference re Alberta Statutes* (1938), [1938] S.C.R. 100, [1938] 2 D.L.R. 81, aff'd (1938), [1938] 3 W.W.R. 337 (P.C.).

92 *Saumur, supra,* note 85 at 329.

printed word."[93] Kellock explicitly rejected the argument that religion fell under the provincial legislative jurisdiction within any of the heads of power of s. 92 of the *British North America Act*.[94] Following the reasoning of Chief Justice Duff in the *Alberta Press Reference*, Kellock concluded that the by-law was *ultra vires* the City of Quebec, and "its officers and agents are restrained from in any way attempting to enforce its provision."[95] Estey remarked that even if the provincial *Freedom of Worship Act*[96] was *intra vires*, "By-law 184 would be in conflict therewith and, therefore, could not be competently passed by the City of Quebec because it was not authorized by the terms of its charter."[97]

Mr. Justice Locke took a somewhat different approach, reviewing in detail the testimony of Watch Tower Society vice-president Hayden Covington, and alluding to the testimony of several other witnesses in the lower court:

> By way of defence, the respondent called a number of witnesses, including a Roman Catholic priest, a Rabbi, a Clergyman of the Church of England and a Professor of Philosophy, to give evidence on such diverse subjects as to what were the elements of a religion, as to whether preaching alone was a religious act, whether the belief of the Jehovah's witnesses, as disclosed in a number of periodicals and pamphlets which it was shown were circulated by them, was in fact a religion, whether the activities of the witnesses were in fact religious activities, what was "the meaning in philosophy" of religious freedom "as regards modern civilization," whether the distribution of religious tracts in the homes of the people was a violation of religious liberty and as to whether they thought is permissible to disobey the law if to obey it was contrary to their religious beliefs.[98]

Combined with the frank admission by the counsel for the City that "the by-law was directed against the contents of the documents,"[99] the purpose of the by-law to impose censorship became crystal clear:

> Among the witnesses called by the City was a Mr. Ohman, described as an Evangelist of the Seventh Day Adventist Church, who had obtained a permit which allowed him to sell the religious literature of his faith

---

93 *Ibid.* at 326–27, 343–49.

94 *Ibid.* at 349, 351.

95 *Ibid.* at 356.

96 R.S.Q. 1941, c. 307, s. 2.

97 *Saumur, supra,* note 85 at 362.

98 *Ibid.* at 367.

99 *Ibid.* at 368.

from house to house. According to this witness, he had received a good reception when he applied for his permit. . . . Apparently, the Chief of Police of the City of Quebec did not object to the teachings of the Seventh Day Adventists while disapproving that of Jehovah's Witnesses.

After reviewing the law, including the *Alberta Press Reference*, Locke concluded that the true purpose of the by-law was not to regulate traffic in the streets "but to impose a censorship on the written expression of religious views and their dissemination, a constititional right of all the people of Canada." This, he said, was tantamount to creating a new criminal offence.

Rinfret and Taschereau stated that in their view the pith and substance of the by-law was to control the use of streets, and pamphlet regulation was secondary:

> Even if the motive of the City was to prevent the Jehovah's Witnesses from distributing their literature in the streets, that could never be a reason to render the by-law illegal or unconstitutional, since the City had the power to pass it.[100]

Furthermore, said Rinfret, freedom of worship is a "civil right within the provinces"; it is not an absolute right, but is subject to provincial control.[101] Cartwright and Fauteau also united in dissent, saying that it is within the competence of the Legislature to authorize a municipality to pass by-laws in relation to "the use of highways" and "police regulations and the suppression of conditions likely to cause disorder."[102]

On the one hand, Rand, Kellock, Estey and Locke were united in stating that the by-law was *ultra vires*, if not of the province then at least of the City of Quebec. On the other hand, Rinfret, Taschereau, Cartright and Fauteau were of the view that the by-law was not only *intra vires*, but totally valid. Once again it fell to Justice Kerwin to cast the deciding ballot. He ruled the matter to be *intra vires* both the City and the province, since in his view "the right to practise one's religion is a civil right in the Province under head 13 of section 92 of the *British North America Act*." He specifically rejected the views of Duff C.J.C. and Cannon J. in the *Alberta Press Reference*, stating that freedom of the press was also a civil right within the province.[103] However, the Province of Quebec had its own mechanism for supporting freedom of religion in *The Freedom*

---

100 *Ibid.* at 300–301.

101 *Ibid.* at 301.

102 *Ibid.* at 388.

103 *Ibid.* at 324.

of Worship Act[104] The Quebec City Charter could not abrogate the terms of this Act by encroaching on "the free exercise and enjoyment" of their religion. By distributing their literature, the Witnesses were not compromising the peace and safety of the Province.

> The above reasons do not justify a declaration that the by-law is ultra vires the City of Quebec since, if not otherwise objectionable, the by-law may have its effect in other cases and under other circumstances; but they do warrant a declaration that the by-law does not extend so as to prohibit the appellant as a member of Jehovah's Witnesses from distributing in the streets of Quebec any book, pamphlet, booklet, circular or tract of Jehovah's Witnesses included in the exhibits and an injunction restraining the City, its officers and agents from in any way interfering with such actions of the appellant.[105]

Ultimately, Kerwin's decision was adopted by the court.

The Quebec government attempted to counter the decision of the Supreme Court of Canada by passing into law on 28 January 1954—less than three months after the *Saumur* decision had come down—*An Act Respecting Freedom of Worship and the Maintenance of Good Order*,[106] which could effectively remove the narrow line of defence identified by Kerwin's reliance upon the *Freedom of Worship Act* of 1941. Buoyed by the success of his action in *Saumur* v. *City of Quebec*, on the day after the new legislation passed into law Laurier Saumur initiated yet another action that was to be heard in the Supreme Court of Canada as *Saumur* v. *A.G. Quebec*.[107]

The Supreme Court of Canada gave a cool reception to what was to become "Saumur's last case." The Superior Court had held that the statute was *intra vires*. When Saumur appealed to the Court of Appeal, the action had been dismissed on the ground that it could not properly be initiated in the province. The Supreme Court of Canada took a position similar to the one it had adopted in *Greenlees*, but this time confined itself strictly to consideration of the law of Quebec as it applies to declarations. A declaratory action does not exist in Quebec, it ruled, since the courts of Quebec deal only with actual, existing disputes. To have a right of action, one must demonstrate an interest in a dispute, in accordance with the *Code of Civil Procedure*, art. 77. Therefore, an action could not be initiated based merely on the fear of future injury.

---

104 R.S.Q. 1941, c. 307, s. 2.

105 *Saumur, supra*, note 85 at 322.

106 S.Q. 1953–54, c. 15.

107 (1964), [1964] S.C.R. 252, 45 D.L.R. (2d) 627, aff'g (1963), [1963] Que. Q.B. 116, 37 D.L.R. (2d) 703 (C.A.).

VII. CHAPUT V. ROMAIN

Only once in all of the cases heard by the Supreme Court of Canada involving Jehovah's Witnesses did the court come to a unanimous decision in their favour, and that was in the case of *Chaput v. Romain*.[108] For once the court was agreed that the police had overstepped their bounds in entering a private home without a warrant, breaking up an admittedly orderly religious meeting, and seizing Jehovah's Witness literature.

The incident occurred on 4 September 1949 in the village of Chapeau, Quebec. The meeting was attended by about 30 people and was being conducted by Albin Gotthold, a resident of Ottawa. About two-thirds of the way through the meeting, Chaput saw three Quebec provincial policemen, in uniform, outside his house in their car. He went outside to see what they wanted. They walked to the house to meet Chaput and one of the policemen, Roger Chartrand, asked if there was a meeting there. When Chaput replied in the affirmative they asked if they might enter, and he consented. Mr. Justice Kellock described what happened next:

> The respondents went inside and, according to them, after observing the proceedings for approximately two minutes, Chartrand told the minister, then reading from the Bible, to discontinue, that the meeting would have to be broken up and those present dispersed. Gotthold's request to be allowed to finish, which he said would take some twenty minutes, met with refusal, and he was compelled to stop. The respondents then seized the Bible Gotthold had been reading, the hymn books, a number of booklets on religious subjects published by Jehovah's Witnesses and the collection box, dispersed the meeting, and conducted Gotthold to the ferry which plies across the Ottawa River between Chapeau and Pembroke, Ontario, upon which they placed him. No charge of any kind was at any time laid against any of the participants in the meeting and none of the items seized have ever been returned.[109]

Mr. Justice Locke, also citing the transcript, pointed out that the Bible—the Catholic Douay Version—was taken out of Gotthold's hand. He quoted Chaput as saying that Gotthold had asked the officers if he was under arrest.

> Mr. Chartrand says no—"Well," he says, "I am not going to stop until I am under arrest," so, as he said that, Mr. Young stepped up and he said, "Let us take Mr. Gotthold"—so they walked back to the people

---

108 (1955), [1955] S.C.R. 834, 1 D.L.R. (2d) 241, 114 C.C.C. 170 [hereinafter *Chaput* cited to S.C.R.].

109 *Ibid.* at 846.

which was in my own home, told them all to get up and get out, of my own home, so they all got up and Mr. Chartrand and Mr. Young took Mr. Gotthold by the arms and took him out and they placed him in the car and took him away to the ferry.[110]

Locke then cited ss 199 and 200 of the *Criminal Code*:

199. Every one is guilty of an indictable offence and liable to two years' imprisonment who, by threats or force, unlawfully obstructs or prevents, or endeavors to obstruct or prevent, any clergyman or other minister in or from celebrating a divine service, or otherwise officiating in any church, chapel, meeting-house, school-house or other place for divine worship. . . .
200. Every one is guilty of an indictable offence and liable to two years' imprisonment who strikes or offers any violence to, or arrests upon any civil process or under the pretense of executing any civil process, any clergyman or other minister who is engaged in or, to the knowledge of the offender, is about to engage in, any of the rites or duties in the last preceding section mentioned, or who, to the knowledge of the offender, is going to perform the same, or returning from the performance thereof.

Locke concluded that the actions of the policemen "were thus wholly unlawful and criminal in their nature and they were liable to prosecution and imprisonment."[111] Their actions were a "flagrant violation" of the right to freedom of worship.[112]

Mr. Justice Kellock cited testimony on the part of Chartrand which alleged that he had received instructions from Montreal. "We were ordered to dismiss the meeting," he said. ". . . That is part of the instructions I had, to go inside of the house and abolish the meeting, *support the public*."[113] According to Edmond Romain, Chartrand had told his fellow officers that there was a meeting of Jehovah's Witnesses which was to be stopped. He added:

Of course we understand that's illegal in Quebec, and that's the reason why there were no other questions necessary.

Q. You understand it is illegal in Quebec?
A. That's what I'm given to understand. . . .

---

110 *Ibid.* at 861.

111 *Ibid.* at 862.

112 *Ibid.* at 864.

113 *Ibid.* at 847, italics in original.

> Q. What gave you the impression it was illegal for Jehovah's Witnesses to hold meetings in Quebec?
> A. Well, I read it in the papers. . . .
> Q. You never bothered about the law, to see if it was illegal?
> A. No; I have nothing to do with that.[114]

In their defence, the policemen stated that 1) Chaput belonged to an organization that had decided to distribute literature which contained seditious libel; 2) he was in possession of pamphlets that contained seditious libel and was "creating animosity and hate between different classes of society"; 3) the policemen were fulfilling their duties as peace officers "for the maintenance of peace, order and public security"; 4) they were acting in good faith and without malice; 5) they had received instructions from their superior officer to do what they did; and 6) Chaput had failed to serve each policeman personally indicating the cause of action, as required by the *Magistrate's Privilege Act*. In addition, Chartrand set up the identical defence used by the policemen in *Lamb*—that the proceedings had not been taken within six months after the events complained of, in accordance with the *Provincial Police Act* and the *Magistrate's Privilege Act*.

Each police officer had made the further "completely frivolous plea" (in the opinion of Kellock) that they "went to see the plaintiff concerning an infraction, which might have been committed by him against the Motor Vehicle Act." Not only was this plea "unsupported by any evidence," but in addition "no evidence was adduced in support of the allegation that the appellant belonged to an organization of the character mentioned, nor that he was in possession of any pamphlets of the description pleaded."

The police expressly admitted that they had not read any of the seized pamphlets either before or after the seizure. When pressed as to why they had embarked on the mission, the third officer, Const. Linden Young, said, "When [Chartrand] gets orders there must be something wrong," and Romain testified, "Just in the fact that we were sent up there to do that, I figured there must be something wrong." Romain further testified that he did not know the meaning of "seditious."[115]

Despite the seemingly blatant violation of civil liberties in this case, both the Superior Court and the Court of Appeal dismissed the action.[116] In doing so, Justice Bisonnette, for the majority, stated that since Chaput had invited members of the public, he had lost any right to complain. He also said that "it was well known . . . that Jehovah's

---

114 *Ibid.* at 848.

115 *Ibid.* at 848–49.

116 (1954), [1954] Q.R. (Q.B.) 794 (Que. C.A.)

Witnesses were carrying on activities of a seditious character."[117] Both Bisonnette and Justice Hyde completely misapplied *Boucher* v. *R.*, according to Kellock. Although he did not go as far as Locke in condemning the police action as "criminal," Kellock said that in effect the policemen were "carrying out an illegal instruction" that was not in the execution of a public duty. Their action therefore did not fall within the protection of the *Provincial Police Act* or the *Magistrate's Privilege Act*.

Perhaps surprisingly, given his traditional position of opposing Jehovah's Witnesses, Taschereau agreed with Chief Justice Kerwin and Justices Estey and Locke that the police had committed an illegal act, violating ss 199 and 200 of the *Criminal Code*. Even Cartwright and Fauteau, also traditionally opposed to the Witnesses, took the position that the police were not responding to a situation that was in any way illegal. Justice Abbott, on the other hand, was of the opinion that the police had acted "in good faith" when they entered Esymier Chaput's house without a warrant, because the meeting being held there had been advertised as a public meeting. However, Abbott J. conceded in a classic understatement that in dispersing the meeting, the police had "exceeded the bounds of good faith."

The various decisions of the Supreme Court of Canada culminating in the 1959 appeals of *Roncarelli* and *Lamb* had revealed to legislators the need to adopt a Bill of Rights with teeth. John Diefenbaker had recently swept into power with a mandate to do exactly that. With Jehovah's Witnesses urging him on with petitions and resolutions garnering nearly half a million names, he introduced in 1960 the *Canadian Bill of Rights*, which to this day is useful as an interpretative statute that in theory protects Canadians from unfair Federal government action or legislation. To the extent that federal legislation violates the *Canadian Bill of Rights*, that legislation must be interpreted in such a way as to avoid the conflict. Weak though it is, the *Canadian Bill of Rights* was a major step towards entrenching in the Canadian Constitution the fundamental freedoms established in *Saumur* and *Boucher* as being so centrally important in a vibrant democracy. But perhaps the most enduring contribution of the *Canadian Bill of Rights* was the preamble, which affirmed "that men and institutions remain free only when freedom is founded upon respect for moral and spiritual values *and the rule of law*." This legacy from *Roncarelli* was reaffirmed in the preamble to the *Canadian Charter of Rights and Freedoms* in 1982, and more recently in draft proposals to change the pivotal *Constitution Act, 1867* by adding a similar preamble.[118]

---

117 *Chaput, supra,* note 107 at 852.

118 *Draft Legal Text; October 9, 1992,* based on the Charlottetown Accord of August 28, 1992.

CHART OF THE FOUR CENTRAL SUPREME COURT OF
CANADA DECISIONS REGARDING JEHOVAH'S WITNESSES

	Boucher (1950)	Saumur (1953)	Roncarelli (1959)	Lamb (1959)
Rinfret	O	O	—	—
Kellock	X	X	—	—
Estey	X	X	—	—
Kerwin	X	X	X	X
Rand	X	X	X	X
Locke	X	X	X	X
Cartwright	O	O	O	X
Taschereau	O	O	O	O
Fauteux	O	O	O	O
Abbott	—	—	X	O
Martland	—	—	X	X
Judson	—	—	X	X

Key: X = in favour; O = opposed; — = not sitting.

4

Towards a Canadian Bill of Rights

I. PETITIONING FOR A CANADIAN BILL OF RIGHTS

News of the arbitrary action against Jehovah's Witnesses by Premier Duplessis as Attorney-General of Quebec was received with umbrage and indignation by the liberal press of English Canada, but in Catholic Quebec the suppression of Jehovah's Witnesses during the late forties was a popular political strategy. Opposition to Duplessis outside Quebec was at least in part generated by the widespread circulation in English Canada of the Watch Tower tract *Quebec's Burning Hate*. Realizing that the majority of Canadians outside Quebec favoured freedom of speech, freedom of religion, and freedom of the press, Jehovah's Witnesses embarked on a new campaign in which they advanced the idea of a nation-wide Bill of Rights that would afford constitutional protection. The proposal was drafted in petition form, and beginning on 2 March 1947, Witnesses across the nation gathered signatures.

The petition to Parliament was designed to show "the necessity for you to make more secure the fundamental liberties of every person in Canada." It pointed out that Canada, by participating in the Atlantic Charter and the United Nations Organization, had declared to the world "that this country stands for full freedom of speech, press and worship." Other nations such as Australia and the U.S. had enshrined such rights in their constitutions, and Canada should follow suit:

> . . . Recent experiences of Jehovah's Witnesses in the Province of Quebec prove that throughout the whole Dominion basic personal rights are open to attack and loss because of a failure to have them guaranteed by a written constitution.
>
> Wherefore, your petitioners humbly pray that your honourable house take immediate steps to enact or cause to be inserted in the British North America Act a federal bill of rights, similar to those of Australia and the United States, in order to secure freedom of speech, press and

worship to all people against municipal, provincial, or national abridgement.

In some instances, the police in Quebec arrested Jehovah's Witnesses for circulating the petition, charged them with "soliciting signatures to a petition," confiscated their petition sheets, and visited persons who had signed the sheets to threaten and intimidate them.[1] But by the time the petition was presented to Parliament on 9 June 1947, more than half a million signatures had been collected.[2]

By then, Parliament had already appointed a joint committee of the Senate and the House of Commons to look into the question of human rights in Canada, thanks largely to the persistence of John Diefenbaker.[3] Diefenbaker, along with T.C. Douglas, had already become the Witnesses' most active advocate in Parliament. Now he turned his attention to the potential of a Bill of Rights:

> What would a bill of rights do? It would establish the right of the individual to go into the courts of this country, thereby assuring the preservation of his freedoms. These great traditional rights are merely pious ejaculations unless the individual has the right to assert them in the courts of law.[4]

Despite the fact that the ban on Jehovah's Witnesses as a seditious organization had been lifted, arrests of Jehovah's Witnesses on charges of seditious libel and seditious conspiracy continued in Quebec. In a four-month period following the arrest of Lamb, Boucher and Saumur, some 843 Witnesses were arrested. These figures did not seem to impress Premier Duplessis, however, and in the spring session, the Duplessis government passed into law legislation that allowed municipalities to require a licence for distribution of literature—parallel to City of Quebec By-law 184 that even at that moment was being challenged in the courts by Laurier Saumur. Violators of the new provision were subject to a $100 fine and three months in jail.[5] It therefore became necessary, from the perspective of Jehovah's Witnesses, to circulate yet another petition advocating the drafting of a Bill of Rights. This time, the petition

---

1 Glen How, "The Case for a Canadian Bill of Rights" (1948), 26 Can. Bar Rev. 759 at 768. See also *Awake!*, 22 July 1947.

2 *Debates*, 1947, Vol. 4 at 3912.

3 *Ibid.* at 3139–83.

4 *Ibid.* at 3197.

5 S.Q. 1947, c. 77, s. 13, art. 371, para. 2; and s. 18, art. 413, para. 11.

garnered a total of 625,510 signatures.[6] Yet these highly successful petitions were only part of the overall strategy of Jehovah's Witnesses.

II. COVINGTON AND HOW ARGUE FOR A BILL OF RIGHTS

Watch Tower lawyers Hayden Covington (at that time Vice-President of the Watch Tower Bible and Tract Society in New York) and Glen How had been busy not only drafting the petitions and defending Jehovah's Witnesses in the courts (How had been counsel in *Greenlees, Boucher,* the *Saumur* cases, *Chaput, Lamb,* and dozens of major cases in the lower courts) but writing articles on the idea of a Canadian Bill of Rights. Two of these articles—Covington's "The Dynamic American Bill of Rights" and How's "The Case for a Canadian Bill of Rights"—were published in *The Canadian Bar Review* in April and May, 1948. These essays were re-printed by Jehovah's Witnesses and circulated to virtually every lawyer, judge and member of Parliament in the country.

There is no doubt that Covington had written his article with a Canadian audience in mind. On the first page he mentioned "the tradi-tional British view" and compared it to Canada's view of the rights of the individual, as opposed to the American view:

> It has been said that, in Canada, there is an entire "absence of any at-tempt to fetter the freedom of our legislatures by fundamental limita-tions such as abound in the United States federal and state consti-tutions." In other words, the appeal of persons injured by ill-considered legislation must be to those who elected the government, *i.e.,* the people. Remedy can be obtained only by long drawn-out political process.[7]

By contrast, the American Bill of Rights had given the American judiciary "extraordinary power"; it was "a dynamic instrument in the hands of the people":

> The insertion of the rights of the individual into the rock-ribbed provisions of the Constitution is in sharp contrast to the Anglo-Saxon custom of relying on vague, unwritten tradition. Traditions can be very elusive when the citizen asks a court to apply them against the government. . . .[8]

Covington reviewed American case law illustrating how the Bill of Rights had been applied in the U.S., inevitably focusing on the issue of freedom

---

6 *Debates*, 1949, Vol. 1 at 371.

7 (1948), 26 Can. Bar Rev. 638.

8 *Ibid.* at 640.

of worship as it applied to Jehovah's Witnesses in such cases as *Gobitis* v. *Minersville School District*.[9] He concluded:

> In some countries such as Canada and Great Britain, where the courts are less able to protect the citizen against legislative or executive denial of his rights, criticism is heard of the constant boiling of litigation under the Bill of Rights in the United States. Opponents of the American system contend that it is a bad thing to allow litigants to challenge in the courts acts or decrees of the government; that such power results in the disintegration of the liberties themselves.
>
> The answer to the contention that civil rights are just as secure in such countries can be found in the facts. Compare the security available to the people in the courts of the United States with the insecurity of those in countries without a Bill of Rights. This insecurity lies entirely in the inability of the courts to perform the same protective function over personal freedoms as do the courts of the United States. It is in the realm of civil liberties, at least, that the sovereignty of the legislatures should not be absolute. In this field the courts should enter and remain. Then, and only then, will there be security.[10]

In his article in the May 1948 issue of *The Canadian Bar Review*, Glen How discussed some of the leading cases pertaining to freedom of the press and other civil liberties, including the *Alberta Press Reference*. He pointed out that quasi-constitutional instruments such as the *Magna Carta* and the *Bill of Rights* of the United Kingdom were vastly overrated as instruments for preservation of civil liberties. In the case of the *Magna Carta*, for example, "freedom of speech, freedom of worship, due process of law, equality before the law—these things were not even remotely dreamed of in the days of John. The press had not even been invented."[11] How described the British *Bill of Rights* as a statute providing freedom of speech in Parliament alone, quite different from the instrument he had in mind in which a Bill of Rights would be fully embedded in the constitution.

How, like Covington, salted his essay with allusions to ongoing Jehovah's Witness litigation. The British *Bill of Rights*, he said, which technically was still in force in Canada, declared that prosecutions for petitioning the King were illegal.

---

9 310 U.S. 586, 60 S. Ct. 1010, 84 L. Ed. 1375 (1940).

10 Covington, *supra*, note 7 at 668.

11 How, *supra*, note 1 at 765.

This provision has not prevented Canadian citizens from being prosecuted within the past year at Verdun, Quebec, for circulating a petition asking the Canadian government to enact a modern Bill of Rights. They were charged with "soliciting signatures to a petition." Despite the fact that the cases have been pleaded, these citizens have been waiting nearly a year for judgment. Prosecutions of this sort are no doubt completely illegal, but until we get some enforceable law that says so, such mediaeval outrages will probably continue.[12]

Such violations of civil liberties, How argued, were commonplace in Canada. He reviewed in detail the arguments in *Saumur* v. *Recorder's Court of Quebec*, which the Supreme Court had refused to hear because the appeal was from a writ of *habeas corpus* in a criminal matter, and observed:

What has been done by the Quebec legislature and by the courts in the *Saumur* case is, I submit, in direct conflict with the law as expounded by the Supreme Court of Canada. Mr. Justice Cannon of the Supreme Court has said that distributing information is something "every citizen of Canada can do lawfully and without hindrance or fear of punishment,"[13] unless in doing so he infringes on the *Criminal Code*.

This statement of the law did not prevent Laurier Saumur from spending three months in the Quebec jail.[14]

Alluding to the propensity of the justice system to wink at principle in favour of technicalities, How said that Mr. Justice Cannon's statement of law in the *Alberta Press Reference* case was satisfactory, but only in an abstract way:

Until legal provisions, with adequate sanctions, permit a citizen to apply to the courts for the protection of his rights, those rights may be no more than a pious hope. A written Bill of Rights, permitting suitable appeals, would invalidate reactionary by-laws and statutes that destroy the liberties upon which the framework of democracy depends.[15]

How also pointed out that a form of business tax was being used unfairly to keep Jehovah's Witnesses off the streets. Despite the fact that the Witnesses offered their tracts for small sums, and often gave them away, a Montreal recorder in *City of Montreal* v. *Furlan* found that the Witnesses were engaged in business, and each Jehovah's Witness was thereupon

---

12 *Ibid.* at 768.

13 *Reference re Alberta Statutes*, (1938), [1938] S.C.R. 100 at 145.

14 How, *supra*, note 1 at 782.

15 *Ibid.*

required to procure a $100 permit. But the cost of the permit was far in excess of the amount of money the average Jehovah's Witness would make from distributing tracts in a given year:

> This decision is much closer to prohibition than to taxation. There is no appeal from the decision of a Quebec Recorder. Whatever he decides is the law, irrespective of the rights denied. Efforts to gain review in the Supreme Court of Canada on a writ of *certiorari* were denied, on the ground that appeals to the Supreme Court must come from the provincial court of appeal.[16] There was no legal remedy whereby this unfair exaction could be prevented.[17]

On the law of sedition in Canada, How pointed out that Canada had recorded more sedition cases since the enactment of the *Criminal Code* in 1892 than all the rest of the British Commonwealth combined, excluding India. Citing Zechariah Chafee's *Free Speech in the United States*,[18] which includes sections on Canadian law, How alluded to an Alberta judge who had remarked in 1916, "There have been more prosecutions for seditious words in Alberta in the past two years than in all the history of England for over one hundred years."[19] How said that the difficulty seemed to be that Canadians were unable to distinguish between writings which were in reality "a menace" and those which were merely distasteful to the majority. "In certain parts of the country there has never been any real acceptance of the idea that the mere expression of objectionable facts and opinions is no crime."[20] He went on to discuss the *Brodie*[21] case and freedom of worship, and concluded:

> In a land such as ours, peopled by so many different racial and ethnic groups, rights depending on tolerance alone are far from safe. In order that every Canadian may walk without fear; in order that all may know the value which Canada sets upon the dignity of the individual; in order that freedom of expression and freedom of worship may be effectively guaranteed and enforced by the courts; the rights of the individual citizen must be written into the constitution. The respect thus shown for the rights of others, and the consciousness of equality for every person and group in every province, would remove divisive fears and be a real

---

16 *Furlan* v. *City of Montreal* (1947), [1947] S.C.R. 216.

17 How, *supra*, note 1 at 784.

18 (Boston: Harvard University Press, 1941) at 512.

19 How, *supra*, note 1 at 789.

20 *Ibid.*

21 (1936), [1936] S.C.R. 188, 65 C.C.C. 289, [1936] 3 D.L.R. 81.

aid to national unity. For the world it would be further proof of Canada's maturity as a nation.[22]

How's article contains several of the arguments he was to make in court on behalf of Jehovah's Witnesses charged with sedition and other offences, and in litigation initiated in protest of the violation of the civil liberties of Jehovah's Witnesses.

III. *BOUCHER* AND THE FREEDOM TO CRITICIZE

In Quebec, pleas such as those of Covington and How for increased civil liberties fell on deaf ears, but the Supreme Court of Canada showed signs of budging from the entrenched position it had demonstrated in *Greenlees*. Clearly freedom of the press, freedom of expression, freedom of association, and freedom of religion were equally jeopardized by the ban on Jehovah's Witnesses, and continued to be jeopardized by the prosecutions in Quebec for seditious libel and seditious conspiracy, both *Criminal Code* offences that tended to trammel civil liberties if misused. The 4–4 split in the Supreme Court in the 1950 *Boucher* decision demonstrated that the Supreme Court had a long way to go in terms of adjusting its attitudes where civil liberties were concerned. True, the win was a vast improvement over the loss in the *Greenlees* case four years before—a loss which shocked Glen How into writing an article critical of the Supreme Court because, in his view, its jurisdiction was too narrow.[23] Several of How's suggestions in that article were adopted by the Canadian Parliament in the revamping of the *Supreme Court Act* in 1949. The *Boucher* case was one of the first major cases on sedition to be heard after the new statute became law. It was in fact first heard by the Supreme Court of Canada in May and June, 1949,[24] and in the second hearing a year later, arguments were heard by the full court. Chief Justice Rinfret continued to dwell on the technicalities of the law governing the Supreme Court, insisting on a rigid limiting of discussion to consideration of the points of dissent.[25] But other Justices of the Supreme Court of Canada were prepared to deliberate on the relevant law of the United Kingdom with respect to seditious libel. In lifting the corner of the rug of sedition, they found beneath it an outmoded tradition that did not bear preservation into the twentieth century.

---

22 How, *supra*, note 1 at 796.

23 How, "The Too Limited Jurisdiction of the Supreme Court" (1947), 25 Can. Bar Rev. 573.

24 *Boucher* v. R. [1951] S.C.R. 265, [1950] 1 D.L.R. 657, 9 C.R. 127, 96 C.C.C. 48 [hereinafter *Boucher* cited to S.C.R.].

25 *Boucher, Ibid.* at 268.

Mr. Justice Rand at least implied that any political authority that would insist on interpreting seditious libel as removing the right to criticize the government was two centuries out of date. "The crime of seditious libel is well known to the Common Law," he said.

> Up to the end of the 18th century it was, in essence, a contempt in words of political authority or the actions of authority. If we conceive of the governors of society as superior beings, exercising a divine mandate, by whom laws, institutions and administrations are given to men to be obeyed, who are, in short, beyond criticism, reflection or censure upon them or what they do implies either an equality with them or an accountability by them, both equally offensive. In that lay sedition by words and the libel was its written form.[26]

In those days, the crime of seditious libel was "a deduction from fundamental conceptions of government"; but during the centuries that followed, attitudes towards government changed:

> Constitutional conceptions of a different order making rapid progress in the 19th century have necessitated a modification of the legal view of public criticism; and the administrators of what we call democratic government have come to be looked upon as servants, bound to carry out their duties accountably to the public. The basic nature of the Common Law lies in its flexible process of traditional reasoning upon significant social and political matter; and . . . the substitution of new conceptions, under the same principle of reasoning, called for new jural conclusions.[27]

Today, no authority would hold that publishing a document merely tending to cause discontent or ill-will or hostility between rival groups (rather than specific illegal acts of violence) would constitute the crime of sedition, said Rand, for the obvious reason that freedom of thought and freedom of speech are the essence of democratic life. However controversial discussions may be in the social, religious or political arenas— however heretical or fanatical those ideas may seem—the compact that underlies a free society "accepts and absorbs these differences," weaving them into the fabric of society on the framework of freedom and order. These very differences become, in fact, the basis for social stability. Controversy is part of our everyday life, and serves to stimulate us "in the clarification of thought and, as we believe, in the search for the

---

26 *Ibid.* at 285–86.
27 *Ibid.* at 286.

constitution and truth of things generally."[28] Although Rand did not mention civil liberties, clearly he had them in mind.

In deference to these important underlying principles of civil rights, the sedition legislation at s. 133A of the *Criminal Code* itself contained a definition of "WHAT IS NOT SEDITION," including the defence of intending in good faith to show that the Crown had been misled or mistaken, to point out errors or defects in the constitution or in government action at various levels, or in the administration of justice. It was legal "to excite" fellow citizens to attempt to procure "the alteration of any matter in the state," as long as the means used was itself lawful. Yet another defence, one now mirrored in the new "hate laws" of Canada, is the defence of the intention in good faith "to point out in order to their removal, matters which are producing or have a tendency to produce feelings of hatred and ill-will between different classes of His Majesty's subjects." Underlying these provisions, said Rand, is the notion of "free criticism as a constitutent of modern democratic government." The provision protects "the widest range of public discussion and controversy, so long as it is done in good faith and for the purposes mentioned. Its effect is to eviscerate the older concept of its anachronistic elements."[29] Rand used the s. 133A provision to find that in publishing their tract *Quebec's Burning Hate*, Jehovah's Witnesses were merely pointing out, to achieve their removal, matters which tended to produce feelings of hatred and ill-will. They were not themselves promoting illegal conduct.

In their parallel decisions, Justices Kellock and Estey took Rand's line of argument in *Boucher* one step further. Kellock observed that the *Code* protects places of worship from acts of violence and disturbance. He cited *Beatty* v. *Gillbanks*[30] as authority for the proposition that those who resort to violence or disturbance are the lawbreakers "rather than those who exercise the right of free speech in advocating religious views however such views may be unacceptable to the former."[31] Estey added that "one may freely and forcefully express his views" even to the point of causing feelings of hatred and ill-will without opening himself up to charges of sedition, as long as he stays within "the limits defined by the law":[32]

> The statements . . . may be objectionable, even repugnant to some and provoke ill-will and hatred. That, however, is not sufficient.[33]

---

28 *Ibid.* at 288.

29 *Ibid.*, at 290.

30 (1882), 9 Q.B.D. 308.

31 *Boucher, supra,* note 24 at 302.

32 *Ibid.* at 308.

33 *Ibid.* at 314.

One of the central issues that the tract had been seeking to demonstrate, Estey pointed out, was that the right to freedom of worship was being denied to Jehovah's Witnesses. Any group in Canada that interfered with the right to worship of any other group, as alleged by Jehovah's Witnesses in *Quebec's Burning Hate*, naturally and quite correctly became the subject of public concern.[34]

Mr. Justice Locke reviewed the history of the case law concerned with sedition, including the two Jehovah's Witness cases from the 1930s, *Brodie* and *Duval*, and came to similar conclusions as Kellock and Estey. The right of free public discussion upon any subject touching the government of the state has long become firmly established. A rule of law by which judges, administrators or Ministers of the Crown are immune from criticism on the ground that to impugn their honesty or capacity might reflect badly upon the government of the day is totally at odds with the fundamental right to criticize the government freely, and the right of public discussion. These fundamental rights are subject only to laws of defamation and contempt of court. This amazingly prescient judgment was delivered by Locke nearly a decade before the *Roncarelli* decision with its even broader implications for the application of the Rule of Law.

Four of the five justices who ruled in favour of dismissing the charges of sedition against Aime Boucher in the course of their decisions canvassed several rights, including freedom of worship, freedom of expression, freedom of the press, freedom of speech, freedom to criticise the government, and freedom to criticise the courts. They did so, however, without departing from the context of the definition of "seditious" or "sedition." In the decisions they do not cite authority for their observations that such rights exist. It would seem that the justices did not regard this as being necessary. They held these rights to be inalienable, underlying the very system of democracy upon which Canada relies for its existence.

Curiously, however, four of the other justices, three of them from Quebec, did not regard the sedition issue as being one concerned with fundamental rights stemming from the British common law. In fact, Chief Justice Rinfret specifically stated that "it is unnecessary in the present case to refer to any pronouncements" from Great Britain, "because here in Canada we have the precise legislation on the issue."[35] That "precise legislation," in the opinion of Rinfret, overrode Boucher's civil liberties.

---

34 *Ibid.*

35 *Ibid.* at 275–76.

IV. *SAUMUR* AND FREEDOM OF WORSHIP

Several of the many issues raised in the *Saumur*[36] case concerned fundamental freedoms, including freedom of speech, freedom of the press, and most centrally of all, freedom of worship. As we have seen, the case revolved around the validity of a Quebec City by-law that required licences for distribution of literature and gave the Chief of Police discretion to refuse to issue the required licences if he objected to the content of the literature. The court decided that the primary object of the legislation was censorship, but in coming to that decision the judges discussed in detail the interplay of federal and provincial legislation and whether freedom of worship and freedom of the press fell under the jurisdiction of the federal government or the provincial government. The majority, including Kerwin J., held that the municipal legislation was *intra vires* the province and the City of Quebec.

Chief Justice Rinfret set the tone by specifying that the pith and substance of the by-law was to control and regulate the streets; literature distribution was a secondary purpose. Taschereau joined the Chief Justice in his dissent, and Cartwright and Fauteau wrote a parallel judgment that assumed that provincial jurisdiction applied. Clearly the Province and the City had jurisdiction to control the streets, all five justices agreed. Kerwin, however, detected a conflict between the legislation designed to control the streets and the principle of freedom of worship, even though "in my view the right to practise one's religion is a civil right in the Province under head 13 of section 92 of the *British North America Act*."[37] So was freedom of the press a civil right within the Province, he said.[38]

Rinfret and Taschereau agreed with the analysis of Kerwin where freedom of worship was concerned. Freedom of worship was not an absolute right, but was subject to control by the province, said Rinfret. Nor could freedom of worship be regarded as falling within the scope of the preamble of s. 91 of the *B.N.A. Act*.[39] Cartwright and Fauteau remarked that a provincial statute was not rendered invalid simply because it interfered to a limited degree with freedom of the press or of religion.[40] Kerwin pointed out specifically that Canada did not have a Bill of Rights

36 *Saumur* v. *City of Quebec* (1953), [1953] 2 S.C.R. 299, [1953] 4 D.L.R. 641, 106 C.C.C. 289 [hereinafter *Saumur* cited to S.C.R.].

37 *Ibid.* at 323.

38 *Ibid.* at 324.

39 *Ibid.* at 311, 315, and 323.

40 *Ibid.* at 386–88.

similar to the one contained in the U.S. Constitution, "and decisions on that part of the latter are of no assistance."[41]

Ivan Rand led the counteroffensive where the issues of freedom of worship and jurisdiction were concerned. He cited statute after statute which had placed safeguards on the freedom of religion, including the *Articles of Capitulation* (1760), the *Treaty of Paris* (1763), the *Quebec Act* (1774), the *Constitutional Act* (1791), the *Union Act* (1840), the *Canada Act* (1852), and the *Confederation Act* (1867). Taken together, certain parts of these statutes could be read as providing Canadians with protection of their civil liberties. But some of the statutes had been repealed and others superseded. Confusing though these provisions might be, "From 1760 . . . to the present moment religious freedom has, in our legal system, been recognized as a principle of fundamental character," said Rand. Furthermore, "That the untrammelled affirmations of religious belief and its propagation, personal or institutional, remain as the greatest constitutional significance throughout the Dominion is unquestionable."[42] In particular, the *Canada Act* of 1852 began with the preamble, "Whereas the recognition of legal equality among all Religious Denominations is an admitted principle of Colonial Legislation . . ." and concluded:

> It is hereby declared and enacted . . ., That the free exercise and enjoyment of Religious Profession and Worship, without discrimination or preference, so as the same be not made an excuse for acts of licentiousness, or a justification of practices inconsistent with the peace and safety of the Province, is by the constitution and laws of this Province allowed to all Her Majesty's subjects within the same.[43]

Interestingly, this wording was retained almost intact in the Quebec *Freedom of Worship Act*,[44] which was still in force in Quebec at the time of the *Saumur* litigation, and which, in the wake of *Saumur*, was to be amended in a transparent attempt to close off any loopholes where Jehovah's Witnesses were concerned.

Rand also alluded to the statutory history of the expression "Property and Civil Rights in the Province" as used in s. 92(13) of the *B.N.A. Act*. This examination "shows indubitably that such matters as religious belief, duty and observances were never intended to be included within that collocation of powers." He went on to discuss civil rights in more general terms:

---

41 *Ibid.* at 324.

42 *Ibid.* at 327.

43 1852 (14 & 15 Vic.), c. 175.

44 R.S.Q. 1941, c. 307, s. 2.

Strictly speaking, civil rights arise from positive law; but freedom of speech, religion and the inviolability of the person, are original freedoms which are at once the necessary attributes and modes of self-expression of human beings and the primary conditions of their community life within legal order. It is the circumscription of these liberties by the creation of civil rights in persons who may be injured by their exercise, and by the sanctions of public law, that the positive law operates. What we realize is the residue inside that periphery.[45]

Most civil rights such as the right to hold property and the right to conduct a business—indeed "most of the legal relationships between persons in Canada,"[46] are provincial in orientation; but many classes of subjects, including various aspects of criminal law pertaining to civil rights, were withdrawn from property and civil rights of the province by their exclusive vesting in the federal parliament. Civil rights against defamation, assault, false imprisonment, the punishments of the criminal law, and other civil rights thus lie within the exclusive jurisdiction of the Dominion.

In argument, Glen How had referred repeatedly to the *Alberta Press Reference*, and Rand dwelt at length on this 1938 decision of Sir Lyman Duff. Whereas Kerwin had been critical of the *Alberta Press* decision,[47] Rand cited the decisions of both Duff C.J.C. and Cannon J. at length, and with approval. Duff had remarked:

Any attempt to abrogate this right of public debate or to suppress the traditional forms of the exercise of the right (in public meeting and through the press) would, in our opinion, be incompetent to the legislatures of the provinces, or to the legislature of any one of the provinces, as repugnant to the provisions of The British North America Act.

Cannon had expressed a similar opinion:

Freedom of discussion is essential to enlighten public opinion in a democratic state; it cannot be curtailed without affecting the right of the people to be informed through sources independent of the government concerning matters of public interest. . . . Democracy cannot be maintained without its foundation: free public opinion and free discussion throughout the nation of all matters affecting the State within the limits set by the criminal code and the common law.[48]

---

45 *Saumur, supra*, note 36 at 329.

46 Peter Hogg, *Constitutional Law of Canada*, 3d edn. (Toronto: Carswell, 1992) at 539.

47 *Saumur, supra*, note 36 at 324.

48 *Ibid.* at 331. See *Reference re Alberta Statutes (Accurate News & Information Act of Alberta)* (1938), [1938] S.C.R. 100.

Kerwin pointed out, also citing Duff, that certain aspects of religion and freedom of speech may indeed be affected, legitimately, by provincial legislation; but where this occurs, "such legislation . . . must be sufficiently definite and precise to indicate its subject matter."[49]

Rand remarked that the Quebec City by-law, in the guise of regulating the roads, was intended in fact to impose censorship. The two apparent functions were inseparable; therefore the entire by-law was invalid, in his view. Kellock added:

> The by-law is not directed to the mere physical act involved in the handing to another of a document but has in view the contents of the document and the desirability or otherwise, in the view of the chief of police, as to its circulation. A document refused a licence would not involve anything more from the standpoint of obstruction of the highway or the impeding of those using it, than one with respect to which a licence is granted, and both documents, if discarded by the recipients, would equally be a source of litter. The by-law, however, is not concerned with such matters. Nothing more is needed, in my opinion, to discern the real nature and character of the by-law, namely, to provide that some material may reach the public using the streets, while the rest may not.[50]

Interestingly, Kellock cited Glen How's article "The Case for a Canadian Bill of Rights" as a source for some of his information, including the details of *Saumur* v. *Recorder's Court of Quebec*.[51]

Following the same line of argument as Rand, Kellock went one step further: he remarked that in his opinion, the by-law was *ultra vires* the province. Estey said the by-law was ultra vires the City of Quebec, and Locke said the by-law created a new criminal offence, and so was in effect *ultra vires* the province, not because it did not fall under the s. 92(13) head (Property and Civil Rights in the Province) but rather because it fell under the s. 91(27) head (the Criminal Law):

> The true purpose of the by-law is not to regulate traffic in the streets but to impose a censorship on the written expression of religious views and their dissemination, a constitutional right of all of the people of Canada, and to create a new criminal offence.[52]

Clearly the Supreme Court of Canada was not totally sure of itself with respect to the "constitutional right of all the people of Canada."

---

49 *Ibid.* at 333.

50 *Ibid.* at 338.

51 *Ibid.* at 349 (fn.) Compare How, *supra*, note 1 at 779–80.

52 *Ibid.* at 379.

There remained a great deal of confusion as to the meaning of "Civil Rights in the Province," several of the justices holding that "civil rights" should be interpreted in the American way to embrace civil liberties such as freedom of the press and freedom of worship. Rand was quick to point out the history of the phrase "Property and Civil Rights in the Province," including its origin in s. 8 of the *Quebec Act* of 1774. Kellock emphasized that "freedom of worship and profession was not a 'civil right' and certainly not a civil right 'within' the province of Lower Canada. It has been decided by the Judicial Committee that 'Property and Civil Rights' in the Act of 1774, although 'used in their largest sense' have exactly the same meaning in the statute of 1867."[53] Kellock J. cited *Citizens Insurance Co. v. Parsons*[54] as authority for the proposition that the term "civil rights" in this context applies to the entire body of law governing relationships between and among subjects: "The law which governs property and civil rights in Quebec is in the main the French law as it existed at the time of the cession of Canada, and not the English law which prevails in the other provinces."[55] Kellock concluded, "Any contention that the right to the exercise of religion is a mere 'civil right' is, therefore, for these reasons, quite untenable in my opinion. Even if such a matter could be so regarded, it would not be a civil right 'within the province.'"[56]

Nevertheless, in *Saumur* the majority, including, surprisingly, Kerwin, held that freedom of worship was precisely a "civil right within the province." It therefore became more imperative than ever to clarify precisely what were the "rights" that implicitly enjoyed constitutional protection. As Rand observed, civil liberties (as opposed to rights) up to that time were not legislated; they existed from the beginning as the residue. Peter Hogg was later to define this concept more succinctly: "Civil liberties exist when there is an absence of legal rules: whatever is not forbidden is a civil liberty."[57]

Like *Boucher*, *Saumur* demonstrated that reliance on an "implied bill of rights" that could be drawn from the *B.N.A. Act* and other constitutional or quasi-constitutional documents resulted in confusion and a rift in opinion even at the highest level of juristic consideration. In *Saumur*, both Kellock and Locke suggested the possibility of an implied bill of rights,[58] but the majority clearly did not agree with this notion. Frank Roncarelli's lawyer, F.R. Scott, supported the "implied bill of rights"

---

53 *Ibid.* at 348.

54 (1881), 7 App. Cas. 96.

55 *Ibid.* at 111.

56 *Saumur, supra,* note 36 at 349.

57 Hogg, *supra,* note 46 at 540.

58 *Saumur, supra,* note 36 at 354, 363.

theory in his book *Civil Liberties and Canadian Federalism*,[59] published not long after the *Roncarelli* decision came down. However, in the same year, Bora Laskin shot down the theory in an article in *The Canadian Bar Review*.[60] Peter W. Hogg remarks in *Constitutional Law of Canada*,

> The implied bill of rights theory was forgotten, or at least was never mentioned, by the Supreme Court of Canada from 1963 until 1978, when the Court decided the *Dupond* case (1978). In that case, Beetz J., for the majority, said that none of the fundamental freedoms that were inherited from the United Kingdom "is so enshrined in the Constitution as to be beyond the reach of competent legislation." This seemed to give the theory its quietus.[61]

Thomas Berger wrote of the *Dupond* decision, "Mr. Justice Beetz' idea of freedom of speech is a truncated one. He severed, for constitutional purposes, some of the essential means of exercising freedom of speech." Not even a statutory Bill of Rights would help reverse the effect of Beetz' decision in *Dupond* v. *Montreal*.[62]

V. THE CANADIAN BILL OF RIGHTS

To this day, Jehovah's Witnesses in Canada consider the adoption of the *Canadian Bill of Rights* as one of their major triumphs. Cases such as *Boucher, Saumur, Chaput, Roncarelli* and *Lamb* are justifiably regarded as stepping-stones along the way to the eventual enshrining of these principles in the *Canadian Charter of Rights and Freedoms*.

Whereas in *Boucher* and *Saumur*, the Supreme Court of Canada discussed questions regarding fundamental freedoms openly, in the other three central cases involving Jehovah's Witnesses the issue revolved around legal rights—the right to be free from police harassment in *Chaput*, the right to be free from persecution at the hands of elected authority in accordance with the rule of law in *Roncarelli*, and the right to be free from arbitrary arrest and malicious prosecution in *Lamb*. All of these issues were grist for the mill for the drafters of the *Canadian Bill of Rights*. The preamble of the Bill reflects these issues in its statement of the principles upon which the Bill is founded—"principles that acknowledge the supremacy of God, the dignity and worth of the human person and the position of the family in a society of free men and free institutions":

---

59 (Toronto: University of Toronto Press, 1959).

60 (1959), 37 Can. Bar Rev. 77 at 103.

61 Hogg, *supra*, note 46 at 775–76.

62 (1978) [1978] 2 S.C.R. 770.

Affirming also that men and institutions remain free only when freedom is founded upon respect for moral and spiritual values and the rule of law. . . .[63]

Section 1 of the *Canadian Bill of Rights* specifies that six enumerated "human rights and fundamental freedoms" would "continue to exist without discrimination by reason of race, national origin, colour, religion or sex." These six rights and freedoms include

(*a*)   the right of the individual to life, liberty, security of the person and enjoyment of property, and the right not to be deprived thereof except by due process of law;

(*b*)   the right of the individual to equality before the law and the protection of the law;

(*c*)   freedom of religion;

(*d*)   freedom of speech;

(*e*)   freedom of assembly and association; and

(*f*)   freedom of the press.

Section 2 focuses more particularly on legal rights. It is very clear under s. 5(2) that the *Canadian Bill of Rights* applies only to the legislation, regulations and other activities of or related to the Parliament of Canada. Nonetheless the model for the various provincial bills of rights and the *Charter* was set.[64]

The *Canadian Annual Review for 1960* gave credit where due with respect to the eventual adoption of the *Canadian Bill of Rights*:

There is great truth in the statement . . . that Jehovah's Witnesses, and not Mr. Diefenbaker, have given Canada her Bill of Rights. Almost without exception, the great decisions on civil liberties given by the Supreme Court of Canada since the war are the legal by-products of the pangs and sufferings of individual Jehovah's Witnesses at the hands of provincial and municipal authorities.[65]

Peter Hogg has stated that the omission of a bill of rights from the *Constitution Act, 1867* "never seems to have been regretted until after the second world war, when concern for civil liberties surfaced publicly and led to suggestions that a bill of rights should be adopted."[66] But the failure of the Diefenbaker government to entrench the *Canadian Bill of*

---

63 S.C. 1960, c. 44.

64 Including, eventually, the *Alberta Bill of Rights*, S.A. 1972, c. 1; R.S.A. 1980, c. A-16; and the Quebec *Charter of Human Rights and Freedoms*, S.Q. 1975, c. 6; R.S.Q. 1977, c. C-12.

65 (Toronto: University of Toronto Press, 1961) at 271.

66 Hogg, *supra*, note 46 at 779.

Rights in the constitution meant that the statute remained ineffectual where provincial legislation was concerned, and accordingly provincial violations of civil liberties, such as those in Quebec, would not have been covered by the *Bill of Rights* in any case. Furthermore, the *Canadian Bill of Rights* was superceded in 1982 by the *Canadian Charter of Rights and Freedoms*, except for two provision of the Bill that are not duplicated by the *Charter*: the protection of property rights in s. 1(*a*) and the guarantee of a fair hearing for determining rights and obligations in s. 2(*e*).[67]

The *Canadian Bill of Rights* was regarded by some authorities as merely a rule of interpretation or construction that would have little weight in countermanding or overruling even federal statutes; but in 1969 the Supreme Court of Canada, in a 6-3 decision, declared in *R. v. Drybones*[68] that s. 2 of the Bill had the effect of rendering inconsistent federal legislation inoperative. *Drybones* overrode s. 94(*b*) of the *Indian Act* which had made it an offence for an Indian to be drunk anywhere outside an Indian reserve. Ritchie J. for the majority declared that s. 94(*b*) flew in the face of s. 1(*b*) of the *Canadian Bill of Rights*, which guaranteed "equality before the law." Thereafter, the Supreme Court declared that the *Canadian Bill of Rights* had special status as a "quasi-constitutional instrument."[69]

Nonetheless, the *Canadian Bill of Rights* was widely regarded as ineffectual and inadequate to the task of protecting civil liberties in Canada, and almost immediately after its passage in 1960 a movement began to rework the Bill of Rights with a view to making it applicable to provincial as well as federal legislation. As Hogg points out, "The most prominent of the advocates of a bill of rights was Pierre Elliott Trudeau . . . , [who] steadily sought to achieve provincial consent to an amendment of the Constitution which would include a new amending formula and a new bill of rights."[70] The *Charter*, adopted in 1981 by the federal government and every province with the exception of Quebec, contains many of the elements of the *Canadian Bill of Rights*.

A comparison of the fundamental freedoms referred to in the *Charter* with those listed in the *Canadian Bill of Rights*, and indeed in the *American Bill of Rights*, is illuminating in terms of the degree to which the fundamental freedoms have expanded in scope in recent years. Section 2 of the *Charter* provides:

---

67 *Ibid.* at 640.

68 (1970), [1970] S.C.R. 282, 71 W.W.R. 161, 9 D.L.R. (3d) 473.

69 *Hogan v. The Queen* (1974), [1975] 2 S.C.R. 574 at 579, 48 D.L.R. (3d) 427, 18 C.C.C. (2d) 65, per Laskin J.

70 Hogg, *supra*, note 46 at 794.

2. Everyone has the following fundamental freedoms:
   (*a*) freedom of conscience and religion;
   (*b*) freedom of thought, belief, opinion and expression, including freedom of the press and other media of communication;
   (*c*) freedom of peaceful assembly; and
   (*d*) freedom of association.

Whereas the *Canadian Bill of Rights* guarantees only "freedom of religion," the *Charter* also guarantees "freedom of conscience" which moves far beyond concerns of religion into more secular beliefs. Furthermore, there is a major distinction between the individual's right to freedom of conscience and religion guaranteed by the *Charter* and the *collective* right implied in the First Amendment of the *American Bill of Rights*, which provides:

> Congress shall make no law respecting an establishment of religion, or prohibiting the free exercise thereof. . . .

In America, the guarantee of the right to worship is provided to the religious *establishment* rather than to the individual. This matter is of considerable consequence to Jehovah's Witnesses, who have argued both in the United States and in Canada that the state has no right to interfere in the relationship between an individual and the religious establishment to which he may have belonged.[71]

Section 2(*b*) of the *Charter* dovetails with s. 2(*a*), which guarantees "freedom of thought, belief, opinion and expression, including freedom of the press and other media of communication." Thus the elements of s. 1(*d*) and (*f*) of the *Canadian Bill of Rights* (freedom of speech and freedom of the press) are incorporated into the *Charter*.[72] "Freedom of

---

71 In America, *"an establishment of religion"* is protected, along with that establishment's free exercise of religion; but the individual is not protected against his religious establishment by the First Amendment. In Canada, it is the *individual* who is protected. To the extent that an individual may be forcibly denied access to the religion of his choice by the vicissitudes of that religion, has that individual's right to freedom of religion been curtailed? This argument was advanced in the Alberta Court of Appeal case *Zebroski v. The Watch Tower Bible and Tract Society*, (1988, unreported; leave to appeal to S.C.C. refused), but the appeal was rejected on other grounds.

72 Despite predictions that freedom of thought, belief and opinion would "have little impact, since even a totalitarian state cannot suppress unexpressed ideas" (Hogg, *supra*, note 46 at 961), the importance of these specific provisions in s. 2(*b*) of the *Charter* has been emphasized in such cases as *R. v. Keegstra* (1990) 3 S.C.R. 697, where defences to statements allegedly promoting hatred against an identifiable group (s. 319 of the *Criminal Code*) include the defence that the statement is "true," that the expression of an opinion was uttered in "good faith," and that the accused made the statement and "on reasonable grounds he believed them to be true"; and *R. v. Zundel* (1987) 58 O.R. (2d) 129 (C.A.), where the Crown conceded that "spreading false news" under s. 181 of

expression" is clearly a broader concept than the "freedom of speech" provided for by the *Canadian Bill of Rights* and would seem to include aspects of communication that go well beyond speech, including symbolic language such as street theatre and protest. Since freedom of expression includes "freedom of the press and other media of communication," innovative dimensions of communication not even invented or anticipated at this juncture will be covered automatically by the *Charter*. On the other hand, although both the *Canadian Bill of Rights* and the *Charter* guarantee the right to freedom of assembly and freedom of association, s. 2(c) of the *Charter* specifies *peaceful* assembly, which is possibly a narrower concept than "freedom of assembly and association" specified in s. 1(e) of the *Canadian Bill of Rights*.[73] Two rights covered by the *Canadian Bill of Rights* but conspicuously absent from the *Charter* are the right to "enjoyment of property" (s. 1(a)) and the right not to be arbitrarily exiled (s. 2 (a)).

Despite the similarities in wording between the *Canadian Bill of Rights* and the *Canadian Charter of Rights and Freedoms*, there is a world of difference between them in terms of applicability and enforcement. The *Canadian Bill of Rights* is at best a "quasi-constitutional" interpretative statute at least equal in weight to the *Interpretation Act* and the *Canada Evidence Act*. Under s. 2, the *Canadian Bill of Rights* allows federal legislation to be "read down" in such a way as to protect the interests, rights and freedoms of those whose rights have been or are liable to be encroached. The *Charter*, by contrast, is a full-fledged constitutional instrument which governs both governmental action and legislation at the federal, provincial and, by extension, municipal levels.

Whereas the *Canadian Bill of Rights* was the brainchild of Progressive Conservative Prime Minister John Diefenbaker, the *Charter* was very much the personal project of Liberal Prime Minister Pierre Elliott Trudeau, who sought the input of legal academics from across the country so that he could incorporate their ideas into the process of constitutional reform. These bright lights of Canadian constitutional law were to be a major influence on the eventual adoption of the *Charter*. It is very interesting, therefore, to note the ways in which they responded to the earlier cases involving fundamental freedoms, especially the Jehovah's Witnesses cases already discussed. A review of how Canada's foremost legal minds responded to the crisis to Canadian civil liberties before and during the process of *Charter* adoption is the subject of the following chapters.

---

the *Criminal Code* would include "a statement, tale or news" presented as "fact" but does not include an "opinion."

73 However, the placement of "freedom of association" under a separate head in the *Charter* may enhance its importance.

5

F.R. Scott and Pierre Elliott Trudeau

I. F.R. SCOTT, BARRISTER

Douglas Sanders has remarked that there were two "exceptional lawyers" involved in the Jehovah's Witnesses cases:

> W. Glen How of Toronto devoted his legal career to defending the Jehovah's Witnesses, of which he was a member. He produced a massive, written argument in the *Saumur* case extensively documenting the history of religious freedom in Canada. The other lawyer who is identifiable in the civil liberties cases is Frank Scott. Like How, he was not appearing as a regular practitioner but as a supporter of the principles involved. For at least some of the cases he was not paid.[1]

It must be remembered that Scott lived and worked in Catholic Quebec, where Jehovah's Witnesses regularly vented their wrath on the Roman Catholic Church, which they regarded as being inspired and controlled by Satan. Indeed, this argument had even been taken forward to the courts in Quebec a decade before by a less subtle lawyer than Scott. The defence factum in the 1938 sedition case of *Duval* v. *R.* outlined one of the main doctrines of Jehovah's Witnesses—one which is still a central tenet of the faith:

> Satan has become the prince of the earth and humanity is in his grip; all human institutions are in his control; the church, the financial bodies, the political governments, the bar, the bench, have become corrupt and serve the purposes of Satan, who has blinded humanity.[2]

---

1 Douglas Sanders, "Law and Social Change: The Experience of F.R. Scott" in Sandra Djwa and R. St J. Macdonald, eds., *On F.R. Scott: Essays on His Contributions to Law, Literature, and Politics* (Montreal: McGill-Queen's University Press, 1983) at 126.

2 *Duval* v. *R.* (1938), 64 Que. K.B. 270 at 279.

Sanders speculated on the reasons why Scott became involved in litigation involving this unpopular group:

> In his writings Scott put forward rather simplistic civil libertarian arguments. The rights of Jehovah's Witnesses and communists must be protected, he argued, or everyone is deprived of rights. The infringement of the rights of any is the infringement of the rights of all. As well, he argued that tolerance of various opinions was necessary so that there could be a winnowing of ideas in society, in order to test their truth. . . . The arguments fail to explain why Scott would have expected positive results in the 1950s. And so I assume that he became involved in litigation that he, himself, saw as unpredictable in outcome.[3]

Scott himself gave a somewhat different explanation for his defending Jehovah's Witnesses. The legal protections afforded by the civil liberties are always needed most by unpopular people, he wrote. Furthermore, the legal profession is obliged to defend individual citizens who have unpopular or even antisocial opinions. Branding them "outlaws" simply because of their unpopular beliefs and then using their unofficial "outlaw" status to rationalize unfair attacks on them by citizens and authorities alike is a fallacy that should not be tolerated by either the courts or the legal profession:

> Even in our supposedly civilized societies we seem capable of developing the concept of outlaw. The outlaw is—outside the law; he has no rights of any kind, and therefore no one can do wrong in attacking, defaming, arresting or assaulting him, or even in destroying his property. It seems that the Witnesses of Jehovah were placed in that category in some parts of Quebec. Because one of their pamphlets was once held to be seditious, it was assumed by some officials that not only were all their other pamphlets seditious but that every member of the sect belonged to a seditious conspiracy though no court had ever held this and no such charge was ever laid. Roncarelli, for instance, was accused of fomenting sedition and had his private business deliberately destroyed when all he had ever done, besides being a member of the Witnesses, was give lawful bail in a lawful court with the lawful approval of the presiding judge. . . . There is no more dangerous concept than this to the cause of civil liberties. Civil liberties are always needed most by unpopular people. . . .[4]

---

3 Sanders, *supra*, note 1 at 127.

4 F.R. Scott, *Civil Liberties and Canadian Federalism* (Toronto: University of Toronto Press, 1959) at 44.

Long before the *Roncarelli* case, Scott was interested in civil liberties and the constitution. Walter Tarnopolsky described him as "an advocate of civil liberties and architect of modern Canadian thought on human rights and fundamental freedoms," and added: "The various writings of Frank Scott on human rights and fundamental freedoms, commencing in the early 1930s and continuing through the 1940s, assured a place for the topic in future works on constitutional law in Canada."[5] By 1933, Scott was already drafting policies for the Co-operative Commonwealth Federation (CCF) Party with a view to demonstrating the Party's viability within the Constitution, and from 1942 to 1950, he served as national chairman of the CCF at a time when the civil liberties of Jehovah's Witnesses were being violated on a daily basis across the country.[6] The CCF became active in attempting to defend Jehovah's Witnesses from government persecution,[7] and after the war was the first political organization to push for a Bill of Rights.[8]

Scott's first overt support of Jehovah's Witnesses came in a *Canadian Forum* article in 1947 called "Duplessis v. Jehovah,"[9] in which he alerted Canadians to the fact that "a small religious sect has been persecuted and indeed martyred in many parts of Quebec." Here, a dozen years before the final Supreme Court of Canada resolution of *Roncarelli* v. *Duplessis*, Scott pointed out that by posting bail for countless Jehovah's Witnesses charged with peddling literature without a licence, Roncarelli was merely trying "to check Mr. Duplessis' mass persecution of the Witnesses." The laying of a charge, Scott said, is not of itself necessarily persecution, but "it becomes so when we learn that the number arrested reaches many hundreds, and particularly when Mr. Duplessis tries to deny the accused the normal right of every citizen to bail." In the *Roncarelli* case, Scott said, there wasn't even a pretence of legal process.[10]

In 1949, Scott published his influential essay "Dominion Jurisdiction over Human Rights and Fundamental Freedoms,"[11] in which he first dis-

---

5 Walter Tarnopolsky, "F.R. Scott: Civil Libertarian," in Djwa and Macdonald, *supra*, note 1 at 133, 140.

6 David Lewis, "F.R. Scott's Contribution to the CCF," in Djwa and Macdonald, *supra*, note 1 at 78–83.

7 See *Debates*, 1940, Vol. 1 at 752–53; Vol. 2 at 1068–71, 1078–79, 1206–07, 1215; 1941, Vol. 2 at 1068–70, 1089, 1188–1201, 1203–17, 1251–52.

8 See Walter Tarnopolsky, *The Canadian Bill of Rights* (Toronto: Carswell, 1966) at 14. Tarnopolsky credits CCF MP Alistair Stewart with introducing the concept into Parliament in 1945.

9 F.R. Scott, *Essays on the Constitution: Aspects of Canadian Law and Politics* (Toronto: University of Toronto Press, 1977) at 193. See also (1947), 26 *Can. Forum* at 222.

10 *Ibid.* at 195.

11 27 Can. Bar Rev. 497.

tinguished between civil rights (as referred to in s. 92 of the *B.N.A. Act*) and civil liberties—which, he concluded, could come under federal jurisdiction if Ottawa desired to pursue the matter. The confusion arose from the fact that the United States used the term "civil rights" to refer to the basic freedoms, and several court rulings in Canada had interpreted the words in s. 92 in the same way.[12] The net effect of these decisions, according to Scott, was that the provinces would become "the chief guardians of our traditional liberties." But the more correct view, he pointed out, was that the words "property and civil rights in a province" applied "only to private law rights between individuals, and not to those public rights, such as freedom of religion, of speech, of the press, of association and of the person, which are really attributes of citizenship and the limits of which are set in the criminal law."[13]

Other authorities interpreted civil liberties to fall outside the subjects listed in ss 91 and 92 of the *B.N.A. Act*, stating rather that they straddled both domains. Freedom of speech, for example, fell into both the domain of the provinces to the extent that it was concerned with civil rights and the domain of the Dominion to the extent that it was concerned with criminal law.[14] A fourth view was that of an "implied bill of rights" beyond the pale of Parliament or the provincial Legislatures. This argument took three different forms. First, the constitution of the United Kingdom included such timeless documents as the *Magna Carta*, the *Petition of Right*, and the *Bill of Rights*, establishing a tradition of civil liberties invoked by the preamble to the *B.N.A. Act*, which provided for a constitution "similar in Principle to that of the United Kingdom."[15] Second, the *B.N.A. Act* contained certain internal remedies entailing continuity and the right to appeal if certain "guarantees" were not met; indeed, the parliamentary system itself could not exist without free speech and freedom of association, and freedom of religion was surely implied by the *B.N.A. Act*'s protection of denominational schools.[16] Third, the principle of "natural law" determined that any natural right could not be abridged by positive law.[17] Scott attempted to resolve these ambiguities in his

---

12 In *Saumur*, Rinfret C.J.C., Taschereau J. and Kerwin J. all adopted this point of view.

13 Scott, *Civil Liberties and Canadian Federalism, supra*, note 4 at 24. See also *Saumur*, per Estey J.

14 In *Saumur*, both Fauteau J. and Cartwright J. expressed this view.

15 This view, discussed in *Saumur*, had first been adopted in *R. v. Hess (No. 2)* (1949), [1949] 1 W.W.R. 586, [1949] 4 D.L.R. 199, 94 C.C.C. 57 (B.C.C.A.), per O'Halloran J.A.

16 A similar point of view was adopted much earlier by Duff C.J. in *Reference Re Alberta Statutes* (1938), [1938] S.C.R. 100 at 135: "The law by which the right of public discussion is protected existed at the time of the enactment of *The British North America Act*."

17 A viewpoint later developed in *Chabot v. School Commissioners of Lamorandière* (1957), [1957] Que. Q.B. 707, 12 D.L.R. (2d) 796 (C.A.).

essay, which Tarnopolsky has called "the first detailed argument to assert that the jurisdiction of Parliament in relation to human rights and fundamental freedoms was extensive and that a comprehensive Bill of Rights was needed."[18]

Scott's contribution to constitutional law became far more direct than the writing of articles, however. According to J.R. Mallory, Scott helped draft the 1949 amendment to the *B.N.A. Act* that was eventually to be incorporated into the *Constitution Act, 1982* as s. 4(2):[19]

> When Frank saw the text he was horrified because it would have enabled a government to bring in legislation at any time extending the life of Parliament beyond the five years provided in the Constitution. At Frank's urging they took the matter up and the government agreed to add at the end of Section 91(1) the following phrase: "provided, however, that a House of Commons may in time of real or apprehended war, invasion or insurrection be continued by the Parliament of Canada if such continuation is not opposed by the votes of more than one-third of the members of such House."

As advisor to the Saskatchewan government, Scott also gave input into the dominion-provincial conference on amending the constitution organized by Louis St. Laurent early in 1950. By this time, Scott had been teaching constitutional law for some 30 years. He saw the need of entrenching a bill of rights in the constitution in such a way that it could not be easily altered.[20] As early as 1946 he had argued, "Any Bill of Rights should be enacted as an amendment to the *B.N.A. Act* rather than as a statute."[21] Since Diefenbaker's *Canadian Bill of Rights* was not entrenched but was merely a federal statute delineating rights that could easily be overruled, Scott referred to that document as the "spurious bill of rights."[22]

But perhaps Scott's greatest contribution to Canadian jurisprudence was his clarification of the "rule of law" in *Roncarelli v. Duplessis*. He had been concerned about the wide-reaching implications of the actions of the Duplessis regime for more than a decade:

---

18 Tarnopolsky, *supra*, note 8 at 8–9.

19 Sandra Djwa, *The Politics of the Imagination: A Life of F.R. Scott* (Vancouver: Douglas & McIntyre, 1989) at 264.

20 *Ibid.* at 266, citing a letter F.R. Scott to T.C. Douglas, 20 February 1950.

21 *Ibid.* at 267, citing Minutes of the Civil Rights Conference, Ottawa, 28–29 December 1946, pp. 1, 3, 7.

22 *Ibid.* at 267.

Mr Duplessis, having helped Mr Drew to wreck the Dominion-Provincial Conference in the name of 'provincial autonomy,' seems now about to wreck all civil liberty in Quebec in the name of 'law and order.' On December 4 [1946] he cancelled the liquor license of Frank Roncarelli, owner of a well-known and highly respectable restaurant in Montreal, because Mr Roncarelli was continuing to put up bail for Jehovah's Witnesses as fast as Mr Duplessis continued to arrest them. And plenty have been arrested: some 800 cases are pending in Montreal.

. . . Mr Duplessis thinks nothing of using his authority as Premier and Attorney-General of the Province to take away the means of livelihood of people whose only crime is that they do not agree with his political views or dare to oppose his policies in a lawful manner. His violent attacks recently upon certain labour leaders, and his issuing instructions to the courts to refuse them bail, are all in keeping with the recent persecution of the Witnesses and of Mr Roncarelli. . . .

It is to be hoped that the Roncarelli affair will provide a rallying point for responsible and organized protest. The issue rises above religious and party lines.[23]

Scott recognized that many persons, especially Catholic residents of Quebec, would have a difficult time focusing on the underlying issues, for "the Witnesses direct their chief attacks—and frequently very scurrilous attacks—upon the Catholic Church." This tendency "confuses the issue for many people and prevents them from protesting the arbitrary action of Mr Duplessis for fear of being thought to sympathize with the ideas which the Witnesses disseminate." To succumb to such fear of appearances, Scott suggested, is to play right into Duplessis' hands:

No doubt Mr Duplessis is relying on this confusion to confine the protest to insignificant proportions, just as he probably imagines that the cancelling of the license will not raise an outcry from the Protestant clergy, many of which are unaccustomed to defending a man's right to sell liquor. Fortunately he seems to have underestimated the number of people who will not be fooled by such tactics. Had he confined himself to laying charges against individual Witnesses the volume of protest would not have been anything like as great as it is now that the larger issue has been raised by the action taken against Mr Roncarelli.[24]

Scott cited an article in the *Montreal Gazette* in which Duplessis gave his reasons for revoking Roncarelli's licence and seizing his stock of liquor:

"A certain Mr. Roncarelli has supplied bail for hundreds of Witnesses of Jehovah. The sympathy which this man has shown for the Witnesses in

---

23 Scott, "Duplessis *versus* Jehovah," *supra*, note 9 at 193–94.

24 *Ibid.* at 194.

such an evident, repeated and audacious manner, is a provocation to public order, to the administration of justice and is definitely contrary to the aims of justice. He does not act, in this case, as a person posting bail for another person, but as a mass supplier of bails, whose great number by itself is reprehensible."[25]

Scott's outrage is readily apparent in his article in the January 1947 issue of *Canadian Forum*:

> Was there ever a more astonishing statement from a Canadian Attorney-General? Mr Roncarelli is a member of Jehovah's Witnesses, and his 'audacious sympathy' for his co-religionists is to be justification for taking away his livelihood! He was not himself distributing pamphlets; he was merely giving bail. And what is bail? Bail is the security given by or on behalf of an accused person to ensure that he will appear to stand trial. Bail aids the administration of justice, and is a traditional part of it. It is for the courts, and the courts alone, to decide whether or not bail should be allowed, and in these cases they had permitted it. Mr Roncarelli was guaranteeing that the Witnesses would duly appear to be tried. What a 'provocation to public order!' For the exercise of his legal right and this ancient guarantee of human liberty Mr Roncarelli has his license cancelled and his restaurant raided by a gang of policemen who, incidentally, carried away his entire stock of liquor.[26]

Rather than promoting disorder, Roncarelli was attempting to check the mass persecution of Jehovah's Witnesses at the hands of Duplessis, said Scott. He went on to analyse further statements made by the Premier, including the argument that Roncarelli held the liquor licence issued by the province as a privilege rather than a right. "'To allow him to continue to have that privilege,' said Duplessis, 'and, because of that privilege, secure the means of encouraging acts leading to public disorder would have been, in effect, to make the Attorney-General an accomplice.'" Scott heaped scorn upon this specious argument, saying that "such excuses as Mr Duplessis gives are an insult to the intelligence":

> On the same basis of reasoning, of course, the City of Montreal is an accomplice because it allows him water, the Quebec Hydro because it supplied electricity and gas, the Bell Telephone Company because it provides him with a telephone, and every diner who eats a meal aids and abets the horrible crime. Yet curiously enough Mr Duplessis does not dare lay any charge of any sort against this man who is such a dreadful menace to our national society. Mr Roncarelli is even allowed to continue in possession of his license to manage a restaurant. Can it be

---

25 *Ibid.*, citing *Montreal Gazette* of 5 December 1946.

26 *Ibid.* at 194–95.

that the restaurant license is continued because to cancel it Mr Duplessis would have to show cause in a court of law, whereas, under the dictatorial powers of the *Alcoholic Liquor Act*, cancellation can be imposed at the mere whim of the Premier?[27]

Scott identified two main issues arising from the Roncarelli incident. First was the need to establish active civil liberties associations across the country, for "the principles at stake concern every Canadian":

Certainly the most Catholic province in Canada should hesitate before it officially supports the idea of religious persecution, even under the provocation which the Witnesses undoubtedly give. There are too many people who might be persuaded that persecution is a good policy, and it might be difficult to confine it to Quebec.[28]

Indeed, in other parts of Canada, especially British Columbia, other more serious breaches of civil liberties had taken place, particularly the persecution of Japanese Canadians who, unlike Jehovah's Witnesses, had not provoked the authorities, nor did they "insult their fellow citizens by calling them evil names in widely distributed pamphlets."[29]

The second issue that Scott identified in his early essay was the need for judicial review of administrative acts. In Scott's view, Roncarelli should have been able to appeal the cancellation to an impartial tribunal; but in Quebec, and possibly elsewhere, there was no such mechanism.[30]

Scott's eloquent defence of Roncarelli in *The Canadian Forum* did not go by the restaurateur, who immediately requested his initial lawyer, A.L. Stein, to contact Scott with a view to engaging the law professor on the Roncarelli defence team. A third lawyer, Lionel Forsyth, was also engaged:

Forsyth assisted Scott and Stein in their first attempt to sue the now former chairman of the Quebec Liquor Commission, Edouard Archambault. Under the Liquor Law of Quebec, Archambault could be sued only with the permission of the Quebec Chief Justice, a position now occupied by Archambault himself. The three lawyers prepared a petition, filed on January 31, 1947, that set out the grounds of complaint and requested the authority to sue. On February 5 Judge Archambault dismissed the petition against himself. The trio understood from this judgment that if they had made their case more clearly, they might be

---

27 *Ibid.* at 195.

28 *Ibid.* at 195–96.

29 *Ibid.* at 196.

30 *Ibid.*

given permission to sue. Accordingly, they made a second submission to Judge Archambault on April 16. It was rejected two weeks later.

Meanwhile, they had concluded that not only the manager but also the Liquor Commission as a legal body could be sued. They wrote to Attorney-General Duplessis requesting permission to sue. The man who had committed the fault, if there was one, was also in a position to judge his own case. Duplessis did not reply. After some time had elapsed, the newspapers reported that the Premier had no intention of allowing the petition.[31]

Within the Faculty of Law at McGill, Scott became aware of increased peer pressure to limit his activities to teaching. Both Forsyth and Stein came under considerable pressure from their other clients to drop the case, and Forsyth caved in to the pressure. With some trepidation, Scott and Stein decided to continue the fight without him—this time suing Duplessis himself.[32]

The initial hearing before Judge McKinnon in May 1950 was barred to the public at Duplessis' behest, and the court house was heavily guarded by provincial police "with pistols in their belts, marching up and down as though some sort of siege were taking place":

Scott felt an initial strangeness as he entered the courtroom. He had borrowed a gown from Charles Lussier and bought a waistcoat and bib. He later remarked that he was "almost more worried about getting my robes in order than I was about the legal argument which I knew I was going to present." The argument continued for three days, and it seemed to him that "in the first day I delivered the entire course I give to the First Year students, on the second day I gave the second course and on the third day I gave the Third Year Administrative Law course, which was then being presented at the Law Faculty." Arguing from Dicey that even a premier was accountable for his actions if he acts outside the limitations of his office, Scott pointed out that the Quebec Liquor Commission had been constituted as an independent body and Duplessis, in commanding Archambault—if he indeed had commanded him—had committed a "fault" and was therefore responsible for subsequent damages to his victim, Roncarelli.[33]

Duplessis took the stand on the third day, stating that "In my opinion a man like Roncarelli was not worthy of holding a privilege from the province," and stating of his relationship to Archambault, "When a superior officer gives an order, an inferior officer obeys."

---

31 Djwa, *supra*, note 19 at 308.

32 *Ibid.* at 309.

33 *Ibid.* at 311.

> At that moment Scott felt the case had been won. Stein had forced Duplessis to admit that he was indeed the *causa causans* of the action, the person who is responsible. And it was so taken later as a fact by the trial judge. . . . However, he awarded damages of only $8,123.53 on the ground that he could not allow for profits lost because of the loss of a liquor licence because "'no licence holder has any inherent right to such a licence'."[34]

Roncarelli, who had sought $118,741 including loss of possible profits, appealed the award, and Duplessis cross-appealed. But it was not until June 1956 that the Quebec Court of Appeal heard the case and promptly overturned the decision of Judge McKinnon, stating that no order had been given by Duplessis.

By then, Roncarelli had been forced into bankruptcy. The Watch Tower Bible and Tract Society, representing Jehovah's Witnesses, decided to withdraw financial assistance from Roncarelli unless he agreed to be represented by their own lawyers, Covington and How. But Roncarelli insisted that Scott and Stein continue with the case when it went before the Supreme Court of Canada in May 1958.[35] The rule of law "is a fundamental principle of the English and Canadian Constitutions," Scott had written in his brief to the Court. "It is the foundation of the supremacy of the law over the state and over every state official. With us, all officials possess a limited jurisdiction only, which some statute or text of law defines."[36] Neither as Attorney-General nor as Prime Minister of Quebec did Duplessis have the right to commit the acts which damaged Roncarelli financially, he added.

When Duplessis' counsel, Dean M. Emery Beaulieu of the University of Montreal Law School, was asked "the real reason why this licence was cancelled," he answered simply that it was to cut the restaurateur's credit. As Scott later remarked in an interview with Elspeth Chisholm,

> It was to cut Roncarelli's credit, meaning to reduce his financial position so he couldn't give any more bail! When I heard that admission from Duplessis's counsel I said to myself, we've won the case. No court in a democratic country can contemplate a public official deliberately destroying a man's credit so he can't give bail. Giving bail is a human right. A tremendous human right. Each bail bond must be approved by the

---

34 *Ibid.* at 312.

35 There, Scott was invited by Kerwin C.J. to stand close to the Bench where only lawyers appointed Queen's Counsel are supposed to go. "He QC-fied me," Scott quipped to Sandra Djwa in 1980. *Ibid.* at 313.

36 Appellant's submission in *Roncarelli* v. *Duplessis*, at 48.

court; it was approved by the court every single time that Roncarelli gave bail. Then where was Roncarelli at fault?[37]

The 6–3 decision of the Supreme Court of Canada came down a year later on 27 January 1959. The *Montreal Star* published the entire text of the decision, citing as its reason the "profound importance in relation to public order and the rule of law." The judgment, the newspaper said in an editorial, "puts a curb on the exercise of arbitrary authority and establishes the supremacy of the rule of law in this country."[38]

During Walter Tarnopolsky's first year as Dean of the University of Windsor Law School, he invited Scott to be the keynote speaker at the official opening of the Law Building. Commenting on the principles at work in the *Roncarelli* case, and specifically the rule of law, Scott pointed out that they consisted really of "two basic rules underlying our constitutional structure":

> The first is that the individual may do anything he pleases, in any circumstances anywhere, unless there is some provision of law prohibiting him. Freedom is thus presumed, and is the general rule. All restrictions are exceptions. The second rule defines the authority of the state, and places the public official (including the policeman) in exactly the opposite situation from the private individual: a public officer can do nothing in his public capacity unless the law permits it. His incapacity is presumed, and authority to act is an exception. Duplessis, for instance, could not find any legal authority to justify his order to cancel Roncarelli's liquor licence: so he paid personally.[39]

These two basic rules, Scott said, entitle us to say that we live in a free society. He emphasized this fact in a lecture at Carlton University in Ottawa:

> No public officer has any power beyond what the law confers upon him, and the courts say what the law is. Thus the law puts a definite boundary around each official beyond which he acts at his peril. I say this, in Ottawa, with all the emphasis at my command. Any citizen—and this is a crucial corollary to which there are few exceptions—can sue any offi-

---

37 Cited in Djwa, *supra*, note 19 at 314.

38 28 January 1959.

39 Cited in Tarnopolsky, "F.R. Scott: Civil Libertarian," *supra*, note 5 at 144. Compare the tripartite definitions of "rule of law" propounded by A.V. Dicey in *Introduction to the Study of the Constitution* (London: Macmillan, 1961) at 202–03, and H.W. Jones in "The Rule of Law and the Welfare State" (1958), 58 Col. L. Rev. 143.

cial in the ordinary courts if that official has damaged him in a manner not permitted by law. No one is immune, not even a Prime Minister.[40]

In *Essays on the Constitution* (1977) Scott pointed out the irony that "though Roncarelli established a great principle, his restaurant was closed, his social status in Montreal undermined, and he was obliged to earn his living elsewhere. The Witnesses of Jehovah, however, now practise their religion unimpeded by Quebec police."[41]

The late Senator Therese Casgrain, former president of the CCF Party in Quebec, recounted Scott's reaction to fighting and eventually winning the *Roncarelli* case:

> As a friend, I watched, with deep interest and admiration, his determination to uphold the liberties of the citizen in the *Roncarelli* case. Those who knew the Duplessis regime in Quebec will understand what it meant to defy the then premier of Quebec, who was also attorney general of the province, or even to be associated with such an attempt at defiance. I remember going to Frank's home after this case had been won. All his friends were there to rejoice, including Roncarelli.[42]

Gerald LeDain made a similar observation regarding Scott's temerity in his essay "F.R. Scott and Legal Education":

> What his participation as counsel in the *Switzman* and *Roncarelli* cases reflected was not just his professional ability but his independence and moral courage. It is difficult for someone who did not live in Quebec at that time to appreciate the atmosphere of psychological intimidation that was created by the Duplessis regime, and the determination that it took to challenge Duplessis in such a direct manner. Prominent counsel felt obliged to decline the *Roncarelli* brief. In my opinion, it is as much for his independence and moral courage, reflected over the years in the strong stands he took on contentious issues, as for his unusual gifts and intellectual achievements, that Frank Scott is so respected in this country.[43]

In the year after his victory in *Roncarelli*, Scott delivered several radio talks and lectures in which he reviewed the Jehovah's Witnesses cases

---

40 Scott, *Civil Liberties and Canadian Federalism, supra,* note 4 at 48.

41 Scott, *Essays, supra,* note 9 at 193.

42 Therese Casgrain, "The Achievements of F.R. Scott," in Djwa and Macdonald, *supra,* note 1 at 4. Also present at Scott's house that night were Pierre Trudeau and Eric Kierans. See Djwa, *supra,* note 19 at 314.

43 In Dwja and Macdonald, *supra,* note 1 at 114.

and tried to put them in perspective. That Jehovah's Witnesses suffered from persecution at the hands of the government went without saying:

> The City of Montreal, for instance, launched over a thousand cases against the Witnesses on petty charges of distributing literature or peddling without a licence, and every single one of the cases had to be withdrawn eventually, as the arrests were without legal foundation. In the Boucher case a liberal definition of sedition by the Supreme Court freed the Witnesses from the charge that their pamphlet *Quebec's Burning Hate* was seditious. In the Chaput case three Quebec provincial policemen, who had broken up a peaceful service being conducted by a minister of the Witnesses in a private house, were compelled to pay damages, though they had acted under orders from a superior officer.[44]

Scott, who had assisted Glen How with the *Boucher* case,[45] emphasized the need to keep authority figures (and especially the police) under control to avoid situations like that manifest in *Chaput*; for "the police state starts to grow in the police force":

> Even the police should know it is a crime to disturb religious worship; here it was the police, and not the Witnesses, who were committing the crime. This case warns us that we shall not be secure in our civil liberties in Canada so long as our police forces contain ignorant, brutal, or high-handed men. . . . We neglect this portion of the state machinery at our peril.[46]

He returned to this theme in his two lectures contained in *Civil Liberties and Canadian Federalism*. *Chaput*, he said, illustrated several important rules of constitutional and administrative law.

> On the administrative law side, the case illustrates the well-known rule that orders from a superior officer are no defence. The lesser official in the governmental hierarchy is not protected in wrong-doing because the superior officer tells him to do something; the illegal order merely makes the superior officer liable too. This rule is essential to the preservation of the rule of law as we have inherited it; it makes each and every public officer personally responsible for right behavior, and unable to hide behind some cloak of authority.[47]

---

44 F.R. Scott, *The Canadian Constitution and Human Rights* (Toronto: Canadian Broadcasting Corporation, 1959) at 40.

45 Djwa, *supra*, note 19 at 311.

46 *Ibid.*

47 Scott, *Civil Liberties and Canadian Federalism*, *supra*, note 4 at 43.

In his 1960 essay "Expanding the Concepts of Human Rights," Scott again referred to the rule of law in regard to *Roncarelli*, *Chaput* and *Lamb*. All three cases, he said, reaffirmed "the great principle of supremacy of the law": "The *Roncarelli* case involved the liability of a Prime Minister, and the *Chaput* and *Lamb* cases involved the liability of constables, and all the officials sued were held liable for acts done without legal justification."[48] But as he noted in *Civil Liberties and Canadian Federalism*, the cases took years of litigation—12 1/2 years in the case of Miss Lamb. "We should be grateful that we have in this country some victims of state oppression who stand up for their rights," remarked Scott. "Their victory is the victory of all of us."[49] Furthermore, despite the obvious risks of social and professional ostracism, it is the responsiblity of legal counsel to defend unofficial "outlaws," because such defence epitomizes the very function of the law, of the judiciary, and of the legal profession:

> It is the function of the law, and of the independent judges who apply it as well as of the independent barristers who practise it on behalf of all clients who need their help, to uphold the notion of legality against the pressures of angry opinion. Should the lawyers be afraid to take unpopular clients, and the judges afraid to give unpopular decisions, all the principles of the law would be worthless.[50]

Similar principles applied to politics, where the rights of the individual had to be balanced with the larger demands of an increasingly complex society. "Can we select the form and shape of our society and move progressively toward it without liquidating all those who stand in the way?" he asked in an unpublished paper "The State as a Work of Art":[51]

> Politics is the art of making artists. It is the art of developing in society the laws and institutions which will best bring out the creative spirit which lives in greater or less degree in every one of us. The right politics sets as its aim the maximum development of every individual. Free the artist in us, and the beauty of society will look after itself.[52]

As Sandra Djwa pointed out, Scott's view of society was two-pronged, "being, above all, directed toward cultivation of the individual,

---

48 Scott, *Essays, supra,* note 9 at 354.

49 Scott, *Civil Liberties and Canadian Federalism, supra,* note 4 at 45.

50 *Ibid.* at 44.

51 Cited in Djwa, *supra,* note 19 at 267.

52 *Ibid.*

and of 'the rule of law' as being necessary for the protection of both individual and society".[53]

> His vision of the good society was, above all, the socialist "just society." And his view of the ideal constitution that would create it—a repatriated *B.N.A. Act* tailored to Canada's needs—was a topic he enjoyed speculating on when meeting with younger lawyers like Trudeau.[54]

Scott developed a "very carefully constructed thesis" which treated the constitution as "a living, dynamic thing"—a thesis so obvious and so well-documented that, while at first it was regarded as being avant-garde or even revolutionary, in the hands of influential persons such as Pierre Trudeau it became "the accepted viewpoint in Canadian law":

> Scott's students, many of whom took an active part in various public policy issues, have been advocates and even extenders of what might be called the "Scott thesis," dramatically so through the repatriation of the constitution in 1982 with its entrenched Charter of Rights.[55]

Scott was not content with leaving such heady issues solely in the hands of his students and acquaintances, however. Throughout the 1970s he continued to advise government committees on the shaping of the constitution, particularly with respect to repatriation and entrenchment of a Charter of Rights. Describing Scott as "a rebel without a pause" (an appellation borrowed from Tarnopolsky) Chairman Mark MacGuigan told the Special Joint Committee on the Constitution of Canada in 1970, "It would be a superfluity to introduce Professor Scott to an audience such as this," and added that Scott had been a witness before a similar committee as long ago as 1935. Scott responded:

> Every time I come to another formal meeting to discuss the Canadian Constitution, I do so with mingled feelings of hope and pessimism. As you have pointed out, I made my first presentation about the Canadian Constitution to a Committee of the House of Comnmons in 1935. I then took part in the federal-provincial constitutional conferences in 1950, at which you may remember we sorted out the provisions of the *B.N.A. Act* into six categories, matters affecting the federal government only, provinces only, common matters, and so forth, but we got no further on that try.
> I then took part in the discussions in 1959 and 1960 where we made little more specific progress because there emerged from those discus-

---

53 *Ibid.*

54 *Ibid.*

55 *Ibid.* at 269–70.

sions the Favreau-Fulton formula, which got very close to being accepted as an amendment to the constitution to provide us with a method of repatriation, as it was called, of the *B.N.A. Act* and procedure for future amendments. However, that failed. Now, here it is 1970 and I find myself in the same kind of position.[56]

Scott emphasized his misgivings with the *Canadian Bill of Rights*, stating that "if you want to limit sovereignty, you do it properly by entrenched clauses in the Constitution, not by one Parliament limiting itself in the future." He therefore did not accept the *Canadian Bill of Rights* "as a substitute for a true Bill of Rights in the Constitution itself"; for the *Canadian Bill of Rights* "did not give us many new rights; they were all more or less around in the law before."[57] He elaborated:

> An argument can be made that the present *B.N.A. Act* does in fact entrench certain of these rights but it is a very flimsy argument. The courts have never wholly accepted it. In other words, the idea that there is an implied Bill of Rights in the present Act is an idea that has some support.
> Take, for instance, the Quebec padlock act. It was held invalid because it invaded the criminal law field. Therefore it could not be passed by the provincial legislature of Quebec. But, by the same argument, it could have been passed by the federal legislature; so their rights could have been taken away. It was only the wrong government that took them away.[58]

Asked if the civil rights cases that he had been involved in would have been much better advanced or better served had the *Canadian Bill of Rights* been entrenched, and whether an entrenched Bill of Rights was still needed to protect civil liberties, Scott replied:

> I certainly am emphatically of that position. It is precisely because they are just floating around and not anchored that I want the Bill. I mean, they can be taken away by somebody else's law. I want them to be put beyond any form of change except by amending the constitution.[59]

"I would keep the entrenched rights—relatively few," he added, and when one of the committee members suggested that he meant only the political and legal rights, Scott responded: "Yes, the good old fundamen-

56 *Proceedings of the Special Joint Committee on the Constitution of Canada*, 1 December 1970 at 17:6.

57 *Ibid.* at 17:12.

58 *Ibid.* at 17:26.

59 *Ibid.* at 17:25.

tal freedoms, what I call the circle of liberty, those things we all have agreed upon for a long time."[60]

Scott's cynicism with respect to the process of revising the constitution came through loud and clear to the committee. "I intend to live another ten years, Mr. Chairman, and I have no doubt I may be back again on that occasion," he said.

> *The Joint Chairman (Mr. MacGuigan)*: I hope that these problems at least will be settled by that time.
>
> *Professor Scott*: But it all goes to show, of course, that there is never an end to the evolution of a constitution, because it is not the kind of document that you can draw up once and for all and have it fixed and permanent. It must combine rigidities with flexibilities, and the dynamism of the modern society just cannot be constrained for long in a particular set of words. [61]

True to his word, exactly ten years later Scott once again made submissions to another Joint Committee on the Constitution. Part of his brief was read into the record on 10 December 1980. It contained a poignant warning of the importance of every word in the proposed Constitution Act. It was perhaps Scott's "last word" on the Constitution, for by then his health was failing:[62]

> The Committee and the Senate and the House of Commons of Canada must, however, bear in mind that every word, indeed every punctuation mark in that proposed resolution will undergo repeated and lengthy process in the courts of this country and this for a time extending indefinitely into the future. Enormous amounts of time and energies of the legal professions in all their branches will be devoted to its scrutiny. Profound consequences may turn on the meaning of any single word. Amendments are likely to be difficult, in some cases impossible, in a practical sense, to obtain. I therefore urge the Committee and, through it, both Houses of Parliament to ensure that the parliamentary examination of this instrument procedes not merely without haste but on the contrary with the most meticulous care and with the greatest deliberation.[63]

---

60 *Ibid.* at 17:31.

61 *Ibid.* at 17:6.

62 He had been using a pacemaker to stabilize tachycardia since 1974, "but by 1980 his whole body was clearly in a state of attrition." Djwa, *supra*, note 19 at 447.

63 *Proceedings of the Joint Committee on the Constitution of Canada*, 10 December 1980 at 23:69.

Scott's involvement in *Roncarelli* v. *Duplessis*, the classic Canadian "rule of law" case, was never far beneath the surface of his deliberations on the need to entrench the Charter in the Constitution.

In 1981, Scott was urged by Mr. Justice Thomas Berger, who 20 years earlier had worked with Scott on the *Oil Workers Case*,[64] to attend a symposium in Scott's honour at Simon Fraser University. Djwa remarked:

> In many ways the Scott symposium was an index to Canadian history and culture of the past sixty years. Certainly there seemed to be no other individual in Canada for whom the Prime Minister of the country, the Chief Justice of the Supreme Court, the first mandarin of the Ottawa civil service, the director-general of the National Arts Centre, and the associate director of the Canada Council would gather to take part in a pre-conference entertainment. But all did so for Frank Scott because he had had such a direct influence on their lives.[65]

Not only did they attend, they themselves became parodied in a skit that Jehovah's Witnesses in all likelihood would have regarded as profane if not heretical:

> One Wilbur Throckmorton, Cherubim Second Class, fired from the Celestial Civil Service for his role in creating Scott, an irritant in the celestial machinery, has appealed to the Celestial Supreme Court. His advocates, the Archclerk Michael (Pitfield) and St. Peter (Trudeau), advise Jehovah, J., the presiding judge, "to hold his nose" and grant the appeal. This comment parodied Prime Minister Trudeau's remark to the British Parliament, whose Kershaw Committee was then suggesting the Canadian federal government was exceeding its power in unilaterally requesting patriation of the *B.N.A. Act* without the provinces' consent. In the skit, Jehovah (Chief Justice Bora Laskin) reinstates Throckmorton, observing the issue turns on the question of "whether or not Scott has been good for Canada."[66]

The proceedings of the symposium were collected and published in *On F.R. Scott: Essays on His Contributions to Law, Literature, and Politics*,[67] featuring articles by such notables of Canadian law and letters as David Lewis, Kenneth McNaught, Gerald Le Dain, William Lederman, Walter Tarnopolsky, D.G. Jones and Thomas Berger. Perhaps the greatest tribute came from Tarnopolsky in "F.R. Scott: Civil Libertarian":

---

64 *Oil, Chemical and Atomic Workers* v. *Imperial Oil* (1963), [1963] S.C.R. 584, 41 D.L.R. (2d) 1, 45 W.W.R. 1.

65 Djwa, *supra*, note 19 at 442.

66 *Ibid.* at 442–43; see also Djwa and Macdonald, *supra*, note 1 at xxi.

67 *Supra*, note 1.

I will illustrate my characterizations of him and, perhaps, even some of the ironies associated therewith, by reference to the following specific propositions, determining our appreciation of human rights and fundamental freedoms in Canada, for which he can claim credit: (1) The topic of human rights and fundamental freedoms is not only a legitimate, but an indispensable component of Canadian constitutional law. (2) Within our federal state, there is an important role for the central government in the field of human rights and fundamental freedoms, despite provincial jurisdiction over 'property and civil rights.' (3) The 'rule of law' is as important a part of our 'Constitution similar in Principle to that of the United Kingdom' as is parliamentary supremacy. (4) Although traditionally in Anglo-Canadian constitutional practice our human rights and fundamental freedoms were realized by restraining governments from interference, increasingly we have recognized that some of our human rights can only be realized through assumption of government responsibility. (5) An essential feature of Canadian federalism, unlike the unitary and homogeneous situation of the United Kingdom, is protection of such group rights as those relating to language and religious schools.[68]

Almost all of these topics arose in connection with Jehovah's Witnesses cases, in particular *Roncarelli*. But Tarnopolsky pointed out that Scott's involvement went far beyond representing individuals in the courts:

Before turning to these topics, I must refer to Scott's role as an advocate and activist in defending the civil liberties of unpopular minorities. This was accomplished not just through legal scholarship, but through more popular writings in such magazines as *The Canadian Forum*, as well as through organizational and counsel work.[69]

Under the heading "FRANK SCOTT, DEFENDER OF THE CIVIL LIBERTIES OF PERSECUTED GROUPS," Tarnopolsky wrote: "Most students of Canadian history, especially students of constitutional law, will be familiar with the contributions of Frank Scott to the defence of the Jehovah's Witnesses in Quebec in the 1950s";[70] and he described Scott's early involvement in the *Roncarelli* case.[71] Under the heading "CIVIL LIBERTIES IS A NECESSARY COMPONENT OF CANADIAN CONSTITUTIONAL LAW," Tarnopolsky stated without qualification that "the various writings of Frank Scott on human rights and fundamental freedoms . . . assured a place for the topic in future works on constitutional law in Canada."[72] Under the heading "THE

68 *Ibid.* at 133–34.

69 *Ibid.* at 134.

70 *Ibid.*

71 *Ibid.* at 138–39.

72 *Ibid.*

ROLE OF THE CENTRAL GOVERNMENT WITH RESPECT TO HUMAN RIGHTS AND FUNDAMENTAL FREEDOMS," Tarnopolsky applauded Scott's essay "Dominion Jurisdiction over Human Rights and Fundamental Freedoms":

> In this essay, not only did Scott set out the argument for an 'implied Bill of Rights' in the *B.N.A. Act*, first hinted at in the *Alberta Press Bill* case, and subsequently picked up by members of the Supreme Court of Canada in the Jehovah's Witnesses cases of the 1950s, but he also provided the basic argument, since referred to and amplified both by authors and judges, distinguishing between the matter of 'civil liberties' and the subject of 'property and civil rights' within section 92 of the *B.N.A. Act*.[73]

Under the heading "THE RULE OF LAW AS IMPORTANT PART OF OUR CONSTITUTION AS PARLIAMENTARY SUPREMACY," Tarnopolsky described in detail the arguments used in *Roncarelli* and alluded to *Chaput* v. *Romain* and *Lamb* v. *Benoit* as being examples of the application of the principle of rule of law.[74]

F.R. Scott's contribution as constitutional lawyer and law teacher went far beyond the four cases he took before the Supreme Court of Canada, only one of which concerned Jehovah's Witnesses. But because of his roles as advisor to Glen How in *Boucher* and dozens of other cases, and as counsel in the *Roncarelli* case, Scott is universally identified as being involved with the Jehovah's Witnesses. He himself stressed again and again the importance of the various Jehovah's Witnesses cases to the development of a tradition of civil liberties in Canada. He recognized that through their constant, often bitter attacks on rival religions and on the political systems of the world, Jehovah's Witnesses asked for much of what they received in terms of persecution at an individual level. Nonetheless, "it is the function of the law . . . to uphold the notion of legality against the pressures of angry opinion"—no matter how unpopular the client may be.[75] This became for F.R. Scott the central motivation for becoming an advocate for causes like Jehovah's Witnesses.

Pierre Elliott Trudeau, who regarded Scott as his mentor and who took a particular interest in the *Roncarelli* case, was inspired to adopt a similar altruistic stance for similar reasons.

---

73 *Ibid.* at 141–42.

74 *Ibid.* at 142–44.

75 Scott, *Civil Liberties and Canadian Federalism, supra,* note 4 at 44.

II. PIERRE ELLIOTT TRUDEAU, PRIME MINISTER

F.R. Scott found an ally in his belief in the necessity of entrenching a Bill of Rights into the Constitution in Pierre Elliott Trudeau, with whom he had had a long acquaintanceship. They had first crossed paths as early as 1938, when Trudeau, then a high school student, joined a crowd of unruly pro-Franco demonstrators in a successful attempt to thwart a socialist fund-raising rally organized by Scott and Norman Bethune on behalf of visiting Spanish loyalists.[76] From that point on, Trudeau followed Scott's career with interest, reading his articles and books and attending his lectures at the University of Montreal on such aspects of constitutional law as patriating the constitution. Trudeau borrowed Scott's concept of "the just society," first espoused in a 1939 essay, almost verbatim.[77] Trudeau began to attend CCF rallies, and in turn Scott began to move in Trudeau's circle of young Quebec intellectuals: "At labour meetings, social gatherings, and through shared interests, Scott and Trudeau began to see more of each other."[78] They both participated in the 1950 Dominion-Provincial Constitutional Conference in Quebec. By then,

> Trudeau had absorbed many of Scott's views on Canada and the constitution as an adjunct to a socialist philosophy. Trudeau had also acquired a healthy respect for Frank Scott as contrasted to Duplessis. Recollecting the Quebec conference, he remembered the striking difference between "the thinking man [Scott] and these politicians."[79]

According to Scott's biographer, Sandra Djwa, "it was in the struggle for a more democratic society in Quebec, in particular in the fight against Duplessis, that Scott and Trudeau found common ground. Scott's jousts against Duplessis in the fifties were followed closely by Trudeau and his group."[80] They became close allies during the 1950s when Trudeau cast about searching for remedies to the economic problems besetting the impoverished: "I found them first of all in the study of socialist thought," Trudeau said in an interview with the *Toronto Star*.[81] Both men attended the founding meeting of *L'Institut canadien des affairs publiques* in 1954.

---

76 Djwa, *supra*, note 19 at 173.

77 *Ibid.* at 319.

78 *Ibid.* at 236.

79 *Ibid.* at 319.

80 *Ibid.* at 320.

81 8 April 1968.

Eventually Trudeau became "a frequent visitor to Scott's office,"[82] and invariably Trudeau was in the courtroom whenever Scott pleaded a case.[83] After the *Roncarelli* victory, for instance, Trudeau went to Scott's home to celebrate with Scott, Roncarelli and others at an impromptu party.[84]

For several years, Scott had been working with Jean-Charles Falardeau on a study of the notorious Asbestos Strike, a study to be called *La Greve de l'amiante*. "Scott asked Trudeau, who as a radical could not find employment in Quebec universities in the fifties, to edit the book. Trudeau agreed."[85] Over the next two years, Trudeau and Scott shepherded the manuscript through to publication.[86]

Perhaps most significantly of all, in 1956 Scott and Trudeau embarked on an extended tour of the Arctic together, taking a barge trip down the Mackenzie Valley. The journey inspired some of Scott's most memorable poems—and some of Trudeau's most influential essays on democracy. Using Scott as his mentor and "sounding board," Trudeau completed "Some Obstacles to Democracy in Quebec," in which he referred to the Jehovah's Witnesses cases,[87] and his *Manifeste democratique* (mirroring Scott's own "Democratic Manifesto" of 1941) in which he urged Quebeckers to form *Le Rassemblement*—a united front in opposition to the *Union nationale*.[88] As Djwa explained,

> It was precisely the lack of democracy in Quebec that had spurred Scott's first efforts for reform in 1931 and informed his battles against Duplessis in the late forties and most of the fifties in the Padlock and Roncarelli cases.
>
> Trudeau had wanted to accompany Scott on his trip down the Mackenzie River, not just because of the adventure but because, as he said, "[Frank] was a great hero of mine. . . . I never studied under him. . . . But he was the man who was taking sides in a courageous way in important causes . . . whether it be Jehovah's Witnesses, [or] in his writings."[89]

---

82 Djwa, *supra*, note 1 at 229, 236, 319.

83 *Ibid.* at 432.

84 *Ibid.* at 314.

85 *Ibid.* at 321.

86 *Ibid.* at 322.

87 Included in Pierre Elliott Trudeau, *Federalism and the French Canadians* (Toronto: Macmillan, 1968) at 112.

88 Djwa, *supra*, note 19 at 318–327; and Michael Oliver, "F.R. Scott as Quebecer," in Djwa and Macdonald, *supra*, at 174.

89 *Ibid* at 326.

Trudeau saw his association with Scott as a way of making up for a perceived deficiency in training in constitutional law at the University of Montreal. "It's been [from] my contacts with Frank in his person and his actions that I absorbed much of my constitutional thinking," he said. "In an intellectual argument he always did me the honour of a fair hearing. So going on the Mackenzie with him wasn't just another adventure . . . it was a chance to be exposed to Frank Scott for days and weeks."[90]

Trudeau, like Scott, had become heavily involved in fighting the influence of Duplessis. But it became painfully obvious to him and his acquantances that *Le Rassemblement* would not work in Quebec. Nor would Tommy Douglas's brand of CCF socialism ever catch on in Quebec. Jean Marchand, Gerard Pelletier and Pierre Trudeau began to look elsewhere for a medium to carry their message.

Not long after the *Roncarelli* decision came down, Duplessis died. Separatism began to rear its head, and Trudeau, along with Pelletier and Marchand, decided that the federal Liberal Party was an appealing route to go. Trudeau was elected in 1966 and the following year became Minister of Justice. By January 1968, Trudeau was deliberating over whether to run for party leader, and Scott wrote him a not unflattering letter urging him to let his name stand.[91] Later, Trudeau offered Scott a seat on the Senate, but Scott declined on principle since both he and the New Democratic Party that he had helped found had gone on record as being opposed to the institution.[92]

Scott and Trudeau now held common views on many constitutional issues, including "the necessity of repatriating the constitution, and, above all, about the need to entrench a Bill of Rights in the constitution," according to Djwa:

> Many of these early views Trudeau carried into his fifteen years in power as Prime Minister of Canada. Indirectly, in the next two decades, Scott may have helped shape the future of Canada, especially as it related to Quebec and the Constitution.[93]

In 1955, Trudeau wrote in a submission to the Tremblay Commission that democracy and civil liberties were inextricably intertwined, and he suggested that even then, Quebec was ready to look at constitutional reform including "repatriating the Canadian constitution" and incorporat-

---

90 *Ibid.*

91 *Ibid.* at 336, where it is cited in its entirety.

92 David Lewis, "F.R. Scott's Contribution to the C.C.F.," in Djwa and Macdonald, *supra*, note 1 at 174.

93 Djwa, *supra*, note 19 at 337.

ing an entrenched Bill of Rights.[94] Yet as he wrote the following year in *La Greve de l'amiante*,[95] ecclesiastical censure was the order of the day for anyone who spoke of secular values, including democratic rights, for such values were regarded by "popular opinion" as eroding the authority of the Roman Catholic Church. Trudeau gave by way of example a dispute that arose between two journalists, one of them employed by Duplessis' newspaper, *Notre Temps*, which regularly attacked "the new religion of democracy." For a while there was a running battle between Leopold Richer of *Notre Temps* and the "libertarian" G. Filion of *Le Devoir*, who in 1956 had the temerity to write, "Freedom is not a gift but something that must be won. The only freedom is that which has been torn from authority." Richer responded that Filion's statement "is defiance of established authority, whether religious or civil. It is sedition."[96] As further evidence of the relationship between political and Church authority, Trudeau pointed to a paid political announcement sponsored by the *Comité interdiocesain d'Action radiophonique* that was aired on 20 June 1956—the very morning of the provincial general election:

> Sovereign authority, by whatever government it is exercised, is derived solely from God, the supreme and eternal principle of all power. . . . It is therefore an absolute error to believe that authority comes from the multitudes, from the masses, from the people. . . . All this explanation about the origin, the basis, and the composition of this alleged [!] sovereignty of the people is purely arbitrary. Moreover, if it is admitted, it will have as a consequence the weakening of authority, making it a myth, giving it an unstable and changeable basis, stimulating popular passions and encouraging sedition.

To which Trudeau added: "Think *that* over before you cast your vote!"[97]

Both Richer's allegations and the radio message, with their willingness to castigate anomalous opinion as "seditious," must have sounded all too familiar to Jehovah's Witnesses in Quebec in 1956. Trudeau the democrat, having been tarred with the same brush of sedition as Jehovah's Witnesses in Quebec, subsequently showed considerable familiarity with their plight, alluding to the sect regularly in his political writings,

---

94 Cited in Trudeau, "A Constitutional Declaration of Rights" (1967). Published in *Federalism and the French Canadians, supra,* note 87 at 53.

95 (Montreal: Editions Cité Libre, 1956).

96 "Some Obstacles to Democracy in Quebec," in *Federalism and the French Canadians, supra,* note 87 at 113–14.

97 *Ibid.* at 110–11.

and referring specifically to *Boucher* v. *R.*,[98] *Saumur* v. *City of Quebec*,[99] *Chaput* v. *Romain*,[100] and *Roncarelli* v. *Duplessis*.[101]

In August 1958, not long before the Supreme Court of Canada hearing of the *Roncarelli* case, Trudeau published his essay "Some Obstacles to Democracy in Quebec,"[102] initially drafted while on his trip down the Mackenzie River with Scott, in which he explained the lack of civic-mindedness among French Canadians in religious terms. "French Canadians are Catholics," he wrote, "and Catholic nations have not always been ardent supporters of democracy":

> They are authoritarian in spiritual matters; and since the dividing line between the spiritual and the temporal may be very fine or even confused, they are often disinclined to seek solutions in temporal affairs through the mere counting of heads.[103]

To Duplessis' Quebec, civil liberties were merely "an alleged right to propagate error" and "democracy, if it is known at all, is known as an evil." Trudeau remarked:

> An unusual approach to civil liberties might also be considered as typical of French Canada. At the time of the decision on the Jehovah's Witness case [i.e., the *Saumur* decision], enforcing freedom of religion, public opinion in Quebec was quick to point out that the judges of the Supreme Court had been somewhat divided along racial and religious lines.[104]

In his 1962 essay "New Treason of the Intellectuals," Trudeau speculated as to how future generations would receive the knowledge that the generation of the 1950s had spent their time indulging in the "new treason" of separatism:

> What! they will say to the judges and lawyers, civil liberties having survived in the province of Quebec thanks only to the Communists, the

---

98 *Federalism and the French Canadians*, supra, note 87 at 171.

99 *Ibid.* at 112, 171.

100 *Ibid.* at 171.

101 *Ibid.* at 171, 205.

102 In *Canadian Journal of Economics and Political Science*, Vol. 24, No. 3 (August 1958). Republished in Mason Wade, ed., *Canadian Dualism* (Toronto: University of Toronto Press, 1960), and in Trudeau's *Federalism and the French Canadians*, supra, note 87 at 103–23.

103 "Some Obstacles to Democracy in Quebec," in *Federalism and the French Canadians*, supra, note 87 at 108.

104 *Ibid.* at 112.

trade unions, and the Jehovah's Witnesses, and to English and Jewish lawyers and the judges of the Supreme Court in Ottawa, and you had nothing better to do than cheer on the coming of a sovereign state for French Canadians?[105]

Trudeau added in a footnote:

Seven times in the last decade alone, beginning in 1951, the Supreme Court in Ottawa has reversed the decisions of the Court of Appeal of the Province of Quebec, decisions which would have spelled disaster for civil liberties: the Boucher case (seditious libel); the Alliance case (loss of union certification); the Chaput case (religious assembly); the Birks case (compulsory religious holidays); the Switzman case (padlock law); the Roncarelli case (administrative discretion). At the moment of going to press we learn that yet an eighth case can now be added to this list: the case of *Lady Chatterly's Lover.*

Later, in another essay on "Separatist Counter-Revolutionaries"[106] Trudeau extolled the virtues of men such as Roncarelli (whose appeal before the Supreme Court of Canada he had attended) and Frank Scott who worked "to advance freedom and democracy" in Quebec. "Around 1960," he wrote, "it seemed that freedom was going to triumph in the end."

From 1945 on, a series of events and movements had combined to relegate the traditional concepts of authority in Quebec to the scrap-heap. . . . So much so that the generation entering its twenties in 1960 was the first in our history to receive fairly complete freedom as its lot. The dogmatism of Church and State, of tradition, of the nation, had been defeated. Authority had returned to its proper place in a free system. A lawyer could head the Lay Movement without losing his clients. Professors could say 'no to the Jesuits' without being barred from the university. Comedians or movie producers could subscribe to Marxism without being discharged by the government corporations. Students could try to impose their views on educational institutions without being kicked out.[107]

Citing the "elementary principle of justice: 'hear the other side'," Trudeau went on to discuss such principles as freedom of the press and freedom of expression:

---

105 "New Treason of the Intellectuals," in *Federalism and the French Canadians, supra,* note 87 at 171.

106 *Federalism and the French Canadians, supra,* note 87 at 204 ff.

107 *Ibid.* at 206.

What can I say to people who have never read John Stuart Mill, *On Liberty*? 'The beliefs which we have most warrant for have no safeguard to rest on, but a standing invitation to the whole world to prove them unfounded.' No man can demand freedom of speech if he finds it a matter of indifference that public debate and free confrontation should be brushed aside as a means of arriving at political truths; these ideas are indissolubly linked.[108]

Trudeau concluded:

No kidding! In the province of Quebec the Jehovah's Witnesses and the Communists, two tiny minorities, have been mocked, persecuted, and hated by our entire society; but they have managed by legal means to fight Church, government, nation, police, and public opinion. . . .[109]

As newly appointed Dean of the Faculty of Law at McGill, Scott remained a very active lobbyist where constitutional matters were concerned, even consulting with Prime Minister Pearson on such matters.

His suggestion regarding expert advice inside the cabinet on constitutional developments was considered helpful by Pearson. Would Michael Pitfield make a good secretary for a group of experts? Scott thought he would. This committee was the nucleus for what later became Senator Carl H. Goldenberg's Committee on the Constitution, which reported directly in 1967 to Minister of Justice Pierre Trudeau.[110]

Shortly after becoming Minister of Justice, Trudeau initiated a "comprehensive review" of the Constitution. The following year he delivered an address to the Canadian Bar Association called "A Constitutional Declaration of Human Rights" in which he described the activities of the advisory body:

We have reached the conclusion that the basis most likely to find a wide degree of acceptance, and one that is in itself a matter calling for urgent attention, is a constitutional Bill of Rights—a Bill that would guarantee the fundamental freedoms of the citizen from interference, whether federal or provincial, and that would have a high degree of permanence in that neither Parliament nor the Legislatures would be able to modify its terms by the ordinary legislative process.[111]

---

108 *Ibid.* at 208.

109 *Ibid.* at 210.

110 Djwa, *supra*, note 19 at 397–98.

111 Trudeau, *Federalism and the French Canadians*, *supra*, note 87 at 54.

He described the new legislation as being broader in scope than the *Canadian Bill of Rights*. While it would include all of the "familiar basic rights (freedom of belief and expression, freedom of association, the right to a fair trial and to fair legal procedures generally)," as well as the familiar guarantees against discrimination contained in the *Canadian Bill of Rights*, the new Bill would go much further in guaranteeing language rights. It would apply to both Parliament and the provincial legislatures so that their powers "would be restrained in favour of the Canadian citizen who would, in consequence, be better protected in the exercise of his fundamental rights and freedoms."[112] But Trudeau could see that many technical difficulties would have to be ironed out:

> Should the rights be declared generally, or defined precisely with exceptions clearly specified? For example, if we guarantee freedom of speech without qualification, will this invalidate some of our laws which deal with obscenity, sedition, defamation, or film censorship? Is freedom of religion compatible with compulsory Sunday-closing legislation? What of a constitutional guarantee of 'due process of law'? . . . Should we avoid the possibility of such an interpretation of 'due process' in Canada by using a more precise term to guarantee the rule of law? What of the right to counsel? Should this 'right' impose a duty on the government to provide counsel for those who cannot afford it? . . .
>
> These are some of the questions which will arise as we try to develop a constitutional Bill of Rights.[113]

Once the fundamental rights were guaranteed, said Trudeau, they would be beyond the reach of government at all levels. This would confer new, important responsibilities on the courts, which would have to interpret the Bill of Rights to decide the scope of the protected rights and the extent of curtailment of government power. But he added: "Let us first agree on the basic freedoms, on the fundamental rights that we wish to guarantee. After that, we will deal with the mechanism."[114]

Less than six months after his presentation to the Canadian Bar Association, Trudeau's team of constitutional experts received the blessing of the provinces for a comprehensive review of the constitution by a joint Senate and House of Commons committee "appointed to examine and report upon proposals, made public, or which are from time to time made public by the Government of Canada, on a number of subjects related to the Constitution of Canada during the course of the comprehensive

---

112 *Ibid*. at 57.

113 *Ibid*. at 56.

114 *Ibid*. at 58–59.

review."[115] Within a year, Trudeau's team had prepared the Federal White Paper "The Constitution and the People of Canada."

The Senate could not have chosen a more poignant date than 8 October 1970 to initiate the setting up of a Special Joint Committee of the Senate and the House of Commons to examine and report upon the proposals of the Government of Canada in the area of the Constitution, for that was the day the C.B.C. broadcast the F.L.Q. Manifesto in response to the kidnapping of British trade commissioner James Cross three days earlier. On 10 October, Pierre Laporte, Quebec's Minister of Immigration and Manpower and Labour, was kidnapped. On 15 October, the day before the invocation of the *War Measures Act* by Pierre Trudeau and two days before Laporte's murder, the House of Commons passed a resolution by which they joined forces with the Senate in establishing a Joint Committee on the Constitution. The joint committee met to take evidence for the first time at the Lord Nelson Inn in Halifax on Monday, 19 October 1970—the day before the funeral of Pierre Laporte. In the succeeding weeks, ironically at a time of grave constitutional crisis when civil liberties in the country had been suspended indefinitely under the *War Measures Act*, the Joint Committee began its work of hearing Canadians' concerns about constitutional reform and civil liberties. In particular, it heard from a wide range of academics with a background in law— including the foremost constitutional experts of the day, F.R. Scott, D.A. Schmeiser, and Walter Tarnopolsky.

Scott continued to correspond with Trudeau directly on constitutional matters during this period, occasionally expressing his outrage at the way some policies were being implemented, especially where bilingualism and biculturalism were concerned. In 1975, he drafted (but did not send) a letter in which he made a personal plea to Trudeau to intervene in the Quebec language issue surrounding Bill 101:

> Every now and then certain elements in Quebec have to be checked, Pierre, and this is one such occasion. We would still have the Padlock Act if the Supreme Court had not saved the day for Quebec liberals. Same with arbitrary executive action but for Roncarelli. Same with terrorism but for your action against the F.L.Q. . . .[116]

Although the letter itself says more about Scott than about Trudeau, it is telling in terms of the close nature of their ongoing relationship.

By August 1978, it had become clear that Bill C–60, which was then being considered by a parliamentary committee, needed substantial re-

---

115 *Proceedings of the Special Joint Committee on the Constitution of Canada*, 19 October 1970 at 1:5.

116 Djwa, *supra*, note 19 at 426.

drafting. Trudeau personally asked Scott to revise and condense the Bill of Rights to be included in the new Constitutional Act.[117] Scott agreed at first, but upon reflection declined, saying that he felt "a profound sense of hopelessness in our constitutional future." He wrote to Michael Pitfield:

> I am afraid I have not recovered from the blow to all my beliefs dealt by Bill C–60. If the previous constitution was unworkable, the one that seems to be emerging will be doubly so. . . . Pierre himself, despite some brave words about the need for a strong government at Ottawa, has aided and abetted the disintegration. I dubbed him a "separatist by abandonment." . . . What I asked myself was, how does a Bill of Rights fit into the new constitution? Will there be a preamble to the revised *B.N.A. Act* different from the preamble to the [Bill of Rights]? I don't want to try to improve the wording of a part of the document in ignorance of the shape and power-distribution in the whole structure.[118]

In Scott's view, the biggest problem with the Charter of Rights, as it was eventually adopted, was the "notwithstanding" clause: "Even Pierre Trudeau himself contributed to this disappearance of the old concept of Canada by his willingness to make concession after concession to the demands of the Quebec nationalists," Scott declared,[119] presciently anticipating the controversy that was to come decades later with Quebec's invocation of the "notwithstanding" clause to protect its language laws.

Djwa remarked that neither Trudeau nor Scott recognized "the profound influence [Scott's] vision of Quebec and his constitutional thinking had on the former Prime Minister":

> As co-editor of *Quebec States Her Case*, Scott undoubtedly read Michael Oliver's introduction where the latter remarked on Trudeau's "novel" idea of entrenching a Bill of Rights in the constitution. But Scott had not reminded Oliver that he had been advocating this idea to Trudeau and others ever since the forties. It is unlikely he thought of it, for, as he so frequently said, "there is no copyright on ideas." Yet the parallel between Scott's forties constitutional writings on Quebec and those of Trudeau in the fifties and sixties seems apparent. However, the validity of this connection was not fully documented until September, 1984, when I read aloud a paragraph on the "just society" from Scott's 1939 essay on "A Policy of Neutrality for Canada" to Pierre Trudeau: momen-

---

117 *Ibid*. at 434.

118 *Ibid*. at 434–35.

119 *Ibid*. at 437 (letter F.R. Scott to Sandra Djwa).

tarily, neither of us could decide whether he or Scott had been the author.[120]

The persecution of Jehovah's Witnesses by Duplessis directly sharpened the focus of the issue of fundamental freedoms for Scott, and possibly for Trudeau. Certainly Trudeau was influenced by the activities and reasoned opinions of Scott on constitutional matters, including the necessity of entrenching a Bill of Rights that would protect the rights of unpopular minorities. Trudeau showed familiarity with the Jehovah's Witnesses cases of the 1950s, socialized with Roncarelli, and regarded Roncarelli's lawyer as a mentor and friend. Indirectly at least, Jehovah's Witnesses through their litigation helped shape the opinion of Prime Minister Pierre Elliott Trudeau, the man who more than anyone else became a driving force behind Canadian constitutional reform. With the passage in Westminster of the *Canada Act 1982 (U.K.)*, Canada's Constitution was safely patriated for the first time, and the *Canadian Charter of Rights and Freedoms* was incorporated into the Constitution as Part I of the Canadian *Constitution Act, 1982*. Further amendments were incorporated under the Constitution Amendment Proclamation of 1983, which became effective on 21 June 1984.

Long after his retirement as Prime Minister, Trudeau continued to influence the unfolding of constitutional reform. An outspoken opponent of the Meech Lake Accord reached between the federal government and the provinces in 1986, Trudeau lobbied tirelessly against special status for Quebec, seeing this as a direct threat to Confederation. Many attribute the ultimate failure of the Meech Lake Accord to Trudeau's behind-the-scenes influence, especially in his support of the position taken by Newfoundland premier Clyde Wells.[121]

On 13 December 1991, Trudeau expressed his concerns about the threat to fundamental freedoms in Canada at a fund-raising dinner for the newly resurrected *Cité Libre*, the magazine he had helped found four decades earlier. Citing the imposition of Quebec's Bill 178, which restricted signs in languages other than French, Trudeau warned that unless the fundamental rights of the individual take precedence over collective rights, Canada could anticipate an increased "tyranny of the majority."[122] He made it clear that his view had not changed that, compared to collective rights, "individual rights are supreme." On October 1, 1992, Trudeau spoke out strongly against voting "yes" in the

---

120 *Ibid.* at 456–57.

121 On the other hand, it is unlikely that the Meech Lake Accord would have survived the solitary negative vote of Elijah Harper in the Manitoba Legislature.

122 Andre Pecard, "Trudeau trumpets individual rights," *Globe and Mail*, Saturday, 14 December 1991 at A5.

constitutional referendum that determined the reshaping of Canada including concessions to Quebec as "a distinct society." Ironically, the publishers of Trudeau's speech on the subject were warned in the following week that the publication might contravene Quebec's referendum law. Quebec's chief returning officer Pierre-F. Côté, wrote to the publishers, Les Editions de l'étincelle, that publication and distribution of the speech would be governed by a spending cap on the No committee. Thus, even Trudeau, the architect of freedom of expression, was subjected to a form of censorship designed to delay publication on his speech until after the 26 October 1992 referendum.

The process of drafting the *Canadian Charter of Rights and Freedoms* took more than a decade, during which time two special commissions and representatives of the Trudeau government ranged across the country seeking advice and input from Canadians of all walks of life. The Commissioners paid especial attention to what was said by law professors and historians, many of whom shared their insights as to the significance and weakness of the existing *Canadian Bill of Rights*. Several of these academics, including D.A. Schmeiser, Walter Tarnopolsky and M. James Penton, all of whom had written books on the struggle for civil liberties in Canada, also shared insights as to the role of Jehovah's Witnesses in developing the rights and freedoms that Trudeau sought to entrench in Canada's refurbished Constitution. Their opinions are worthy of examination, since they indubitably helped shape the *Canadian Charter of Rights and Freedoms* into its current form.

6

The Critical Reception of the Jehovah's Witnesses Cases

I. D.A. SCHMEISER'S *CIVIL LIBERTIES IN CANADA*

The first detailed analysis of the role of fundamental freedoms and human rights, especially vis-à-vis the Canadian constitution and the implications of the newly passed *Canadian Bill of Rights*, was D.A. Schmeiser's *Civil Liberties in Canada* (1964).[1] Schmeiser was at that time a professor of law at the University of Saskatchewan and a colleague of Walter Tarnopolsky. Schmeiser clearly regarded *Saumur* v. *Quebec* as the quintessential Canadian civil liberties case, and the central theme of his book was the protection of religious freedom. After all, as Rand J. had remarked in *Saumur*,

> Religious freedom has, in our legal system, been recognized as a principle of fundamental character. . . . That the untrammelled affirmations of religious belief and its propagation, personal or institutional, remain as of the greatest constitutional significance throughout the Dominion is unquestionable.[2]

Schmeiser excuses his relatively limited treatment of civil liberties other than freedom of religion by arguing that the first five of the "seven distinct but closely interrelated freedoms" identified by Anson Phelps Stokes in *Church and State in the United States*[3] are not a problem for Canadians. He lists these five as 1) freedom of conscience, 2) freedom of worship, 3) freedom of association, 4) freedom of propaganda, and 5) freedom from civil disability:[4]

---

1 London: Oxford University Press, 1964.

2 [1953] 4 D.L.R. 641 at 668.

3 New York: Harper, 1950.

4 Schmeiser, *supra*, note 1 at 54.

The first five freedoms do not present much difficulty in Canada, although the fourth was severely strained by the controversy involving the Jehovah's Witnesses in the Province of Quebec. No responsible Canadian advocates the denial of any of these, and so it is unnecessary at this stage of our development to justify them. The sixth and seventh cannot be dismissed so easily, however.[5]

The remaining two freedoms, freedom from discrimination by the state on the basis of religion, and freedom of the church from control by the state, constitute the focus of the first two-thirds of Schmeiser's study.

His analysis of *Saumur* starts with the question of jurisdiction. It will be recalled that Chief Justice Rinfret, with Mr. Justice Taschereau concurring, held that "property and civil rights" should be "used in their largest sense,"[6] and Mr. Justice Kerwin held that the right to practice one's religion was a civil right in the Province under head (13) of s. 92.[7] Arguments by the City of Quebec that head (16) might also apply in *Saumur* were shot down by Mr. Justice Rand, who regarded it as self-evident that legislation in relation to the profession of a religion or to religion itself was neither a local nor a private matter but had national dimensions appertaining to a sensitive yet "boundless field of ideas, beliefs and faiths with the deepest roots and loyalties."[8] Schmeiser notes that Rand was joined by Justices Kellock and Locke in finding that the s. 92 "civil rights" did not include fundamental freedoms such as freedom of religion, and that the subject was beyond provincial competence.[9] Mr. Justice Estey also found the municipal by-law *ultra vires* by virtue of the fact that freedom of religion, in his view, fell under the "criminal law" power.[10] Two of the Justices, Cartwright and Fauteau, avoided the constitutional issue altogether. Schmeiser concluded:

> To summarize, three judges held that religious freedom was a civil right; four held that it was not (one of the four holding that it came under the criminal law power); and two did not deal with the problem. Four judges held the by-law in question to be *ultra vires*; five held the by-law to be *intra vires*, but one of the five held that the by-law did not operate so as to prohibit Saumur from distributing his tracts. The final result of the litigation, accordingly, was that Saumur won his case, but the by-law stood.

---

5 *Ibid.* at 54–55.

6 [1953], 4 D.L.R. 641 at 660.

7 *Ibid.* at 664.

8 *Ibid.* at 670.

9 *Ibid.* at 717–18.

10 *Ibid.* at 699–700.

> With such result, and with such variation in the judgments, it is indeed difficult to cite the decision as authority for very much.[11]

Nonetheless, the individual arguments, especially those of Rand J., have been cited again and again as clarifying the law in the area of civil liberties, and subsequent cases adjudged by the same justices on similar issues were nowhere nearly as inconclusive.[12]

Schmeiser points out that Canada's leading constitutional authorities, including F.R. Scott, Bora Laskin and Louis-Philippe Pigeon, concluded that "religious freedom is within federal competence under the criminal law power." But such an argument leads to another conundrum: although Laskin has suggested that religious discrimination could be made a criminal offence,[13] when would such a putative "offence" encroach upon the other freedoms, such as freedom of speech or freedom of the press? What is "discrimination?" Could such a law really be enacted in a meaningful way? Can one really legislate absence of discrimination in a criminal sense? The better view, according to Schmeiser, seems to be that of Mr. Justice Rand:

> Despite the present trend towards including religious freedom in the criminal law power, it might nevertheless be better to follow the cautious approach of Rand J. in the *Saumur* and *Birks* decisions in denying provincial competence over religious freedom without handing it to Parliament. The day might well arrive when our Courts would like the power to deny the competence of both Parliament and the legislatures to interfere with religious freedom.[14]

Like Scott, Schmeiser treated *Chaput v. Romain, Lamb v. Benoit* and *Roncarelli v. Duplessis* as a trilogy providing "strong precedents" for anyone deprived of a basic right.[15] But Schmeiser focused more on the implications of the decisions on statutory interpretation. In *Chaput* and

---

11 Schmeiser, *supra*, note 1 at 82. Compare Bora Laskin's analysis in "An Inquiry into the Diefenbaker Bill of Rights" (1959), 37 Can. Bar Rev. 77 at 116–17:"The awkward result of the case was that while six justices denied provincial competence at least in some circumstances, five justices affirmed provincial competence, at least in some circumstances; and while four justices denied federal competence at least in some circumstances, five justices denied federal competence at least in some circumstances; and yet only three justices denied any federal power, while four justices denied any provincial power."

12 In particular *Henry Birks & Sons* v. *Montreal* (1955), [1955] S.C.R. 799, [1955] 5 D.L.R. 321, 113 C.C.C. 135.

13 "An Inquiry into the Diefenbaker Bill of Rights" (1959), 37 Can. Bar. Rev. 77 at 100–122.

14 Schmeiser, *supra*, note 1 at 87.

15 *Ibid*. at 117.

Lamb the statutes concerned were the *Magistrate's Privilege Act*[16] and the *Provincial Police Act*,[17] which protected any policeman who "has exceeded his powers or jurisdiction, and has acted clearly contrary to law" provided he acted in good faith and in the execution of duty. As we have seen, the Supreme Court ruled that the fact that the police were operating under orders of a superior officer was irrelevant. Furthermore, in *Chaput* the *Magistrate's Privilege Act* did not grant total immunity, especially where the police had themselves broken the law by interfering in a religious service in what Rand called a "flagrant violation" of Chaput's rights. The police could not claim to have acted in good faith; nor on the facts could they show any justification for behaving the way they did in breaking up the private meeting and escorting the minister to the ferry.[18] Similarly in *Lamb*, the six-month limitation period provided by statute was held to be inapplicable since Benoit had acted outside his official capacity and the initial arrest was not justified.[19]

In the *Roncarelli* case, a clear majority of the Court found that the discretionary power held by the one-man Liquor Commission to cancel liquor permits could only be exercised in relation to the administration or enforcement of the *Alcoholic Liquor Act*.[20] Since Duplessis acted totally outside his legal capacity as Attorney-General and Premier, the notice normally required by art. 88 of the *Code of Civil Procedure* was unnecessary.[21]

Schmeiser concluded regarding the trilogy:

> In effect, the Supreme Court ignored the express words of the statutes, and forcefully indicated that it would construe away any limitation sections if the offending person had acted illegally. Any error of law, no matter how involved the point of law was, could be sufficient to remove a claim of good faith. It may well be that the authority of these decisions will provide a stronger basis for respect of the basic liberties than any prohibitive statute ever could.[22]

---

16 R.S.Q. 1941, c. 18, s. 7.

17 R.S.Q. 1941, c. 47.

18 Schmeiser, *supra*, note 1 at 87.

19 Per Kerwin C.J., Cartwright, Rand, Judson, Locke and Martland JJ. Note that Taschereau, Fauteux and Abbott JJ. took exactly the opposite position, stating that Benoit had acted in his official capacity and that therefore the statutory limitation did apply.

20 R.S.Q. 1941, c. 255.

21 Per Kerwin C.J., Locke, Martland, Rand, Judson and Abbott JJ. Fauteau J., by contrast, held that even though the actions were illegal, failure to give notice barred the action.

22 *Supra*, note 1 at 117.

In these three cases, said Schmeiser, "the Supreme Court of Canada has shown how far it is prepared to go in construing statutes so as to allow civil remedies in the event of any infringement on basic human rights."[23]

With the exception of James Penton's specialized treatment of Jehovah's Witnesses,[24] Schmeiser critically examines more Jehovah's Witnesses cases than any other writer on civil liberties, and naturally covers a wide ground. He deals with the issue of Jehovah's Witnesses students refusing to salute the flag, as in *Ruman* v. *Lethbridge School Board Trustees*,[25] an administrative law case in which the central question was "whether the board acted within their powers under the School Act";[26] and *Donald* v. *Hamilton Board of Education*,[27] in which the Witnesses argued that saluting the flag and standing for the national anthem were "exercises of devotion or religion, objected to by his parent or guardian" in which students could not be forced to participate despite a statute which required obedient compliance with prescribed patriotic exercises. The Witnesses lost both cases at trial. Donald won on appeal to the Ontario Court of Appeal, and in Alberta the legislature hastily amended the *School Act*[28] to accommodate Ruman by requiring students whose parents objected to saluting the flag merely to stand to attention during the flag-raising ceremony.[29] School children also figured prominently in *Perron* v. *Rouyn School Trustees*, where the Protestant school board prevented Jehovah's Witnesses from entering a school because they were not technically Protestant, and *Chabot* v. *School Commissioners of Lamorandière*, where the Catholic school board refused to accept Jehovah's Witness children into a school unless they took part in Roman Catholic religious exercises. The Witnesses won both cases, the first because the Protestant board relied on a semantic argument (the court ruled that to be considered Protestant one only had to be a Christian who repudiates the authority of the Pope), and the second because it was the natural right of any parent "to give one's children the religious education of one's choice."[30] Schmeiser also refers to *R.* v. *Naish*,[31] which held that

---

23 *Ibid.* at 115.

24 *Jehovah's Witnesses in Canada: Champions of Freedom of Speech and Worship* (Toronto: Macmillan, 1976).

25 (1943), [1943] 3 W.W.R. 340.

26 *Ibid.* at 345.

27 (1945), [1945] O.R. 518, [1945] 3 D.L.R. 424, O.W.N. 526 (C.A.), rev'g (1944), [1944] O.R. 475, [1944] 4 D.L.R. 227, O.W.N. 559 (H.C.).

28 S.A. 1944, c. 46, s. 9.

29 Schmeiser, *supra*, note 1 at 88.

30 (1957), [1957] Que. Q.B. 707, 12 D.L.R. (2d) 796 at 802 (C.A.).

31 (1950), [1950] 1 W.W.R. 987, 10 C.R. 65, 97 C.C.C. 19.

passing out religious tracts was an activity protected by the Saskatchewan Bill of Rights.[32]

With respect to specifically religious rights, Schmeiser concluded:

> In effect the main protection afforded by our law to a person whose religious freedom has been violated is his right of civil action. The most likely actions available to an aggrieved person would be for assault, trespass, false arrest, false imprisonment, or malicious prosecution. In such a case, the Courts have power to award exemplary or punitive damages—a deterrent potentially as strong as the threat of criminal prosecution.[33]

Schmeiser turns once again to *Saumur* in his discussion of "The Communicative Freedoms," citing Abbott J. as authority for the proposition that "as our constitutional Act now stands, Parliament itself could not abrogate this right of discussion and debate."[34] Here, says Schmeiser, "we have the first clear judicial denial of Parliament's absolute control over basic human rights. In so doing, Abbott J. undoubtedly gained for himself a niche in the history of civil liberties in Canada."[35] After reviewing the relationship between *Saumur*, the Padlock Act case[36] and the much earlier but highly influential *Alberta Press* case,[37] Schmeiser remarks that as a result of these decisions, "any provincial claim over freedom of speech is very shaky, but the same reasoning comes uncomfortably close to applying to Parliament as well."[38]

In his discussion of criminal sanctions applied against freedom of expression, Schmeiser focuses on the two main Jehovah's Witnesses cases in which the appellants had been charged with sedition, *Duval v. R.*[39] and *Boucher v. R.*,[40] and points out the opposite approaches taken by the Courts. He begins his analysis by comparing the tracts that the two accused were alleged to have been circulating, Duval in 1938 and Boucher ten years later. Duval's tracts declared that "the clergy, the profiteers and

---

32 Schmeiser, *supra*, note 1 at 91.

33 *Ibid.* at 114.

34 7 D.L.R. (2d) 337 at 371.

35 Schmeiser, *supra*, note 1 at 203.

36 *Switzman v. Elbling* (1957), [1957] S.C.R. 285, 7 D.L.R. (2d) 337, 117 C.C.C. 129.

37 *Reference re Alberta Statutes* (1938), [1938] S.C.R. 100, [1938] 2 D.L.R. 81.

38 Schmeiser, *supra*, note 1 at 203.

39 (1938), 64 Que. K.B. 270 (C.A.), leave to appeal to S.C.C. refused (1938), [1938] S.C.R. 390, [1938] 4 D.L.R. 747 [hereinafter *Duval* cited to Que. K.B.].

40 (1950), [1951] S.C.R. 265, [1951] 2 D.L.R. 369, 99 C.C.C. 1, 11 C.R. 85, rev'g (1949), 95 C.C.C. 119, 8 C.R. 97 (Que. C.A.), and replacing after re-argument [1950] 1 D.L.R. 657, 96 C.C.C. 48, 9 C.R. 127.

the politicians are in an alliance to govern the peoples of earth, and their god or invisible ruler is Satan the Devil, the prince of evil." This sentiment was repeated in various ways in three separate tracts.[41] Boucher's tract, *Quebec's Burning Hate*, protested the widespread persecution of Jehovah's Witnesses in the "benighted, priest-ridden province" of Quebec:

> All the facts unite to thunderously declare that the force behind Quebec's suicidal hate is priest domination. Thousands of Quebec Catholics are so blinded by the priests that they think they serve God's cause in mobbing Jehovah's Witnesses. . . .
>
> Quebec, Jehovah's witnesses are telling all Canada of the shame you have brought on the nation by your evil deeds. . . . You crush freedom by mob rule and gestapo tactics. . . . Quebec, you have yielded yourself as an obedient servant of religious priests, and you have brought forth bumper crops of evil fruits.[42]

In convicting Duval, Judge Barclay declared that the pamphlets encouraged condemnation of and contempt for "all forms of organized authority, whether civil or ecclesiastical." Even though the belief is sincerely held, he said, "no remedy is suggested, the only remedy being the complete destruction by Jehovah of all existing institutions." In the view of Barclay J., this did not constitute "fair criticism."[43] Similarly, in affirming the conviction of Boucher, the Quebec Court of Appeal noted that the pamphlet not only promoted feelings of ill-will and hostility between different classes of subjects, but also brought the government and the administration of justice into contempt.[44]

As we have seen, the Supreme Court of Canada required two hearings to decide the *Boucher* cliff-hanger in an eventual 5–4 split. Schmeiser's brief but interesting analysis of the appeal shows just how complex—and how close—was this pivotal civil liberties decision:

> The full Court with only Rinfret C.J.C. dissenting, held that the writings complained of must, in addition to raising discontent or disaffection among subjects or promoting ill-will or hostility between different classes, be intended to produce disturbance of or resistance to established authority. The Court was more divided on the question of bring-

---

41 To this day the notion that Satan is literally in control of the clergy, big business and politics remains a central tenet of faith for Jehovah's Witnesses. See Heather and Gary Botting, *The Orwellian World of Jehovah's Witnesses* (Toronto: University of Toronto Press, 1984) at 13; see also *You Can Live Forever in Paradise on Earth* (New York: Watch Tower Bible and Tract Society, 1982) at 18.

42 [1950] 1 D.L.R. 657 at 672–73.

43 *Duval, supra,* note 39 at 279–80.

44 95 C.C.C. 119. See Schmeiser, *supra,* note 1 at 210.

ing the administration of justice into hatred or contempt, or exciting disaffection against it. Kerwin, Kellock, Estey and Locke JJ. held that there must also be an intention to incite people to violence against or to defeat the functioning of the administration of justice. Taschereau, Cartwright and Fauteux JJ. held that an intention to bring the administration of justice into hatred and contempt was sufficient to constitute a seditious intention. Rinfret C.J.C. and Rand J. did not express any opinion on this question, although there is no doubt that Rinfret C.J.C. would have denied that an intention to incite to violence was necessary, whereas Rand J. would probably have held the opposite. The majority of the Court found no evidence on the record sufficient to convict the accused, whereas the minority would have ordered a new trial.[45]

It therefore became necessary in sedition cases for the Crown to establish beyond a reasonable doubt "an intention to incite to rebellion"—a difficult test to meet, although Schmeiser speculates that some courts may try to get around the "*Boucher* test" by "inferring the intent to incite to rebel from the words used."[46]

Schmeiser compares the charge of sedition in *Boucher* to the charge of spreading false news in *R. v. Carrier,*[47] which also arose from the distribution of *Quebec's Burning Hate*. Here, Drouin J. of the Quebec Court of King's Bench stated that since the aim of both the false news provision and the sedition provision of the *Criminal Code* was to suppress "seditious offences," the offences were "substantially the same."[48] Schmeiser concluded from this observation that the "spreading false news" section of the *Code*[49] is "completely redundant":

> Under the existing authorities, accordingly, any group, organization, nationality, race or religion may be attacked in intemperate and abusive language. The individual who baits any of these groups, stirring up unrest and hatred, or who brings governmental institutions into contempt and disrespect is legally untouchable. The fact that what he says is a complete falsehood does not matter. In considering whether this situation should be changed, attention should be drawn to the large body of opinion holding that these occasional transgressions are the price one must pay for freedom of speech.[50]

---

45 Schmeiser, *supra*, note 1 at 211.

46 *Ibid.*

47 (1951), 104 C.C.C. 75, 16 C.R. 18.

48 *Ibid.* at 85–86.

49 Former s. 166, now s. 181.

50 Schmeiser, *supra*, note 1 at 214.

Like F.R. Scott, Schmeiser was invited to address the Joint Committee on the Constitution when it met in Saskatchewan in February 1971. Schmeiser submitted a lengthy brief in which he reviewed American law indicating that entrenchment of a Bill of Rights into the Constitution could lead to increased litigation, much of it frivolous.[51] Judicial decisions, he said, were by nature political or based on purely personal values, and judicial review was by nature undemocratic, for it amounted to shifting from, if not destruction of, popular or democratic responsibility, judicial appointments not being democratic.[52] He warned that there would be attendant loss of prestige in the courts owing to loss of independence; the spectre of judicial review leads to judges being "labelled" liberal or conservative on the strength of a few judgments, and respect for law and order might be undermined by a few judicial errors.[53] Judicial review is destructive to the Federal principle, he added, and simply would not work in a bicultural Canada, especially where there are two legal systems. "On occasion the Supreme Court has split along civil law–common law lines," he wrote, citing as examples the decisions in *Roncarelli* and *Lamb*, "and many people have questioned the propriety of a system which makes that possible."[54] The principle of *stare decisis* may be threatened by entrenchment, judicial protection may be rendered ineffective, and judicial review may raise false hopes among the populace. Furthermore Canadian identity may be threatened by a system similar to the American system, cases from which Schmeiser cited again and again to demonstrate his thesis. "If Canadians entrench fundamental rights," he concluded, "they will be rejecting a system which has worked reasonably well in Canada in favour of a system that is working badly in the United States."[55]

Schmeiser was even more adamant in his oral presentation. "I think that entrenchment would be a very great mistake," he said. "It seems to me that not enough study and attention has been given to the other side of the story."[56] Asked his position on freedom of conscience and freedom of thought, Schmeiser agreed that there were certain things a state should not do, "but the problem is who is to decide in a difficult social issue." Once again he turned to Jehovah's Witnesses for an example, this time alluding to a blood transfusion case:

---

51 *Proceedings of the Joint Committee on the Constitution of Canada*, 23 February 1971 at 49:47–50.

52 *Ibid.* at 49:40–42.

53 *Ibid.* at 49:44–45.

54 *Ibid.* at 49:50–52.

55 *Ibid.* at 49:56.

56 *Ibid.* at 49:6.

We had an experience in Western Canada in the last few days involving a Jehovah's Witness child, where the parents took the child from a hospital to avoid an operation which might involve a blood transfusion. It is fine to talk about religious freedom there—because I personally think society is right in saying that a child, at a stage where the child cannot decide for itself, must be given the transfusion over the wishes of the parent. There comes a time when you realize that on every social issue there will be differing opinions. The problem is not the question of what the ideal is, because I would support the rights of others as much as I possibly could.

The real issue is this: In the final analysis who makes the judgment whether or not the child gets a blood transfusion? In my judgment, Parliament should be deciding that basic policy issue. Obviously, we all agree that we are in favour of freedom of religion. Obviously, we all agree that we are in favour of freedom of speech and assembly and association. The question is who decides what that means.[57]

In Schmeiser's opinion, with the entrenchment of the Bill of Rights, the Supreme Court of Canada would be making decisions that more properly were the prerogative of an elected Parliament. Thus democracy would be thwarted.[58]

Although Schmeiser has not distinguished himself in the area of constitutional law as markedly as Scott and Tarnopolsky, his recognition of religious freedom as a paradigm for all the other fundamental freedoms is of major significance. He was perhaps the first to recognize that religious liberty by its nature entails freedom of speech, freedom of peaceful assembly, freedom of association, freedom of the press and other media of communication, freedom of expression, freedom of conscience, freedom of thought, freedom of belief, freedom of opinion—in short all of the fundamental freedoms now listed in s. 2 of the *Charter*. The Jehovah's Witnesses cases that Schmeiser described in such detail define, indeed epitomize, the essence of freedom of religion. Freedom of religion, in turn, epitomizes the rights and freedoms embodied in the *Charter of Rights and Freedoms* now solidly entrenched in the Canadian Constitution.

II. WALTER TARNOPOLSKY'S *THE CANADIAN BILL OF RIGHTS*

The second important book to be published on Canadian civil liberties subsequent to the adoption of the *Canadian Bill of Rights* was written by Professor Schmeiser's colleague at the University of Saskatchewan, Professor Walter Tarnopolsky, who currently sits as a Justice of the Ontario Court of Appeal. In his popular study *The Canadian Bill of Rights*

---

57 *Ibid.* at 49:17.

58 *Ibid.* at 49:20.

(1966),[59] Tarnopolsky covered much of the same ground as Schmeiser's book of two years earlier, but his approach was far more balanced; indeed, freedom of religion gets relatively short shrift compared to broader constitutional issues and the political, economic, legal and egalitarian civil liberties issues which are pivotal chapter headings in his study. Tarnopolsky unabashedly borrowed the notion of four main categories of civil liberties from Bora Laskin.[60]

Tarnopolsky called the *Saumur* case "the first post-war case in which a substantial majority of the Supreme Court dealt with the problem of jurisdiction in relation to freedoms of speech, assembly and religion."[61] Indeed, jurisdiction often became the primary issue, and civil liberties themselves decidedly secondary:

> Nearly all decisions of Canadian courts which can be said to touch on civil liberties have been rendered on other grounds, and where civil liberties were discussed, the main attention was focussed on the question of constitutional validity in accordance with the distribution of legislative power under the *B.N.A. Act*. The great Canadian civil liberties cases such as the . . . *Saumur* case . . . were more concerned about legislative jurisdiction than with the question of the existence or extent of certain liberties.[62]

The leading Canadian constitutional law experts in 1959—including Professors Scott, Laskin and Pigeon—concurred in the notion that freedom of religion at least was within federal jurisdiction. But "infringements of civil liberties usually involve several rights and freedoms at once":

> Thus, when police prevent the holding of a service by Witnesses of Jehovah they may be interfering not only with freedom of religion, but with freedom of speech and of assembly as well, and if they seize any of the literature on the premises they may be infringing on freedom of the press.[63]

How does the jurisdiction question affect these closely related but very different issues? Is it possible, for example, for an individual charged with distributing tracts to be protected under one liberty but not pro-

---

59 (Toronto: Carswell, 1966).

60 *Ibid.* at 3. See also his remarks to the 1970 Joint Committee on the Constitution at 8:14. Compare Bora Laskin, "An Inquiry into the Diefenbaker Bill of Rights" (1959), 37 Can. Bar Rev. 77, and "Note on Civil Liberties and Legislative Power," in *Canadian Constitutional Law*, 2d ed. (Toronto: Carswell, 1960) at 938.

61 *Ibid.* at 11.

62 *Ibid.* at 114.

63 *Ibid.*

tected under another? Did it not make sense to lump the various "liberties" together and treat them similarly rather than placing one liberty under one jurisdiction and another under the other?

Bora Laskin was among the first to support Scott in the distinction between civil liberties and civil rights that was pivotal in making the federalist argument with respect to jurisdiction in civil liberties cases.[64] Tarnopolsky pointed out that an important consideration for determining the proper distribution of powers in relation to civil liberties was the application of the "pith and substance" rule originating with *Union Colliery of British Columbia Ltd. v. Bryden*.[65] In *Saumur*, for example, it became necessary for the Court to ascertain the "pith and substance" of the legislation that purported to regulate the activities of Jehovah's Witnesses:

> Is it, for instance, legislation providing for regulation of streets and sidewalks, or is it legislation attempting to interfere with freedom of speech? Is it possible that the distribution of handbills in the streets may for one purpose and in one aspect be subject to municipal by-laws preventing obstruction of public places, while for another purpose and in another aspect such distribution may be included under freedom of religion as being the right to distribute and disseminate information on one's religious beliefs?[66]

To the extent that free speech and the press can be limited by the criminal law of sedition, these freedoms too should fit under federal jurisdiction, as was made clear in "the important case of *Boucher v. The King*."[67] To the extent that defamation has a criminal component, it is a federal offence, but any tort action in defamation is of provincial concern.[68] Censorship, including film censorship, says Tarnopolsky, is properly within federal jurisdiction, especially in light of the *Alberta Press* case.[69]

In the *Padlock* case[70] F.R. Scott used the same arguments as had been used by Glen How in *Saumur* with respect to the relationship between "civil rights" and "civil liberties" and their respective jurisdictions. Since the rights of free opinion and free discussion of opinion are essential to the survival of the Parliamentary system, those rights extended to every

---

64 See Laskin, *supra*, note 60.

65 [1899] A.C. 580. This case was the first to use the term, but *Russell v. R.* (1882), 7 App. Cas. 829, was the first to address the question of ambiguity in statutes and whether the "civil rights" provisions of s. 92 of the *B.N.A. Act* would apply.

66 Tarnopolsky, *The Canadian Bill of Rights, supra*, note 59 at 25.

67 *Ibid.* at 27.

68 *Ibid.*

69 *Reference re Alberta Statutes, supra*, note 37.

70 *Switzman v. Elbling, supra*, note 36.

part of Canada, and are therefore not "matters of a merely local or private nature."[71] Thus municipal censorship authorized by the provincial legislature was *ultra vires* the province. It is interesting to note that four years earlier, four of the justices in *Saumur*,[72] the "leading case" of those concerned with censorship through municipal regulation, had adopted this same position.[73] Tarnopolsky admitted that the *ratio decidendi* of *Saumur* was exceedingly obscure, and concluded, "Perhaps the most important result of the case was that the Witness of Jehovah involved did not have to get prior police approval for the distribution of his pamphlets."[74]

Tarnopolsky pointed out that not long after the *Saumur* decision came down, the Quebec government amended the *Freedom of Worship Act* to state that the distribution of tracts attacking other religious groups was not religious worship.

> The day after the statute came into force, its constitutionality was challenged by Jehovah's Witnesses who contended that they were threatened with prosecution under the statute. The case went to the Supreme Court of Canada as *Saumur et al.* v. *Procureur General de Quebec et al.* [1964] S.C.R. 252, where the action for a declaration was dismissed unanimously on the grounds that under Quebec law, in the circumstances, a private citizen has no right to sue for a declaratory judgment. In this case there was neither a wrong nor a dispute, and so there was no necessity for a consideration of the constitutional question.[75]

Beside *Saumur* and the *Padlock* cases, Tarnopolsky lists *Lamb* v. *Benoit*, *Roncarelli* v. *Duplessis* and *Chaput* v. *Romain* as "the famous civil liberties cases of the 1950's." Of these, "the famous Quebec case of *Roncarelli* v. *Duplessis*" strikingly illustrated "the answerability of the executive for its acts done without legal justification."[76] Several years later, Tarnopolsky gave a succinct impromptu summary of the *ratio decidendi* of *Roncarelli* to the Joint Committee on the Constitution of Canada, and especially its constitutional ramifications:

> . . . The protection provided statutorily for Mr. Duplessis was a protection in his office and . . . his action vis-à-vis Mr. Roncarelli was an action that he took outside his office and, therefore, he was not protected under

---

71 *British North America Act*, 1867, s. 92, head 16.

72 Rand, Kellock, Estey and Locke JJ.

73 Tarnopolsky, *The Canadian Bill of Rights*, *supra*, note 59 at 30–31.

74 *Ibid.* at 31.

75 *Ibid.*

76 *Ibid.* at 104.

the special procedural protection involved. . . . Under the rule of law, one is presumably, as a public officer, as subject to the law as anyone else. Therefore, if you act outside your duties and you cause someone wrong, at that point that person has a right to claim.

There is a rather interesting part of it which may not apply to the common law provinces and that is that under the Quebec law of delict, as you know, Senator, one does not have to show that one suffered a specific tort, but one suffered wrong in the circumstances and the other person acted unjustifiably, therefore, one has the right to damages. . . . However at the same time [it] is a constitutional case because it deals with the whole question of an office holder acting for a purpose not connected with the legislation and, therefore, acting outside his sphere and, therefore, not protected.[77]

In *Civil Liberties in Canada*, Tarnopolsky also indicated a possible link between *Roncarelli* and the *Canadian Bill of Rights*, which in its preamble refers to the rule of law, a central theme in *Roncarelli*:

Roncarelli v. *Duplessis* is perhaps the most striking of the Supreme Court decisions which uphold the "rule of law" in Canada. The various concepts discussed above [i.e. in connection with the *Roncarelli* case] indicate what the preamble to the *Bill of Rights* means in its reference to "freedom founded upon . . . the rule of law." These concepts must influence the interpretation that will be given to such provisions in the *Bill of Rights* as the "due process" clause in s. 1(*a*). To ignore this, and to interpret such a clause as being synonymous with a phrase like "according to law," would be too restrictive, and contrary to the intention of Parliament as expressed in the preamble.[78]

Hence the decision in *Roncarelli*, according to Tarnopolsky, could have a far-reaching effect in interpreting the *Bill of Rights*.

If *Roncarelli* was the leading case in the area of the rule of law, and *Saumur* was the leading case in the area of censorship by municipalities, *Boucher* v. *R*. was the leading case in the area of the crime of sedition. Prosecutions for this crime had been "one of the greatest restrictions on freedom of speech and the press in Canada," according to Tarnopolsky, and *Boucher* "set clear limits to excessive prosecutions for this offence":[79]

By a majority of five to four the Supreme Court held that strong words are not enough, and not even an intention to promote ill-will and hostility between subjects . . . is enough: there must be an intention to incite

---

77 *Proceedings of the Special Joint Committee on the Constitution of Canada* (Ottawa, 1970) at 8:22–23.

78 Tarnopolsky, *The Canadian Bill of Rights, supra*, note 59 at 106.

79 *Ibid.* at 127.

the people to violence and to create public disorder or disturbance, or unlawful conduct against Her Majesty or an institution of the state.[80]

After citing the classic judgment in which Rand J., bemoaning the fact that "heresy in some fields is again a mortal sin," stated that "freedom in thought and speech and disagreement in ideas and beliefs, on every conceivable subject, are of the essence of our life," Tarnopolsky concluded:

> There is no doubt that the Supreme Court decision in *Boucher* v. *The King* would preclude a successful prosecution against the dissemination of what has come to be known as "hate" literature, for the literature under scrutiny in that case could well be placed in the same category. Indeed, it is difficult to see how a provision could be framed which would ban "hate" literature and yet not restrict freedom of speech more severely than the Supreme Court would have it restricted. Perhaps the Committee appointed by the former Minister of Justice, the Hon. Guy Favreau, and headed by Dean Maxwell Cohen, will be able to suggest a formula which is workable, effective, and yet not too vague.[81]

But after seeing the recommended additions to the *Criminal Code* forbidding "group hatred," Tarnopolsky was not optimistic:

> If we believe that "freedom of thought and speech and disagreement in ideas and beliefs, on every conceivable subject, are the essence of our life," we should also believe that "our compact of free society" will be able to accept and absorb these differences and be the stronger for rejecting them rationally, rather than suppressing them arbitrarily. It is not suggested that racial discrimination cannot be proscribed effectively, or that "morality" cannot be legislated. Rather, it is here suggested that the most effective method of opposing those who would publish material calculated to bring into hatred, ridicule or contempt, any person or group of persons by reason of race, national origin, colour or religion is through Human Rights Commissions such as that in Ontario, and the active co-operation of educational authorities to educate a new breed of Canadian immune to the effects of "hate" literature.[82]

Tarnopolsky refers to several other Jehovah's Witnesses cases to illustrate specific civil liberties covered by the *Canadian Bill of Rights*, including *Chabot* v. *School Commissioners of Lamorandière and A.G. Quebec* (where there is only one available school, freedom to attend schools of a different faith without being required to participate in the religious

---

80 *Ibid.* at 128.

81 *Ibid.* at 128.

82 *Ibid.* at 128–29.

exercises of that faith); *Donald* v. *Hamilton Board of Education* (where individuals regarded the singing of the national anthem or saluting the flag to be a religious exercise, they would not be required to perform those functions when a statute specified that students would not be forced to participate in religious exercises); and *Ruman* v. *Lethbridge School Board Trustees*, of which Tarnopolsky commented:

> The court dealt with a provincial statute which provided that local school boards could require compulsory patriotic exercises. Since no provision was made for exemption the court held that the children involved would have to comply or be expelled. This is in marked contrast with the American view that schools' legislation requiring patriotic observances is an infringement of freedom of religion.[83]

He also alludes to Jehovah's Witnesses cases dealing with conscription and conscientious objectors.[84] Finally, he turns his attention to Jehovah's Witnesses cases that illustrate protections of civil liberties through litigation or legislation. *Chaput* v. *Romain* and *Lamb* v. *Benoit*, for example, "illustrate that civil action may be a potent weapon in enforcing people's rights, if the legislation giving those rights does not set out specific remedies."[85] *Chaput* also illustrates that the *Criminal Code* offence of obstructing a minister officiating at a religious meeting, or even disturbing such a meeting, gave real protection to freedom of religion in Canada:

> In the Supreme Court of Canada the appeal was unanimously allowed on the grounds that the respondents had committed an illegal act, and that there was no provincial statute rendering them immune from action. Three of the justices (Kerwin C.J.C., Taschereau and Estey JJ.) decided that the conduct of the respondents was in clear violation of the *Criminal Code*. Five of the the judges (Rand, Kellock, Locke, Cartwright and Fauteux JJ.) agreed that the action of the respondents was illegal, *inter alia* for contravention of the *Criminal Code*, and therefore the appellant was entitled to succeed in his action for damages either in delict or quasi-delict under Article 1053 of the Quebec *Civil Code*. Abbott J. concurred as to the illegality, but he did not refer specifically to the *Criminal Code*. In effect, then, the Supreme Court gave unanimous protection to the appellant's freedom of religious worship.[86]

Tarnopolsky was clearly of the view that the influence of the Jehovah's Witnesses cases of the 1950s outlasted the adoption in 1960 of

---

83 *Ibid.* at 120.

84 *Ibid.*

85 *Ibid.* at 182.

86 *Ibid.* at 122.

the *Canadian Bill of Rights*. Partly because the *Bill of Rights* was merely a federal statute applying to the narrow range of federal statutes, actions and initiatives, it did not assume the stature of a constitutional document, and Tarnopolsky was among the first and most vocal of those who saw the need to entrench a Bill of Rights in the Constitution. He distinguished between fundamental rights (including political and legal rights) and egalitarian rights (including the "human rights" of minorities), and initially suggested that these two very different kinds of rights should be kept separate. But by 1970 he had given up on the notion of two separate Bills of Rights in favour of keeping fundamental and egalitarian rights in two separate sections of the same Bill of Rights.[87]

Not long after the publication of *The Canadian Bill of Rights*, Walter Tarnopolsky was appointed Dean of the University of Windsor Law School. One of his first duties was acting as host to F.R. Scott, as we have seen. Then late in 1970, he testified before the Special Joint Committee on the Constitution of Canada on the ways in which the Bill of Rights could be enshrined in the Constitution. Alluding again and again to the Jehovah's Witnesses cases, Tarnopolsky pushed for the idea of entrenchment of a Bill of Rights that would bind both Parliament and the provinces. This was important, he said, for four reasons. In the first place, there was disagreement with respect to legislative jurisdiction, mostly arising in the wake of the work of Professors Scott and Laskin, who showed that civil liberties did not fall under s. 92 of the *B.N.A. Act* and therefore were not strictly a provincial domain: "Nevertheless there is great dispute now. I would put forth the argument . . . that the fundamental freedoms, except for assembly and association, are largely within federal jurisdiction." Secondly, divided jurisdiction with respect to civil liberties required uniformity of standards in the administration of justice which would be difficult to achieve without an entrenched, binding Bill of Rights. Third, there had been many civil liberties cases, those in wartime often involving the federal government, and those in peacetime often involving the provincial governments, including "the infringement if not necessarily the abrogation of fundamental freedoms and human rights." Fourth, the absence of an entrenched Bill of Rights diminished provincial power:

> I do not believe that any Supreme Court with the calibre of men which we now have on it, could have come to different conclusions with respect to the important civil liberties' cases of the nineteen-fifties.
>
> I realize that is an arguable proposition. If one accepts that proposition, then one has to take the further step that the Supreme Court, in the absence of a bill of rights, could only invalidate the

---

87 *Proceedings of the Special Joint Committee on the Constitution of Canada* (Ottawa, 1970) at 8:25.

provincial legislation on the basis that the matter concerned was one within federal jurisdiction.

In other words, the case of *Saumur* v. *City of Quebec*, the case of *Switzman* v. *Elbling*, and, to quite an extent, the much earlier Alberta Press Bill case involved extensions of federal jurisdiction. And I think that the same would happen in the future. I do not see that a Supreme Court faced with similar invasions of civil liberties could come to different conclusions. If it were to do so, it could only do so on the basis that the matter involved was beyond the jurisdiction of the provincial legislature.

Therefore I would have thought that it would be in the interests of the provinces to favour a constitutionally-entrenched charter of human rights.[88]

Tarnopolsky concluded by saying that any bill of rights is by nature concerned with minorities. Whereas governments necessarily reflect the interests of the majority, a bill of rights provides the necessary balance by protecting minorities of various kinds:

Here I include minorities not only of race and religion but minorities which are quite often unpopular and for whom there is little sympathy in the community. In these circumstances, I believe that a bill of rights has to protect everyone or it will protect no one.[89]

Under questioning by the Joint Committee, Tarnopolsky identified "the two really important parts of a bill of rights" as being 1) the fundamental freedoms of speech, press, religion, assembly and association, and 2) the legal rights. Asked whether Parliament and the legislatures were not better equipped to decide policy in these areas than the judiciary, Tarnopolsky replied that the "democratic nature of Parliament makes it more subject to contravening the rights of a minority." Such a minority requires "the protection of an independent body, which a judiciary is."[90]

> *The Joint Chairman (Mr. MacGuigan)*: Is the most basic part of your response to this question the fact that fundamental to our type of society is not only democracy but also liberty?
>
> *Dean Tarnopolsky*: Yes. The point that I have been trying to make throughout is that the important part of a bill of rights is really to ensure protection of minorities. We always speak of the will of the majority and the protection of the minority, and I think the bill of rights is complementary to the electoral process to ensure a

---

88 *Ibid.* at 8:9–10, 5 November 1970.

89 *Ibid.* at 8:13.

90 *Ibid.* at 8:27.

protection of the minority. The electoral process attempts to ensure the will of the majority and I think the bill of rights is really complementary to it, to ensure the liberal democratic state.

The Joint Chairman (Mr. MacGuigan): So we have a minority protection principle as well as a majority rule principle.

Dean Tarnopolsky: This is what I think a bill of rights does, yes.

The Joint Chairman (Mr. Lamontagne): It is a nice combination of authority and freedom.[91]

Any encroachment on or intervention in the fundamental freedoms should be "only in extreme situations," said Tarnopolsky:

At that point, again, I am not sure that the democratic argument overrides the argument of liberty and the fundamental protection necessary where a legislature does go to the extreme of interfering with the fundamental liberties of speech, press, religion, assembly and association.[92]

Repeating a theme that he had initially raised in *Civil Liberties in Canada*, Tarnopolsky said he did not think the question of hate literature was one that could be solved through a bill of rights: ". . . The judiciary will still have to set limits to what is freedom of speech. . . . I do not think hate literature is necessarily only a group protection question, it involves the question of speech. . . ."[93] On the one hand, "everyone can assert the right to freedom of speech or the right to counsel regardless of his membership in a particular group in society." But on the other, where rights are asserted because one is a member of a certain group, a fundamental contradiction arises. The two kinds of rights are "jurisprudentially incompatible," said Tarnopolsky, and should be separated at least into different parts of any bill of rights, if not into two separate bills.[94]

Ten years later, Tarnopolsky appeared before the second Joint Committee on the Constitution, this time on behalf of the Canadian Civil Liberties Association and, like Scott and Schmeiser, took a rather negative view of the proposed Charter:

We are going to draw to your attention several provisions in this charter, which, in our opinion, make it so defective that we have come to the conclusion that we would be better remaining with the present Canadian

---

91 *Ibid.* at 8:28.

92 *Ibid.* at 8:27.

93 *Ibid.* at 8:20–21.

94 *Ibid.* at 8:21, 25.

Bill of Rights than enacting this charter unless these provisions are removed by amendment.[95]

Sections 1, 25 and 26 would "actually set us back from whatever small advances we have made with the present Canadian Bill of Rights," he said.[96] "If you are going to have a bill of rights, make it a bill of rights which cannot be just over-ridden any time that a court is convinced, which we are suggesting would be relatively easy, that the limits are those which are generally acceptable."[97] The clause that most gave offence, according to Tarnopolsky, was s. 1, which "permits Parliament to take away everything that Parliament gives by the rest of the Charter":

> I think . . . it would be very difficult to argue that whatever Parliament enacts is not generally acceptable in that society. I do not know how one could argue that members of this House do not represent what is generally accepted in society.
>
> I therefore, have no doubt that the treatment of the Japanese Canadians in World War II, that the results concerning Mrs. Laval in 1973, that the Jehovah's Witnesses in Quebec in the 1940's and 1950's, would all be measures which would be generally accepted in our society. I have no doubt also that this is [a] clause which has to be removed or there really is no limit, and again, it finds no counterpart that I know of in any Commonwealth or International bills.[98]

Unfortunately, the position that Tarnopolsky adopted before the Joint Committee was almost diametrically opposed to what he had suggested in an article in the *Canadian Bar Review* in 1975, where he had remarked:

> I believe that Parliament . . . should be able to decide that the legislation should operate notwithstanding the Bill of Rights. I do not believe that a Supreme Court, even with a written Bill of Rights in the constitution, can ultimately stand in the way of a legislature determined to take certain action.[99]

Pressed for an explanation for the discrepancy in his position, Tarnopolsky somewhat lamely replied, "I am not at liberty to express my

95 *Proceedings of the Special Joint Committee on the Constitution*, 32nd Parliament, 1st Session (1980–81), 18 November 1980 at 7:8 [hereinafter *Proceedings*].

96 *Ibid.* at 7:16.

97 *Ibid.* at 7:27.

98 *Ibid.* at 7:9.

99 Walter Tarnopolsky, "The Supreme Court and the Canadian Bill of Rights," *Canadian Bar Review* (December 1975). Cited by Perrin Beatty in *Proceedings, supra,* note 95 at 7:27.

own views. I am presenting the views of the Canadian Liberties Association."[100]

It was perhaps a classic case of "united we fall, divided we stand." After Tarnopolsky's admission that the views he had presented on behalf of the Canadian Civil Liberties Association were diametrically opposed to his own, the committee noticeably lost interest in the submission and quickly wrapped up the day's activities, smug in the belief that the proposed draft of the Charter would suffice after all. As Ron Irwin, then Parliamentary Secretary to both the Minister of Justice and the Attorney-General, later pointed out, there had already been ample discussion:

> In 1968 a discussion paper was published . . . , in 1968 to 1971 they were widely published. There was a constitutional conference continuing over that period in which they discussed this Charter of Rights. There were two Special Joint Committees of Parliament in the seventies had public hearings. They studied all aspects including the Charter of Rights, the Bill of Rights, and reported supporting a Charter both in 1972 and 1978.
>
> Similarly, with the Pepin-Roberts task force, they heard evidence and they supported the Bill of Rights and the Canadian Bar Association had a constitutional committee that reported in 1977 and 1978 in favour of the Bill of Rights.[101]

Despite all this discussion, said Irwin with some indignation, critics of the Joint Committee had the temerity to say that "we are ramming these things through and there has been a lack of discussion."[102] The Joint Committee made up its collective mind to leave the resolution more-or-less intact. Thus was born the new *Constitution Act, 1982*, containing the enshrined *Canadian Charter of Rights and Freedoms*—complete with its controversial, but for now intact, "notwithstanding" clause.

Tarnopolsky, perhaps more than any other critic, had a deep appreciation for the role of the Jehovah's Witnesses cases in shaping fundamental freedoms in Canada. Again and again he referred to the cases in both his writings and his speeches. He, like Trudeau, was an admirer of F.R. Scott and the role that he played as barrister for Roncarelli. Furthermore, his writing did not stop with the adoption of the Charter; in a very real sense his contribution to literature on civil liberties and human rights had only just begun. Not long after the *Constitution Act, 1982* became law, he and Gerald-A. Beaudoin published *The Canadian Charter of Rights and Freedoms: Commentary*,[103] to which a distinguished group of scholars contri-

---

100 *Proceedings, supra,* note 95 at 7:30.

101 *Ibid.* at 34:151–52.

102 *Ibid.*

103 Toronto: Carswell, 1982.

138 ▸ FUNDAMENTAL FREEDOMS AND JEHOVAH'S WITNESSES

buted, including Peter W. Hogg, Irwin Cotler and Dale Gibson. Although
Tarnopolsky had turned his attention to the "Equality Rights" rather than
those rights that both he and Scott had identified as being "fundamental,"
he nonetheless referred to *Roncarelli* as "one of the most famous
applications of this view of 'equality before the law' as part of 'the rule
of law'":

> The essence of this decision was probably most concisely set out by one
> of Roncarelli's counsel, Frank Scott, who suggested that the essence of
> the "rule of law," which includes "equality before the law," could be
> stated in "two basic rules underlying our constitutional structure, which
> entitles us to say that we live in a free society."[104]

In all, there are some 40 references to Jehovah's Witnesses cases in this
first major post-Charter study, most of them contained in Cotler's penetrating chapter, "Freedom of Assembly, Association, Conscience and
Religion."[105] Following the lead set by Schmeiser and Tarnopolsky,
Saumur and *Roncarelli* in particular are cited again and again in post-
Charter literature for their enduring relevance to Canadian constitutional
and administrative law.[106]

III. M. JAMES PENTON'S *JEHOVAH'S WITNESSES IN CANADA*

In January 1971, the Special Joint Committee on the Constitution was
informed yet again about the role of Jehovah's Witnesses in pushing for
the original Bill of Rights—this time from a leading spokesman for
Jehovah's Witnesses, University of Lethbridge history professor James
Penton. Penton reminded the committee that Parliament had received
several major petitions supportive of a bill of rights containing "hundreds
of thousands of signatures," and that in response to these demands Prime
Minister John Diefenbaker had pushed through the present *Canadian Bill
of Rights*. He emphasized that this show of power on the part of Jehovah's
Witnesses had come after years of persecution and frustration:

> In particular, I refer to the banning of Jehovah's Witnesses . . . from July
> 4, 1940 to October 12, 1943 in spite of the fact that a Select Committee of

---

104 *Ibid.* at 400. He went on to cite Scott's description of the "rule of law" at length.

105 *Ibid.* at 123–211.

106 *Saumur* is alluded to 13 times in Tarnopolsky and Beaudoin, *supra.* Peter W. Hogg
makes about 20 references to the Jehovah's Witnesses cases in *Constitutional Law in
Canada*, 3d edn. (Toronto: Carswell, 1992). For a study of the relationship between pre-
Charter and post-Charter adjudication using many Jehovah's Witnesses cases see Neil
Finkelstein, "The Relevance of Pre-Charter Case Law for Post-Charter Adjudication"
(1982), 4 Sup. Ct. L. Rev. 267.

the House of Commons asked that the bans on these organizations be lifted as early as the summer of 1942, after a long study had proven to the satisfaction of all members of the Committee that there had been no good reason to ban them in the first place.[107]

In wartime, said Penton, the RCMP had broken up a meeting in Montreal in the spring of 1943 and arrested Witnesses for possessing copies of the King James Bible that happened to have been printed by the Watch Tower Bible and Tract Society. Two women were imprisoned for two weeks without bail for offering French versions of the Catholic Crampon Bible, again because they were Witnesses. After the War, both provincial governments and the federal government had been guilty of violations of civil liberties: "I refer, of course, to the long and notorious list of the violations of human rights that occurred in Quebec under the Duplessis regime and which were only held in some cases, although not all, to be unconstitutional after long struggles through the courts."[108] Noting that more people were charged with sedition in Alberta during 1914–16 than in England during the entire previous century, Penton added: "Either Albertans were a very seditious lot or governmental officials were overly rigorous and illiberal in their attitudes."[109]

At the time of his presentation, Dr. Penton was already deeply involved in research for his book *Jehovah's Witnesses in Canada: Champions of Freedom of Speech and Worship*,[110] which was to receive critical acclaim from the legal as well as the academic establishment. Penton was to become something of a *cause célèbre*, and some jurists, not least of whom was Thomas Berger, cited Penton again and again as the definitive work on the interface between Jehovah's Witnesses and civil liberties.[111] Penton's book is by far the most thorough history of Jehovah's Witnesses in Canada.

A member of a fifth-generation family of Jehovah's Witnesses, Penton soon found upon embarking on his study that much of the documentation of Jehovah's Witnesses cases had been lost as a result of the ban of the sect during World War II. He had to resort to archives previously not open to historians, including archival materials in the headquarters and branch offices of the Watch Tower and Bible and Tract Society and public records in the Public Archives of Canada. He found that some "public"

---

107 *Proceedings of the Special Joint Committee on the Constitution*, 28th Parliament, 3d Session (1970–71) at 32:51.

108 *Ibid.* at 32:51–52.

109 *Ibid.* at 32:52.

110 (Toronto: Macmillan, 1976).

111 Thomas Berger in *Fragile Freedoms: Human Rights and Dissent in Canada* (Toronto: Clarke Irwin, 1982) gives high praise to Penton's text, which Berger cites liberally.

records remained closed even to historians, however, and some government departments in Ottawa were not in the least enthused about helping him compile a "reasonably complete account of what may well be Canada's most controversial religion."[112] By contrast, the Jehovah's Witnesses' lawyer, Glen How, was particularly helpful in providing background information about the various cases he had represented.[113]

Penton begins his study with an analysis of the state of the law with respect to freedom of religion in Canada in the 1970s, as expressed by D.A. Schmeiser in *Civil Liberties in Canada* and the *Canadian Bill of Rights*. Although the *Canadian Bill of Rights* declares firmly that Canada respects and has always respected the principle of freedom of religion, "There is quite another side to Canadian religious history, which many Canadians have been willing to ignore or overlook."[114] He said that the federal and provincial governments "have been guilty of violating the spirit and letter of the Freedom of Worship Statute and the high-sounding words of the Canadian Bill of Rights, by imposing specific disabilities on certain religions" such as the Doukhobors, the Hutterites, and in particular the Jehovah's Witnesses:[115]

> Jehovah's Witnesses have played a unique role in Canadian religious history. No other religious group has challenged the theological, social, national, and even scientific values of the larger society to the same extent or with the same vehemence. . . . They regard the world around them as satanically ruled, and the religious, political, and economic institutions which support it as deserving of destruction. Such beliefs have caused them to speak out sharply and condemn many of the doctrines, institutions, and practices dear to others. As a result, Jehovah's Witnesses have undergone more consistent opposition and both legal and popular persecutions than members of any other religion, church, sect or denomination in Canada since Confederation.[116]

After outlining the origins of Jehovah's Witnesses in the United States as the "Bible Students,"[117] Penton describes the incursion of the sect into Canada and its fall into disfavour with its pacifist stance during World War I.[118] Vitriolic literature, especially *Bible Students Monthly* and *The Finished Mystery*, led to formal banning of Bible Student literature in 1917

---

112 Penton, *supra*, note 110 at ix–x.

113 *Ibid.* at xi.

114 *Ibid.* at 2.

115 *Ibid.* at 5–6.

116 *Ibid.* at 7–8.

117 *Ibid.*, chapter 1, at 7–34.

118 *Ibid.*, chapter 2, at 35–55.

and subsequent raids by the police on Bible Students' residences and businesses.[119] The ban was followed by forced conscription of Jehovah's Witnesses for military service despite their arguments that they were conscientious objectors.[120]

After the First World War, the Bible Students declared war of their own against the clergy, whom they regarded as being behind the wartime ban.[121] Many Bible Students were charged with licence infractions for "peddling" literature, and many others were charged under the *Lord's Day Act*.[122] Penton devotes a chapter to censorship of the radio programming of the Bible Students in Canada during the 1920s.[123] He then describes the first serious charges of "distributing seditious literature" and "seditious conspiracy" during the 1930s,[124] providing a brief analysis of *Brodie* v. *R.*[125] and *Duval* v. *R.*[126] Although the Supreme Court of Canada overturned the conviction of George Brodie and G.C. Barrett for seditious conspiracy, "it was, at most, a rather hollow win," says Penton:

> Both had been held guilty at trial level and their conviction was affirmed by the Court of King's Bench. Fortunately for Brodie and Barrett, the original indictment against them had never specified the nature of their supposed conspiratorial actions. When the Quebec King's Bench denied a defence contention that the Crown had been obliged to do so, it had ruled contrary to a 1932 decision of the Ontario Appeals Court in a similar case. The Witnesses were therefore allowed to appeal for a final judgment to the Supreme Court of Canada, which reversed the decision, maintaining that the defence was right in insisting that the indictment must clearly specify the nature of seditious conspiracy.[127]

However, *stare decisis* did not seem to apply in Quebec, where immediately after the Supreme Court decision, Duval was convicted of an identical charge for distributing pamphlets that, in the words of the Court of King's Bench decision, "appeal to all to condemn and have a supreme contempt for all forms of organized authority."[128]

---

119 *Ibid.* at 54–55.

120 *Ibid.*, chapter 3, at 56–80.

121 *Ibid.*, chapter 4, at 81–93.

122 *Ibid.* at 90–92.

123 *Ibid.*, chapter 5, at 95–110.

124 *Ibid.*, chapter 6, at 111–28.

125 (1936), [1936] S.C.R. 188; 65 C.C.C. 289, [1936] 3 D.L.R. 81.

126 (1938), 64 Que. K.B. 270.

127 Penton, *supra*, note 110 at 120.

128 *Ibid.* at 121, citing *Duval*, *supra*, note 126.

The ban on Jehovah's Witnesses during the Second World War, including the attendant *Defence of Canada Regulations*, is the subject of Chapter 7, "Banned as Seditious,"[129] in which Penton documents some of the more than 500 arrests of Witnesses reported during the three years of the ban,[130] including *R.* v. *Leeson*,[131] a flag-salute and national anthem case in which the parents were jailed and the children put in the hands of the Children's Aid Society (a precedent for the blood transfusion cases of the 1950s and 1960s), and *R.* v. *Clark*,[132] also a flag-salute case. Penton also described several American and Australian cases that have since had an influence on Canadian Law, such as *Murdock* v. *Commonwealth of Pennsylvania*[133] and *Jones* v. *City of Opelika*[134] on licensing, *Taylor* v. *Mississippi*[135] on the meaning of "sedition," *West Virginia Board of Education* v. *Barnette*[136] on saluting the American flag, and *Adelaide Company of Jehovah's Witnesses, Inc.* v. *The Commonwealth*[137] on the unconstitutionality of a ban on Jehovah's Witnesses in Australia.

Penton's chapter on "Reconstruction and Alternative Service" documents the continued persecution of the Witnesses even after the ban was lifted.[138] He cites the Canadian "patriotic exercises" cases, including *Ruman* v. *Lethbridge School Board Trustees*,[139] in which the Alberta Supreme Court ruled that the trustees had acted within their power under the Alberta *School Act* in expelling Jehovah's Witnesses for refusing to salute the flag and sing the national anthem, and *Donald* v. *Hamilton Board of Education*,[140] in which Robert Donald Jr. was expelled for refusing on religious principle to salute the flag, sing "God Save the King" and repeat the Pledge of Allegiance. Penton suggested that the decision in the *Barnette* case[141] motivated the Witnesses in Canada to

---

129 *Ibid.* at 129–55.

130 *Ibid.* at 156.

131 County Police Court for County of Middlesex, 6 November 1940 (unreported).

132 (1941), [1941] 3 W.W.R. 228 (Man. Police Ct.), rev'd (1941), [1941] 3 W.W.R. 567, [1941] 4 D.L.R. 299 (Man. C.A.)

133 319 U.S. 105, 63 S. Ct. 870, 87 L. Ed. 1292 (1943).

134 316 U.S. 584, 62 S. Ct. 1231, 86 L. Ed. 1691 (1942).

135 319 U.S. 583, 63 S. Ct. 1200, 87 L. Ed. 1600 (1943).

136 319 U.S. 624 63, S. Ct. 1178, 87 L. Ed. 1628 (1943).

137 (1943), 67 C.L.R. 116.

138 Penton, *supra*, note 110, chapter 8, at 156–81.

139 (1943), [1943] 3 W.W.R. 340, [1944] 1 D.L.R. 360 (Alta. T.O.).

140 (1945), [1945] O.R. 518, [1945] 3 D.L.R. 424, [1945] O.W.N. 526 (C.A.), rev'g (1944), [1944] O.R. 475, [1944] 4 D.L.R. 227, [1944] O.W.N. 559 (H.C.).

141 *Supra*, note 136.

appeal the *Donald* case.[142] Australian and Scottish precedents were also cited in the conscription cases, including *Greenlees* v. *A. G. Canada*,[143] which found that Jehovah's Witnesses were not a denomination that could have "ministers":

> W. Glen How, a young Witness attorney soon to become known as one of Canada's most brilliant constitutional lawyers, attempted to appeal the *Greenlees* case to the Supreme Court of Canada. But it refused to hear the case, since that court could not accept cases in which no monetary interest was involved. When How pressed to have the matter heard before the Privy Council in London, the government ended the matter by withdrawing the National War Services regulations. By that time the war had long since ended, and the issue was settled, at least as far as the government was concerned.[144]

In the chapter headed "Quebec's Burning Hate,"[145] Penton documents a number of violent actions initiated by the populace in Quebec against Jehovah's Witnesses, and unwarranted and arbitrary arrests. "Premier Maurice Duplessis decided to suppress them through the most sweeping series of arrests ever carried out against any religious movement in Canadian history," says Penton.[146] The Witnesses fought back. On 3 November 1946, at an assembly convened in Montreal, Jehovah's Witness lawyer Hayden Covington and the president of the Watch Tower Society, Nathan Knorr, launched "a propaganda war to make Jehovah's Witnesses' struggle with Quebec officialdom known from one end of Canada to the other, with little credit to Quebec."[147] Covington pointed out that Quebec's *Freedom of Worship Act* constituted as strong a guarantee of religious freedom as the American Constitution. Knorr followed with a speech introducing the leaflet *Quebec's Burning Hate for God and Christ and Freedom Is the Shame of All Canada*, describing the organized persecution of Witnesses and attributing it to the Roman Catholic Church and the Quebec government. Duplessis called a press conference on 21 November at which he called the leaflet "intolerable and seditious," and there were calls from various officials to "get rid of Jehovah's Witnesses once and for all" and "to free the streets of Jehovah's

---

142 Penton, *supra*, note 110 at 159–60.

143 (1945), [1945] O.R. 411, [1945] 2 D.L.R. 641 (H.C.), aff'd (1946), [1946] O.R. 90, [1946] 1 D.L.R. 550 (C.A.), leave to appeal to S.C.C. refused (1946), [1946] S.C.R. 462 (S.C.C.).

144 Penton, *supra*, note 110 at 177.

145 *Ibid.* at 182–201.

146 *Ibid.* at 185.

147 *Ibid.* at 186.

Witnesses."[148] The tempo of violence in concert with arbitrary police action increased, culminating in the actions against Boucher, Lamb, Carrier, Chaput, Saumur, Roncarelli and hundreds of others.

The revoking of Roncarelli's liquor licence, however, led the English press to cry foul. Penton describes the reaction of F.R. Scott in his article "Duplessis v. Jehovah" in the *Canadian Forum*, but points out that *Maclean's Magazine* and *Saturday Night* were equally vocal. *Saturday Night* even published five stanzas of doggerel called "Destruction of Roncarelli":

> Duplessis came down like a wolf on the fold,
> And his edicts were gleaming in purple and gold;
> And the sheen of his padlocks was hid by the pall
> Of the laws that hang heavy o'er French Montreal.
>
> Like the leaves of the forest when Summer is green,
> The Witnesses lying in prison were seen:
> Like the leaves of the forest when Winter doth rail,
> That host on the morrow was delivered on bail.
>
> For a restaurateur spread his money about
> And silenced Duplessis and got them all out.
> But the eyes of Duplessis waxed deadly and chill,
> Took aim for the liquor, moved in for the kill.
>
> There lay Roncarelli, distorted and pale,
> His food all intact, but vanished his Ale;
> The Witnesses silent at this sudden act
> To discredit the Prophet, suppress every tract.
>
> And the faithful of Rutherford despair at the wreck
> For their steps are now dogged through the whole of Quebec;
> Their champion is curbed by provincial police,
> And his standard is down by the sword of Maurice.[149]

Capitalizing on their sudden apparent popularity, Jehovah's Witnesses began to circulate throughout Canada two petitions urging Parliament to adopt a Bill of Rights.[150]

In Chapter 10, "Victory in the Courts,"[151] Penton describes the attempts of Covington and How to reach a wide academic audience through their articles on the concept of a Bill of Rights and the

---

148 *Ibid.* at 188–89.

149 *Ibid.* at 190, citing *Saturday Night*, 8 February 1947.

150 *Ibid.* at 197–200.

151 *Ibid.* at 202–223.

jurisdiction of the Supreme Court of Canada.[152] He then reviews the facts and basic breakdown of the decisions in the central Jehovah's Witnesses cases (*Boucher, Saumur, Chaput, Roncarelli* and *Lamb*), giving helpful background information surrounding the cases. He notes, for example, that the decision in the *Boucher* case had little immediate effect in Quebec:

> Only nine days after the Supreme Court handed down its decision . . . , two young female pioneer evangelists, Olive Lundell and Winnifred Parsons, were kidnapped and driven out of Joliette, Quebec. The experience was not new to them: along with two other pioneers, Mr. and Mrs. Cecil Jones, they had been expelled from Edmundston, New Brunswick, by a mob aided by the local police only ten months earlier. Yet the situation in Joliette more openly demonstrated the contempt of Quebec public officials, the Catholic clergy, and the general public for the rights of Jehovah's Witnesses and the feelings of English Canadians, including at least two members of the Supreme Court.
>
> According to the two young women, their kidnappers chanted Catholic prayers, threatened to throw them into one of the ice-covered lakes near the city, and frightened them with the possibility of rape. The worst they did was take them to Montreal where they attempted to have the two women jailed as undesirables. But the story did not end there. The police refused to take action against the kidnappers, and when Glen How and another Watch Tower representative, Paul Couture, showed up at a Joliette town meeting the next week, they too were nearly mobbed. Again the two female missionaries were forcibly expelled from the community.[153]

He also notes that the case now known as *Saumur* v. *City of Quebec* was an action initiated by Damase Daviau, another Jehovah's Witness, who just prior to the appeal to the Supreme Court of Canada "became disheartened and refused to proceed with the case":

> For that reason it was taken forward in the name of Laurier Saumur, who, with over one hundred charges against him, was perhaps the most frequently arrested man in Canadian history. Since Saumur was involved in litigation identical to that involving Daviau, he was accepted by agreement as a substitute plaintiff. Thus his name became attached to the constitutionally important case of *Saumur* v. *Quebec*.[154]

Immediately after the *Saumur* decision came down, Penton writes, Duplessis rose in the provincial legislature to introduce Bill 38, an

---

152 *Ibid.* at 203–206.

153 *Ibid.* at 208.

154 *Ibid.* at 211.

amendment to the Freedom of Worship Act designed to nullify the effects of *Saumur*. The Bill

> provided stiff penalties in the form of fines from one hundred to one thousand dollars, and sentences from thirty days to six months in prison, for distributing printed matter of any kind, making speeches, lectures, or remarks, in any fashion which 'insulted members or adherents of a religious profession within the province.' Furthermore, the bill contained a provision for the seizure of all books containing such insults throughout the province by the police, enabling them to search without warrants. And to the shock of civil libertarians throughout Canada, charges could be laid for the offence of simply contemplating the act of insulting the members or adherents of a religious profession 'upon petition supported by the oath of a credible person.' Any of the insults or contemplated insults were, of course, no longer to constitute the free exercise or enjoyment of religious profession and worship.[155]

This legislation, which became law on 22 January 1954, Jehovah's Witnesses sought to nip in the bud with the action of *Saumur v. A. G. Quebec*.[156] In the Quebec Superior Court, How was able to interrogate Premier Duplessis for some three hours, spending most of that time hammering away at the legislative intention of Bill 38 to determine whether the Bill was directed against Jehovah's Witnesses. Duplessis claimed parliamentary privilege and argued that the questions were outside the scope of the court. Mr. Justice Lizotte agreed. How could only appeal once again:[157]

> Though taken before the Supreme Court, again in Saumur's name, the matter was never adjudicated. That body ultimately held that since no one was ever charged under the terms of Bill 38, there was no legal issue. Nevertheless, by opening another long legal battle the Witnesses were able to forestall the enforcement of Duplessis's statutory thunderbolt.[158]

The Supreme Court's ruling in the original *Saumur* case curbed the mass arrests of Jehovah's Witnesses in Quebec, says Penton, but it was *Chaput v. Romain* which finally conveyed to the Quebec police that their interfering with the services of Jehovah's Witnesses was illegal, if not a

---

155 *Ibid.* at 213.

156 (1964), [1964] S.C.R. 252, 45 D.L.R. (2d) 627 aff'g (1963), [1963] Que. Q.B. 116, 37 D.L.R. (2d) 703 (C.A.), [1963] Can. Abr. 249.

157 Penton, *supra*, note 110 at 220.

158 *Ibid.* at 214.

criminal offence.[159] The persecution of Jehovah's Witnesses in Quebec became more subtle. When their children were prevented from attending Protestant schools in Rouyn because the sect was not considered Protestant, Jehovah's Witnesses took the matter to court,[160] eventually appealling to the Quebec Court of Queen's Bench, where Brissonet J. for the court defined "Protestant" as a Christian who repudiates the authority of the Pope. Witness children were thereafter allowed to attend Protestant schools.[161] A similar issue with respect to Roman Catholic schools arose in *Chabot* v. *School Commissioners of Lamorandière*:[162]

> The Chabot boys had originally been expelled from the Catholic school in the parish of Lamorandière. Their crime had been the refusal to make the sign of the cross, kneel, or recite Catholic prayers. Chabot thereupon sought a writ of *mandamus* from the Superior Court at Amos, Quebec, to have his children readmitted to class without taking part in Catholic religious exercises. Glen How, arguing on Chabot's behalf, claimed that since there was no Protestant school in the area, and the plaintiff paid taxes to the Catholic system, he had a right to send his children to a Catholic school which must recognize his right to raise his children in the faith of his choice.[163]

Regulations under the *Quebec Education Act* stipulated that pupils of Catholic schools must take part in Catholic religious exercises. Glen How argued that the regulations were *ultra vires* the province and a violation of the *Freedom of Worship Act*. Since there was no other school in the area, How argued that the school should be regarded as "common in sight of the law." Eventually, on appeal to the Court of Queen's Bench, Pratt J. agreed with How, saying that a child had a "natural right" not to be "obliged to to follow a religious teaching to which their father is opposed."[164] "To all intents and purposes," said Penton, "the *Chabot* case brought an end to what both Jehovah's Witnesses and the higher courts considered to be official persecution."[165]

Penton discusses the facts and decisions of *Roncarelli* and *Lamb*, noting that both cases were "decided on the same day." As with the other cases, he describes the reaction in the English-speaking press, including, for example, an editorial in the *Ottawa Citizen*:

---

159 *Ibid.* at 215–16.

160 *Perron* v. *Syndics d'Ecoles de Rouyn* (1955), [1955] Que. Q.B. 841, 1 D.L.R. (2d) 414 (C.A.).

161 Penton, *supra*, note 110 at 218.

162 (1957), [1957] Que. Q.B. 707, 12 D.L.R. (2d) 796 (C.A.).

163 Penton, *supra*, note 110 at 218.

164 *Ibid.* at 219.

165 *Ibid.*

"Mr. Duplessis' laws for discouraging opinion of which he disapproves have taken quite a battering. In 1950 in the Boucher case the Supreme Court of Canada rejected Quebec's claim that a Jehovah's Witness pamphlet was 'seditious libel.' In 1953 in the Saumur case it ruled that a Quebec City bylaw used to stop distribution of Jehovah's Witnesses' publication contravened the Quebec Freedom of Worship Act."[166]

Penton added: "The English-Canadian press hailed the Roncarelli and Lamb decisions for what they were—final proof that the Supreme Court of Canada would not permit the victimization of even an unpopular minority such as Jehovah's Witnesses."[167]

It is ironic that Jehovah's Witnesses, whom Penton had heralded as being "champions of freedom of speech," should subsequent to the release of his tome decide to muzzle the historian to the point of excommunicating him. As he explained in his preface to a later, more critical study of Jehovah's Witnesses,[168] although the Witnesses, as an oppressed minority, were "occasionally sincerely concerned about the civil liberties and rights of others, . . . [they] were equally willing to be tyrannical to dissenters within their own ranks":

As I travelled throughout Canada and the United States carrying on my research, I became more and more aware of the severe chastisement to which individual Witnesses everywhere were being subjected by their leaders when they dissented in any way from official organizational doctrines or policies, or even when they fell afoul personally of someone in a position of organizational authority.

. . . Upon returning home, in August 1979, I determined to express my concerns and criticisms of what was transpiring within the larger Witness community to the Witness leadership as a whole in writing—a decision which, after over a year's great personal travail, led to my public disfellowshipment or excommunication from Jehovah's Witnesses on what amounted to charges of heresy.[169]

Largely because Penton's more recent study deals with international aspects of the sect, he does not deal with Canadian legal or constitutional issues; of the central Canadian Jehovah's Witnesses cases, only *Boucher* rates a brief mention. Penton restates the truism enunciated by the Su-

---

166 *Ibid.* at 222.

167 *Ibid.*

168 *Apocalypse Delayed: The Story of Jehovah's Witnesses* (Toronto: University of Toronto Press, 1985) at xiv.

169 *Ibid.* at xiv–xv.

preme Court of Canada in *Boucher* that Jehovah's Witnesses "were innocent of sedition" all along.[170]

Innocent but nonetheless persecuted, it is little wonder that Jehovah's Witnesses, including James Penton and Glen How, were at the forefront of pushing for reform along the lines of a "Constitutional Bill of Rights." More than a decade after How first proposed such a reform in *Canadian Bar Review*, the *Canadian Bill of Rights* became law. It was to take another two decades before fundamental freedoms were to be entrenched in the Canadian Constitution in the form of the *Canadian Charter of Rights and Freedoms*. In the interim, the Jehovah's Witnesses cases remained among the most important precedents referred to by the courts in the ongoing struggle to preserve civil liberties in Canada.

---

170 *Ibid.* at 136.

7

The Advent of the Charter

I. THE JEHOVAH'S WITNESSES CASES IN THE PRE-*CHARTER* PERIOD OF TRANSITION

1. The Limitations of the *Canadian Bill of Rights*

For twenty years after the passage into law of the *Canadian Bill of Rights*, the Supreme Court of Canada waffled on whether the Bill should be treated as a simple federal statute, a codification of rights existing prior to its adoption, a quasi-constitutional document, or all of the above. Certainly John Diefenbaker had intended the Bill to have lasting significance, as he indicated at the time of his introducing it into the House of Commons:

> Why is it now necessary to state explicitly in the constitutional document what is already implicit? . . . Experience has shown that what is only implicit in part is in fact endangered by lack of recognition and acceptance, and that an explicit statement of rights is not only advisable to create public recognition of the fundamental basis of our society, but also to prevent infringement of those rights.[1]

In his autobiography *One Canada*, Diefenbaker elaborated:

> A Bill of Rights for Canada is the only way in which to stop the march on the part of the government towards arbitrary power, and to curb the arrogance of men 'clad in little brief authority'. . . .
> Some say that it is unnecessary and our unwritten constitutional rights protect us.
> They have not in the past.[2]

---

1 Cited in *Proceedings of the Special Joint Committee on the Constitution* (1980–81) at 17:41–42.

2 *Ibid.*, 5 December 1980, at 20:23, citing John Diefenbaker, *One Canada* at 254.

The fact remains, however, that the Supreme Court of Canada accepted the overriding authority of the *Canadian Bill of Rights* without major qualification in only one case—*R. v. Drybones* (1969).[3] Although *Drybones* seemed to imbue the *Canadian Bill of Rights* with new life for a short time, with one or two exceptions[4] succeeding judges confined it to its own facts.[5] Still, *Drybones* remains authority for the proposition that the *Canadian Bill of Rights* transcends other federal statutes in power in the sense that a court can use it to override and render inoperative any inconsistent federal legislation. As Mr. Justice Bora Laskin remarked in *Hogan v. R.* (1975),[6] the *Canadian Bill of Rights* is "a quasi-constitutional instrument."[7]

Two Supreme Court decisions—*Robertson v. R.* and *Dupond v. City of Montreal*—served to ring the death knell of the *Canadian Bill of Rights* as anything more significant than a footnote to the study of constitutional law, at the same time confining the Jehovah's Witnesses cases—in particular *Saumur*—to their facts. At most, the *Canadian Bill of Rights* was regarded as a simple summary of the state of civil liberties in Canada—and more specifically the state of religious freedom—prior to its passage. Both *Robertson* and *Dupond* generated a degree of criticism, and both were in effect eventually overridden by the advent of the *Charter*.

2. From *The Sunday Bowling Case* to *Big M Drug Mart*

Robertson v. R.,[8] was popularly known as *The Sunday Bowling Case* because it pertained to the rights of a bowling alley to open for business on a Sunday. The Supreme Court upheld the *Lord's Day Act*, effectively shutting down Sunday bowling for another 20 years. Mr. Justice Ritchie, speaking for the majority, quoted s. 1 of the *Canadian Bill of Rights*, and remarked:

> It is to be noted at the outset that the *Canadian Bill of Rights* is not concerned with "human rights and fundamental freedoms" in any abstract sense, but rather with such "rights and freedoms" as they existed in Canada immediately before the statute was enacted. . . . It is therefore

---

3 [1970] S.C.R. 282, 71 W.W.R. 161, 9 D.L.R. (3d) 473.

4 See, for example, *R. v. Hayden* (1983), [1983] 6 W.W.R. 655, 3 D.L.R. (4th) 361 (Man. C.A.).

5 See *A. G. Can. v. Lavell* (1973), [1974] S.C.R. 1349, 38 D.L.R. (3d) 481; and *A.-G. Can. v. Canard* (1975), [1976] 1 S.C.R. 170, 52 D.L.R. (3d) 548.

6 (1974), [1975] 2 S.C.R. 574, 48 D.L.R. (3d) 427.

7 *Ibid.* at 579.

8 (1963), [1963] S.C.R. 651, 41 D.L.R. (2d) 485 [hereinafter *Robertson* cited to S.C.R.].

the "religious freedom" then existing in this country that is safe-guarded by the provisions of s. 2. . . .

It is accordingly of first importance to understand the concept of religious freedom which was recognized in this country before the enactment of the *Canadian Bill of Rights* and after the enactment of the *Lord's Day Act* in its present form.[9]

In order to ascertain the state of "the concept of religious freedom" prior to passage of the Bill, Ritchie J. cited as authority the decisions in both *Chaput v. Romain*[10] and *Saumur v. City of Quebec*.[11] First, he quoted Mr. Justice Taschereau, who had remarked in *Chaput v. Romain*: "All religions are on an equal footing, and Catholics as well as Protestants, Jews, and other adherents to various religious denominations, enjoy the most complete liberty of thought. The conscience of each is a personal matter and the concern of nobody else."[12] Then Ritchie cited Mr. Justice Rand, who had said in *Saumur*:

> From 1760, therefore, to the present moment religious freedom has, in our legal system, been recognized as a principle of fundamental character; and although we have nothing in the nature of an established church, that the untrammelled affirmations of 'religious belief' and its propagation, personal or institutional, remain as of the greatest constitutional significance throughout the Dominion is unquestionable.[13]

According to Ritchie, these two comments supplied the requisite evidence that "complete liberty of religious thought" and "the untrammelled affirmation of 'religious belief' and its propagation, personal or institutional" had been recognized by the Supreme Court of Canada as existing prior to the passage of the *Canadian Bill of Rights*, and notwithstanding the existence of the *Lord's Day Act*. Ritchie concluded that that Act therefore in no way abrogated, abridged or infringed upon religious freedom.[14]

In 1964, Bora Laskin published a penetrating but scathing analysis of Ritchie's judgment in *The Canadian Bar Review*, saying that Ritchie's "self-imposed horizon of reference is not calculated to inspire much confidence in the depth analysis of the issues confronting the court":

9 *Ibid.* at 654–55.

10 (1955), [1955] S.C.R. 834, 1 D.L.R. (2d) 241, 114 C.C.C. 170.

11 (1953), [1953] 2 S.C.R. 299, [1953] 4 D.L.R. 641, 106 C.C.C. 289 [hereinafter *Saumur* cited to S.C.R.].

12 *Supra*, note 10 at 840.

13 *Supra*, note 11 at 327.

14 *Robertson, supra*, note 8 at 655, 657.

Taschereau J.'s observations on the equality of religions and "complete liberty of thought" in *Chaput* v. *Romain* were a satisfying *obiter* arising in the course of a judgment holding police officers liable in damages for breaking up a peaceful religious meeting conducted by a Jehovah's Witness in a private home. Neither constitutional nor statutory guarantees of religious freedom were involved, and all that the learned Justice (now Chief Justice) was doing was politely reminding the Quebec police and others that persons are entitled to pursue their religious devotions, especially in private premises, without interruption.[15]

Laskin went on to allege that Ritchie had taken statements from Rand's judgment completely out of context:

The context of this passage was provided by a challenged by-law of the city of Quebec forbidding the distribution of books or tracts in its streets without the permission of the police chief. Although Rand J. was concerned with constitutional power in respect of the political freedoms, this was only in the negative sense of determining whether, if the by-law concerned freedom of speech or of religion, it was within or outside of provincial competence to authorize it. He was no more concerned to explore the full meaning of freedom of religion in *Saumur* than was Taschereau J. in *Chaput* v. *Romain*.[16]

Ritchie had reached his conclusion "on the basis of two snippets, torn from their contexts," said Laskin:

With respect, the two passages culled from the two judgments do not in any way lead to such a conclusion. If anything, they express values which, in any constitutional sense, could only be regarded as standards to be applied against challenged legislation, and not propositions limited in their range by existing legislation. It hardly helps to strengthen the chain of reasoning for Ritchie J. to rely on the cliché that the freedoms in an organized society are not absolute but are freedoms under law.[17]

Ritchie had also taken out of context a statement from the dissenting judgment of U.S. Supreme Court Mr. Justice Frankfurter in *West Virginia Board of Education* v. *Barnette*,[18] which Ritchie cited with approval as being "directly applicable to the 'freedom of religion' existing in this country both before and after the enactment of the *Canadian Bill of*

---

15 Bora Laskin, "Freedom of Religion and the Lord's Day Act" (1964), 42 Can. Bar Rev. 148 at 152.

16 *Ibid.*

17 *Ibid.* at 153.

18 319 U.S. 624 at 653, 63 S. Ct. 1178, 87 L. Ed. 1628 (1943) [hereinafter *Barnette* cited to U.S.].

Rights."[19] This statement of American law was examined in depth by Laskin, who concluded that Ritchie had misconstrued the concept of "law" as Frankfurter had used the term. Frankfurter had stated:

> The constitutional protection of religious freedom terminated disabilities, it did not create new privileges. It gave religious equality, not civil immunity. Its essence is freedom from conformity to religious dogma, not freedom from conformity to law because of religious dogma.[20]

Laskin argued that Mr. Justice Cartwright was correct in his dissent in *Robertson and Rosetanni* when he stated that the passage from *Barnette* quoted by Ritchie "presupposes that the word 'law' . . . means law which has a constitutionally valid purpose and effect other than the forbidding or commanding of conduct in a solely religious aspect. In my opinion a law which compels a course of conduct, whether positive or negative, for a purely religious purpose infringes the freedom of religion."[21] In his dissenting judgment in *Robertson and Rosetanni*, Cartwright could not accept "the argument that because the *Lord's Day Act* had been in force for more than half a century when the *Canadian Bill of Rights* was enacted, Parliament must be taken to have been of the view that the provisions of the *Lord's Day Act* do not infringe freedom of religion."[22]

The *Lord's Day Act* remained in effect for another 20 years, when similar arguments were made once again before the Supreme Court of Canada in *R.* v. *Big M Drug Mart*.[23] Here, Mr. Justice Dickson cited the identical passages from *Chaput* and *Saumur* that Justice Ritchie had quoted in *Robertson and Rosetanni*—and, applying the *Canadian Charter of Rights and Freedoms*, reached opposite conclusions from those reached by Ritchie:

> In my view the meaning attributed by the majority in *Robertson and Rosetanni supra* to the concept of "freedom of religion" under the *Canadian Bill of Rights* depends on the majority's view of the distinctive nature and status of that document. An examination of the reasoning that underlies the majority's interpretation demonstrates that it cannot easily be transferred to a constitutional document like the *Charter* and the fundamental guarantees it enshrines.[24]

19 *Robertson, supra*, note 8 at 656.

20 *Ibid.*, citing *Barnette, supra*, note 18 at 653.

21 *Robertson, supra*, note 8 at 660.

22 *Ibid.* at 661.

23 (1985), [1985] 1 S.C.R. 295, [1985] 3 W.W.R. 481, 18 D.L.R. (4th) 321 [hereinafter cited to S.C.R.].

24 *Ibid.* at 342.

The language of the *Canadian Bill of Rights* was "merely declaratory," said Dickson, and "it is on this basis that the excerpts from *Chaput* v. *Romain* and *Saumur* v. *City of Quebec* were seen to be significant, since they articulate descriptions of religious freedom . . . existing in Canada before the *Canadian Bill of Rights*." By contrast, the language of the *Charter* was imperative; it was intended "to set a standard upon which *present as well as future* legislation is to be tested."[25]

By applying the same arguments that had been used in *Robertson* in the context of the *Canadian Bill of Rights* to the application of the *Charter* in *Big M Drug Mart*, Dickson J. reached the conclusion that the *Lord's Day Act* infringed upon freedom of conscience and religion guaranteed by s. 2(*a*) of the Charter:

> The definition of freedom of conscience and religion . . . including freedom from compulsory religious observance, corresponds precisely to the description of religious freedom in Canada offered by Taschereau J. in the passage in *Chaput* v. *Romain, supra,* when he noted that all adherents of various religious faiths are entirely free to think as they wish.[26]

Furthermore, taken in context, the remarks of Justice Rand in *Saumur* lend support to the proposition that, under the *Charter*, religious liberties should not be circumscribed. Rand J. had stated in *Saumur*, "Freedom of speech, religion and the inviolability of the person, are original freedoms which are at once the necessary attributes and modes of self-expression of human beings and the primary conditions of their community life within a legal order."[27] But Dickson pointed out that Rand also recognized that "'*it is in the circumscription of these liberties* by the creation of civil rights in persons who may be injured by their exercise, and by *the sanctions of public law, that the positive law operates. What we realize is the residue of that periphery*'."[28] Dickson could therefore assert, "In my view, the guarantee of freedom of conscience and religion prevents the government from compelling individuals to perform *or abstain from performing* otherwise harmless acts because of the religious significance of those acts to others." The *Lord's Day Act* was therefore of no force or effect, because it provided for "the compulsory observance of the religious institution of the Sabbath."[29] The effect of *Robertson* was in this way neutralized by the majority of the Supreme Court of Canada in *Big M Drug Mart*.

---

25 *Ibid.* at 342–43. Emphasis that of Dickson J.

26 *Ibid.* at 347.

27 *Ibid.* at 348, citing *Saumur, supra,* note 11 at 329.

28 *Ibid.* Emphasis that of Dickson J.

29 *Ibid.* at 348.

3. The *Dupond* Case

Dupond v. *City of Montreal* (1978)[30] was the second major Supreme Court of Canada decision that served to cripple the effectiveness of the *Canadian Bill of Rights* while alluding to *Saumur*, but this time the court confined *Saumur* to its facts. In 1969, Montreal passed an ordinance prohibiting "the holding of any assembly, parade or gathering on the public domain for a time-period of thirty days." Claire Dupond, a Montreal ratepayer, contested the by-law, arguing that it was *ultra vires* the city and indeed the province. She cited *Saumur* as authority for this proposition. Mr. Justice Beetz, speaking for the majority, refused to consider the question of whether the by-law was *ultra vires* on the technicality that although Dupond had included this argument in her affidavit, it had not be argued before the Court.[31] He added that the Quebec Court of Appeal had correctly concluded that the *Canadian Bill of Rights* did not apply to provincial and municipal legislation,[32] and he found that s. 5 of the enactments did not deal with the same subject matter as related provisions in the *Criminal Code*.[33] Furthermore, he rejected the argument that the enactments were "*ultra vires* under the doctrine of *Saumur* v. *City of Quebec*":[34]

> I cannot see anything in the Ordinance which interferes with freedom of religion, of the press or of speech, or which imposes religious observances, in such a way as to bring the matter within the criminal law power of Parliament. The Ordinance prohibits the holding of *all* assemblies, parades or gatherings for a time period of thirty days, irrespective of religion, ideology, or political views.[35]

Beetz distinguished *Saumur* as referring to the case of "uncontrollable discretion given to a municipal officer," whereas in *Dupond* the power was vested in the Executive Committee of the City in accordance with the City charter. Beetz asked: "What is it that distinguishes a right from a freedom and a fundamental freedom from a freedom that is not fundamental?"[36] But the question remained rhetorical. After alluding to the

---

30 (1978), [1978] 2 S.C.R. 770, 84 D.L.R. (3d) 420 [hereinafter cited to S.C.R.].

31 *Ibid.* at 788, 790.

32 *Ibid.* at 789–90.

33 *Ibid.* at 793.

34 *Ibid.* at 794.

35 *Ibid.* at 795.

36 *Ibid.* at 796.

various freedoms, including freedom of speech and freedom of assembly, he concluded:

1. None of the freedoms referred to is so enshrined in the Constitution as to be above the reach of competent legislation.

2. None of those freedoms is a single matter coming within exclusive federal or provincial competence.

3. Freedom of speech, of assembly and association, of the press and of religion are distinct and independent of the faculty of holding assemblies, parades, gatherings, demonstrations or processions on the public domain of a city. This is particularly so with respect to freedom of speech and freedom of the press as considered in *Reference re Alberta Statutes*. Demonstrations are not a form of speech but of collective action. They are of the nature of a display of force rather than of that of an appeal to reason; their inarticulateness prevents them from becoming part of language and from reaching the level of discourse.

4. The right to hold meetings on a highway or park is a right "unknown to English law."

5. The right to have such meeting in the public domain may be governed by federal or provincial legislation, depending on its aspect, including the impugned By-law and Ordinance.

6. The Canadian Bill of Rights, assuming it has anything to do with the holding of assemblies, parades or gatherings on the public domain, does not apply to provincial and municipal legislation.[37]

Now the Chief Justice of Canada, Bora Laskin registered a strong dissent in *Dupond*, in which he was joined by Justices Dickson and Spence. He remarked that in effect the City of Montreal "has enacted a mini-Criminal Code," since the Ordinance dealt "with apprehended breach of the peace, apprehended violence and the maintenance of public order." He added: "We are urged to sustain this incursion into the field of criminal law—a matter exclusively for the Parliament of Canada—because it is a matter of a local or private nature in the Province":

We are left in no doubt here as to the scope of operation of the By-law. In *Saumur* v. *City of Quebec*, Kellock J. noted that the challenged by-law there was 'not to be judged from the standpoint of matters to which it might be limited but upon the completely general terms in which it in fact is couched'. Here, persons who might seek to associate or gather for innocent purposes are to be barred . . . because of a desire to forestall the violent or the likely violent. This is the invocation of a doctrine which should alarm free citizens even if it were invoked and applied under the authority of the Parliament of Canada, which has very wide

---

37 *Ibid.* at 796–97.

power to enact criminal law. To find it invoked by a delegated authority like a municipality . . . appears to me to be an aggravation of its intrusion into the field of criminal law.[38]

Peter W. Hogg has stated the opinion that Laskin's view that the criminal law power should act as a substantial limitation on delegated authority or provincial powers "finds little support in the numerous cases upholding provincial laws."[39] He also expressed the view that Beetz in his judgment in *Dupond* in all likelihood did not intend to reject "the 1950s cases" because Beetz had gone on to hold "that the by-law's prohibition did not involve a denial of free speech." Hogg was of the view that the majority decision in *Dupond*, like the decision in *Robertson and Rosetanni* before it, could not have survived the advent of the *Charter*:

> Civil libertarian concerns about the extensive powers ceded to the provinces by the *McNeil* and *Dupond* decisions are now of primarily historical interest. Such laws would now have to survive Charter review based on freedom of expression and assembly.[40]

In the wake of the *Charter*, "municipal by-laws restricting public meetings or parades will be limitations on s. 2(c) that will have to be justifed under s. 1," he said.[41]

4. Neil Finkelstein's "The Relevance of Pre-Charter Case Law for Post-Charter Adjudication"

Indirectly, then, the Jehovah's Witnesses cases of the 1950s came to the forefront of attention in post-*Charter* analysis both by the courts and by academics. It was perhaps predictable that the cases would continue to have this kind of influence in post-*Charter* decisions and treatments of the law, especially during the transition period before a body of case law pertaining to the *Charter* could be built up. Neil Finkelstein pointed out this fact in 1982 in his article "The Relevance of Pre-Charter Case Law for Post-Charter Adjudication,"[42] in which he referred repeatedly to the Jehovah's Witnesses cases, especially with regard to s. 1 of the *Charter*, to which he confined himself almost exclusively. Finkelstein said that the *Charter* did not affect cases founded upon "common law civil libertarian doctrines or the doctrine of *ultra vires*" for at common law "an individual

---

38 *Ibid.* at 774–75.

39 Peter W. Hogg, *Constitutional Law of Canada*, 2nd edn. (Toronto: Carswell, 1985) at 419.

40 *Ibid.* at 708–709.

41 *Ibid.* at 721.

42 (1982), 4 Sup. Ct. L. Rev. 267 at 268.

is free to do as he pleases vis-à-vis the State unless restrained by a positive rule of law." The State must first demonstrate the existence of a law that circumscribes individual liberty, and then show "that the power conferred by the law is exercised by an authorized official," said Finkelstein.[43] He cited as examples of this principle the *Chaput, Lamb* and *Roncarelli* cases, and remarked, "In *Roncarelli*, not even the most powerful Premier in Quebec's history could take it upon himself to review Roncarelli's liquor licence, notwithstanding that another State official occupying a different (and subordinate) position had the authority to do it."[44] Finkelstein pointed to the *Boucher* case as authority for the proposition that courts tend to construe restrictive statutes narrowly where possible: "More than an intention to create ill-will between groups was necessary to constitute the *Criminal Code* offence of sedition, even though that was enough interpretation under a historical and traditional common law of the crime."[45]

Finkelstein argued that pre-*Charter* cases can be used in the characterization of the "matter" or primary thrust of an impugned statute when applying s. 1 of the *Charter*. Examples that he gave included the "obvious" ones: the *Alberta Press Case, Switzman* v. *Elbling*, and *Saumur* v. *City of Quebec*:

> In *Saumur* v. *City of Quebec*, a municipal by-law prohibited the distribution of any literature without the written permission of the Chief of Police. A member of the Jehovah's Witnesses challenged its validity. While the Supreme Court was badly divided on the *ratio decidendi* of the case, the characterization of the by-law did not pose a real difficulty. Five judges characterized it as being in relation to religion, and two others easily admitted its adverse effect on freedom of the press and religion. While one may wonder about the authority of *Saumur* on the jurisdictional point in light of *A.G. Can.* v. *City of Montreal; Dupond* v. *City of Montreal*, the case is clearly good law on the characterization issue.[46]

Compared to *Saumur, Dupond* is "highly suspect," said Finklestein, and does "not measure up to the standard of good common sense":

> The Supreme Court must be wary of importing such cases as *Dupond* v. *City of Montreal* into post-Charter law. By a by-law, the City of Montreal provided that its Executive Committee could prohibit *"any or all* assemblies, parades or gatherings [that might lead to] tumult or disturbance."

---

43 *Ibid.* at 267.

44 *Ibid.* at 267–68.

45 *Ibid.* at 268.

46 *Ibid.* at 269–70.

It thus authorized the imposition of "content-based" restrictions on the right of assembly. An ordinance was passed pursant to the by-law banning all demonstrations on the public domain for thirty days.

Dupond should be considered with *Saumur* v. *City of Quebec*, where a municipal by-law prohibited the distribution of pamphlets, handbills or other literature on the streets of Quebec City without the written permission of the Chief of Police. The Supreme Court struck down the *Saumur* by-law. The impugned by-laws in both cases were vehicles for censorship, empowering municipal authorities to screen messages and exclude certain of them from transmission in the public domain. Notwithstanding the apparent similarity in the cases, Beetz J, speaking for a majority of the Supreme Court, upheld the *Dupond* by-law.[47]

After reviewing Justice Beetz's characterization of the by-law in *Dupond* (in which Beetz stated that demonstrations are not a form of speech but a display of action, not an appeal to reason but an inarticulate display of force), Finkelstein concluded:

> This cannot be right. People demonstrate to convey a message. They do so peacefully in groups rather than individually to show solidarity and a common desire for a certain outcome or state of affairs, not to display force. Far from being inarticulate, a demonstration's message is usually short, to the point, and very clear.[48]

Finkelstein described *Robertson* as "another example of mischaracterization." By holding that the practical effect of the *Lord's Day Act* was secular and financial rather than religious, a penalty was exacted on any whose religion demanded that they rest on some day other than Sunday:

> It is obvious that the true effect of the legislation is to put an economic clog on the exercise of those religions whose holy day is not Sunday. Members of those religions are put to a test that Christian observers are not: they may earn five days' income and observe their religion, or they may earn six days' income at the expense of their religious observance.
>
> In my view, this type of legislation cannot survive the Charter. Any non-religious purpose that may be argued here is belied by the legislation.[49]

Finkelstein emphasized that the direction to the courts to characterize legislation or determine its pith and substance came from the Charter itself, and the standard was one of common sense. "If a law is in relation to expression, as I believe *Dupond* was, or in relation to religion, as

---

47 *Ibid.* at 271–72.

48 *Ibid.* at 272.

49 *Ibid.* at 272–73.

Robertson was, both as to purpose and effect, the courts should characterize it that way."[50]

Less clear, in Finkelstein's view, were borderline characterization
cases such as *Donald v. Hamilton Board of Education*,[51] which in Finkelstein's view was "at the cutting edge of civil liberties adjudication":

> The issue in *Donald* was whether a student could claim a religious
> exemption from saluting the flag and singing the national anthem. Al-
> though the majority of the population might consider these activities to
> be symbols of patriotism that are devoid of religious significance, free-
> dom of religion is always best preserved where the courts accept a com-
> plainant's contention of religious principle at face value (assuming good
> faith), and move on to the next stage of weighing whatever competing
> public interest might be involved. The Ontario Court of Appeal in
> *Donald* adopted this approach. Gillander J.A., speaking for the Court,
> cast a very uncritical eye on the student's religious claim and, accepting
> it, in effect held that whatever countervailing state interest might exist
> did not override it.[52]

Once the burden under the initial part of s. 1 is satisfied, it shifts to
the government to demonstrate that its actions are justified in a free and
democratic society. This entails a weighing or balancing of the competing
interests, said Finkelstein. Two cases that he cites to demonstrate this
process are *Switzman* v. *Elbling* and *Boucher* v. *R.* In *Switzman*, the restriction imposed by the Duplessis government was the notorious Padlock
Act, a statute that, by means of penalties, prevented what, in the words
of Mr. Justice Rand, "is considered a poisoning of men's minds, to shield
the individual from exposure to dangerous ideas, to protect him, in short,
from his own thinking propensities."[53] In *Switzman*, the law itself was
ruled unconstitutional as not being justified in a free society.

In the case of *Boucher*, however, the charge was sedition. Boucher was
acquitted not because the law was invalid (it was legitimately concerned
with preservation of public order and state security) but because Boucher
did not intend to incite anyone to use force against the State—an essential
element of the offence. Intention to create ill-will between groups is not
enough:[54]

---

50 *Ibid.* at 273.

51 (1945), [1945] O.R. 518, [1945] 3 D.L.R. 424 (C.A.).

52 Finkelstein, *supra*, note 42 at 270.

53 (1957), [1957] S.C.R. 285, 7 D.L.R. (2d) 337 at 357.

54 Finkelstein, *supra*, note 42 at 274.

Boucher does not tell us how close the nexus between the speech and the danger to State security must be, or whether mere intention to incite violence, even without the element of danger, is enough. However, section 1 gives the courts guidance by directing them to ask what interest the State has in suppressing speech if there is little potential for harm. If there is not a close connection between the speech and actual danger, then suppression of the speech is not justifiable under the Charter.[55]

Finkelstein regarded cases in the area of religion as being "the best examples of competing legitimate public and private interests" to arise prior to the *Charter*, and he gave as a central example the case of *Chabot v. School Commissioners of Lamorandière*.[56] *Chabot*, he said, stands for the proposition that "State interest is subordinate to the interests of people holding different religious beliefs, and that they must be exempted from participation in religious exercises in schools if they so choose."[57] He again cited *Donald* as an example of a case where "the State interest in fostering loyalty must yield to religious observance"—a "flag salute" situation similar to that dealt with in the American *Barnette* case cited in *Robertson*.[58] By 1982, it seemed likely that the Jehovah's Witnesses cases would hold their own in the post-Charter era. Although Finkelstein's essay was at best speculative, it was indicative of the scholarship that was to follow—particularly in the works on constitutional law and the Charter that were to be published by such eminent constitutional authorities as Tarnopolsky, Gibson, Cotler and Hogg. It also served to complement a less formal treatment of the relationship between fundamental freedoms and Jehovah's Witnesses at the hands of the prominent Canadian jurist Thomas R. Berger.

5. Thomas Berger's *Fragile Freedoms*

Thomas Berger devotes a full chapter of *Fragile Freedoms: Human Rights and Dissent in Canada*[59] to Jehovah's Witnesses, calling that chapter "Jehovah's Witnesses: Church, State and Religious Dissent."[60] He describes the Roman Catholic Church in Quebec as being "a monolithic presence" that had a major influence in politics, since politicians such as Duplessis sought "to ally themselves with the Church."[61] While "intel-

---

55 *Ibid.*

56 (1957), [1957] Que. Q.B. 707, 12 D.L.R. (2d) 796 (C.A.).

57 Finkelstein, *supra*, note 42 at 278.

58 *Ibid.*

59 Toronto: Clarke, Irwin, 1982.

60 *Ibid.* at 163 ff.

61 *Ibid.* at 163.

lectuals such as Pierre Trudeau, trade unionists such as Jean Marchand, and journalists such as Gerard Pelletier urged the adoption of liberal and democratic ideas" in Quebec, denouncing "clerical domination of provincial life," Jehovah's Witnesses cut even deeper to the quick by actively challenging Roman Catholic doctrine:

> No one suggests that the struggle of the Witnesses was one of the hinges on which events turned in Quebec, but the clash between the Catholic Church and the Witnesses, the confrontation between Duplessis and Jehovah, heralded the arrival of secularism in Quebec. That clash laid bare competing ideas of freedom of speech and freedom of religion.
>
> The Jehovah's Witnesses were unlikely protagonists of secularism, but they were determined to establish their right to seek converts from Catholicism in a province where none had successfully contested the Church's control of its flock.[62]

Their accomplishments were also "secular" in the sense that they used the secular courts to establish their right to distribute religious tracts, an act which Berger termed "political" since it attacked the "obscurantism and repression" of Maurice Duplessis and his curious brand of Quebec nationalism:

> During the Duplessis era, between 1936 and 1959, Church and State joined in persecuting Jehovah's Witnesses, who carried their struggle for freedom of speech and freedom of religion to the Supreme Court of Canada again and again. The Charter of Rights and Freedoms enshrined freedom of speech and of religion as inalienable rights of its citizens in every province. The fervour of this small Protestant sect had more than a little to do with establishing the intellectual foundations for the Charter.[63]

After reviewing several of the more controversial Witness doctrines and the early history of the sect, Berger goes on to review, favourably, James Penton's *Jehovah's Witnesses in Canada: Champions of Freedom of Speech and Religion*,[64] which he calls "an authoritative account . . . of the persecution (for that is what it was) of the Witnesses during the First and Second World Wars and between the wars."[65] He describes the ban on Witness literature during the First World War, the censorship of Witness radio stations, and the Witnesses' response, in which they "demonstrated for the first time their astonishing capacity to obtain signatures on

---

62 *Ibid.* at 164.

63 *Ibid.* at 164–65.

64 Toronto: University of Toronto Press, 1976.

65 Berger, *supra.* note 59 at 167.

petitions."[66] Their attacks on rival churches of Christendom earned "the detestation of the clergy throughout Canada," said Berger, for "their brochures were anti-clerical and anti-Catholic." Even as early as 1933, the Witnesses were charged with a variety of offences, including sedition. "Many were convicted; some were fined, and some were imprisoned."[67]

Once Duplessis came to power in 1936, the campaign against Jehovah's Witnesses intensified, and Duplessis used "not only existing laws but also his new Padlock Act against them, for the legislative net that statute provided was wide enough to catch a Witness as easily as a Communist."[68] But during the war years, the federal government was even more of a threat than Duplessis, who had lost the election in 1939. The Watch Tower Bible and Tract Society's property came to be regarded as "enemy property" and was seized by the Custodian of Enemy Property; their literature was seized, their meeting halls closed, and the Witnesses themselves were arrested—some 500 of them out of a total 1941 population of 7,007. Those Witnesses who remained active despite the ban managed to garner 223,448 signatures on a successful petition to Parliament to lift the ban.[69]

Berger describes the renewed struggle between Jehovah's Witnesses and Maurice Duplessis, who had returned as Premier of Quebec. By November 1946, 800 Witnesses faced trial for sedition or distributing literature without a licence. The Witnesses responded with their vitriolic tract *Quebec's Burning Hate for God and Christ and Freedom Is the Shame of All Canada*, which, said Berger, was "calculated to incense any Catholic":[70]

> Duplessis described the pamphlet as 'intolerable and seditious,' and more Witnesses were arrested. In taking these measures, Duplessis was supported by the French-Canadian press, the Roman Catholic hierarchy, and the people of Quebec. The Witnesses, they agreed, had brought their troubles on themselves. Those who openly attack the faith of a righteous majority must expect to be punished for their insolence.
>
> This way of looking at freedom of religion is of course at odds with the principles of democracy, an essential aspect of which is religious toleration.[71]

---

66 *Ibid.* at 169.

67 *Ibid.* at 170.

68 *Ibid.*

69 *Ibid.* at 171.

70 *Ibid.* at 172.

71 *Ibid.* at 174.

After describing the petitions of Jehovah's Witnesses for a bill of rights, he turns his attention to the Supreme Court of Canada cases, beginning with *Boucher*, pointing out that the trial judge erred when he "virtually directed the jury to convict Boucher. He did not tell the jury they could decide for themselves whether or not Boucher had acted in good faith under s. 138A [of the *Criminal Code*]. Not surprisingly, the jury convicted Boucher."[72] The Quebec Court of Appeal denied his appeal, but the Supreme Court of Canada, only recently made the final court of appeal for Canada, did not:

> Boucher's appeal to the Supreme Court of Canada was the first of the Witnesses' appeals to reach it, and his appeal was heard just after the abolition in 1949 of appeals to the Privy Council in Britain. The Supreme Court of Canada was now the final court of appeal for Canada. Its first decade as Canada's court of last resort was its greatest. During the 1950s no other tribunal in the English-speaking world showed as ardent a concern for fundamental freedoms.[73]

The most powerful judgments of this powerful court, says Berger, were those of Mr. Justice Ivan Rand. "He was profound, learned, eloquent, and he was unyielding in his devotion to civil liberties."[74]

Unfortunately, the decisions of the Supreme Court during its first decade as the highest court of appeal in Canada "are little known, except to lawyers, and they are not well enough known even to them," writes Berger.

> The legal profession took no great interest in these important cases, the judgements were hardly discussed in law schools, and neither the media nor the public comprehended their significance. But they provide for us today uniquely Canadian insights into questions of freedom of speech and freedom of religion, and flesh out the bare bones of the guarantees of the Charter.[75]

After reviewing the *Boucher* and *Saumur* decisions of Mr. Justice Rand, Berger concludes that since the 1950s "there have been solid legal grounds for saying that only Parliament can legislate to curtail the fundamental freedoms" under its criminal law powers:

> Only Parliament, in the exercise of its power to make criminal law, could pass laws in relation to the fundamental freedoms. Rand, however, did

---

72 *Ibid.* at 175.

73 *Ibid.* at 175.

74 *Ibid.*

75 *Ibid.* at 176.

not stop there. It was not enough merely to say that the provinces could not legislate in relation to fundamental freedoms. He wished to state the issue affirmatively:

> ... freedom of speech, religion and the inviolability of the person, are original freedoms which are at once the necessary attributes and modes of self-expression of human beings and the primary conditions of their community life within a legal order.

In this, he foresaw the lineaments of the Charter of Rights, and he provided a firm philosophical basis for the idea that the fundamental freedoms lie beyond the reach of legislative authority, federal or provincial.[76]

This effect is achieved, finally and irrevocably (subject to the *non obstante* clause) by the *Canadian Charter of Rights and Freedoms*, which has enshrined "fundamental freedoms as independent constitutional values," says Berger. But it was Mr. Justice Ivan Rand who "did most to clarify Canadian thought about our fundamental freedoms," and who had first declared that not even the federal government, let alone a provincial government, should have the power to take away the fundamental freedoms of any citizen. This declaration was first made in the context of the Jehovah's Witnesses cases. Berger concludes:

> The Witnesses' clashes with authority provided the occasion for elaborating the constitutional values which undergird Canadian federalism. Freedom of speech and freedom of religion are fundamental aspects of Canadian democracy, and may be claimed by dissenters, whether or not their views affront the beliefs of the majority. No government may take away these rights, and even the highest officials may not abuse the power of their office to deprive dissenters of these rights.[77]

Yet curiously, after the advent of the *Charter*, jurists and legal academics across the nation quickly seemed to lose sight of these high ideals.

---

76 *Ibid.* at 181.

77 *Ibid.* at 189.

II. THE JEHOVAH'S WITNESSES CASES IN THE POST-*CHARTER* PERIOD OF TRANSITION

1. *Canadian Charter of Rights and Freedoms: Commentary*

Perhaps more than any other work, *The Canadian Charter of Rights and Freedoms: Commentary*,[78] edited by Walter S. Tarnopolsky and Gerald-A. Beaudoin, established a patterned procedure in its approach to *Charter* issues using pre-*Charter* cases. Although most of this collaboration of 15 prominent constitutional scholars was prepared before the enactment of the *Constitution Act, 1982*, some of the chapters were subsequently revised.[79] Interestingly, the six authors whose contributions were made in French—Professors Beaudoin, Blache, Chevrette, Garant, Morel and Tremblay—did not so much as allude to the Jehovah's Witnesses cases, even though the most significant of these cases originated in Quebec. In fact, Professors Cotler, Gibson and Tarnopolsky were the only contributors to mention the Jehovah's Witnesses cases.

Tarnopolsky described *Roncarelli* v. *Duplessis* as "one of the most famous applications" of the doctrine of A.V. Dicey that "equality before the law" is part of "the rule of law."[80] He also pointed out that the preamble to the *B.N.A. Act*, which refers to the constitution of Canada as being "similar in Principle to that of the United Kingdom," had been used by the Supreme Court not only as one of the reasons for declaring the Alberta Press Bill invalid, but also "in restraining the Quebec Government of Maurice Duplessis in his battle with the Jehovah's Witnesses and Communists, which has provided us with some of our most important civil liberties cases. Thus, the importance of a preamble, or an 'aims' clause, cannot be minimized."[81]

Dale Gibson alluded to the *Boucher* case to illustrate the firmly established interpretative presumption that courts faced with ambiguous legislation often choose "the meaning most consonant with individual rights and freedoms."[82] He referred to *Saumur* v. *A.-G. Quebec*[83] as a classic example of the restrictive approach to gaining standing before the

---

78 Toronto: Carswell, 1982.

79 *Ibid.* at iv.

80 *Ibid.* at 400.

81 *Ibid.* at 441.

82 *Ibid.* at 32.

83 (1964), [1964] S.C.R. 252, 45 D.L.R. (2d) 627.

court in constitutional matters that had existed prior to the *Thorson* case (1974).[84] In the second *Saumur* case, said Gibson,

> the Supreme Court of Canada denied a member of the Jehovah's Witnesses sect standing to challenge the constitutional validity of a law prohibiting the distribution of certain sect literature. It was held that until he actually broke the law in question and was prosecuted for doing so, the plaintiff would lack standing to seek judicial relief.[85]

Gibson noted that s. 24(1) of the *Charter* had a serious weakness that would not remedy the difficulty raised in *Saumur No. 2*:

> Probably the most serious weakness in the draftsmanship of s. 24(1) is that by restricting its protection to "anyone whose rights or freedoms, as guaranteed by this Charter, *have been* infringed or denied [emphasis Gibson's]," it could be construed as excluding judicial consideration of impending infringements which have not yet come into force or have not yet been applied to the complainant.
>
> Several different types of possible impending infringement come to mind. One is the sort of situation that gave rise to the *Saumur* case referred to earlier: a law prohibiting the exercise of some freedom that the complainant would like to exercise, but not at the cost of criminal prosecution.[86]

Gibson also alluded to *Chaput* v. *Romain* in connection with his analysis of remedies arising from s. 24(1). Where the civil law allows for compensation for "moral damages" as in *Chaput*, which was tried in a civil law jurisdiction, can a court of competent jurisdiction outside Quebec apply civil law remedies to common law cases? Are the courts prepared "to permit unlimited remedial innovation by the courts where Charter violations are involved"? Can each system "borrow the best features of the other"?[87]

But by far the most penetrating study of the role of the Jehovah's Witnesses cases in shaping an approach to the *Charter* is the sixth chapter of the *Commentary* by Irwin Cotler, "Freedom of Assembly, Association, Conscience and Religion."[88] Cotler referred to *Saumur v. City of Quebec*

---

84 *Thorson* v. *A. G. Can.* (1974), [1975] 1 S.C.R. 138, 43 D.L.R. (3d) 1. The issue of standing was further clarified by *Nova Scotia Board of Censors* v. *McNeil* (1975), [1976] 2 S.C.R. 265, 55 D.L.R. (3d) 632; and *Minister of Justice (Canada)* v. *Borowski*, (1981), [1982] 1 W.W.R. 97, 130 D.L.R. (3d) 588 (S.C.C.).

85 Tarnopolsky and Beaudoin, *supra*, note 78 at 494.

86 *Ibid.* at 498.

87 *Ibid.* at 504.

88 *Ibid.* at 123.

as being one of the sources of the developing notion of "'original freedoms'—freedoms so basic that they could not be trenched upon without grave cause." In such cases, an "implied bill of rights was as necessary to self-realization as it was to the social order."[89] But Cotler pointed out that even in those cases where an "implied bill of rights" thesis was developed by Mr. Justice Rand, such as *Saumur* and *Switzman*, "legal federalism remained the organizing motif of judicial review."[90] The *dicta* of Rand support the notion of fundamental freedoms rooted organically in the constitution and the Parliamentary system itself:

> Fundamental freedoms tend to travel together, so that violations or abrogations of them have usually engaged several at the same time. Accordingly, where, as in *Saumur*, a municipal by-law effected a prior restraint on the dissemination of religious tracts by Jehovah's Witnesses, the action may abridge the free exercise of religion, as in the singling out of differential application of prior restraint to Jehovah's Witnesses. It may also, in its prior restraint, particularly if there is a seizure of materials, abrogate the right to freedom of the press; abrogate the freedom to assemble in its prohibition of the use of the public domain; violate freedom of association in its punitive application to members of a religious group and, in its totality, be violative of the incidence of citizenship, of the "critical mass" of "original freedoms" which Rand J. regarded as expressive of a 'generic' notion of fundamental freedoms.
>
> Similarly, where, as in *Chaput*, police officers invade a religious gathering and order the persons assembled to leave, and seize the material on the premises, the action will equally engage freedoms of religion, press, assembly, speech, and association.[91]

The clustered fundamental rights alluded to by Cotler as emerging in *Saumur* v. *City of Quebec* and *Chaput* are part of a mosaic of rights that could fall under the rubric of what has been described as a "system of freedom of expression." Rand J. defined this emerging system most eloquently in *Saumur*:

> Freedom of speech, religion, and the inviolability of the person are original freedoms which are at once the necessary attributes and modes of self-expression of human beings and the primary conditions of their community life within a legal order.[92]

---

89 *Ibid.* at 132.

90 *Ibid.* at 125–26.

91 *Ibid.* at 133.

92 *Saumur, supra*, note 11 at 329.

Thus Rand regarded the fundamental rights as "not only essential for democratic society, they are integral to self-fulfillment and group development."[93]

Unfortunately Rand's remarks, however eloquent, remain only *obiter*, and aside from his "legacy" (as Thomas Berger has described Rand's contributions to the preservation of the fundamental freedoms[94]) the courts prior to the *Charter* failed to confront the "system of freedom of expression" directly, apparently having higher regard for the "double override" described by Mr. Justice Cartwright in *Saumur*:

> Under the *B.N.A. Act* . . . the whole range of legislative power is committed either to Parliament or the Provincial Legislatures and competence to deal with any subject matter must exist in one or other of such bodies. There are thus no rights possessed by the citizens of Canada which cannot be modified by either Parliament or the Legislature.[95]

Cartwright went on to admit that "it may often be a matter of difficulty to decide which of such bodies has the legislative power in a particular case."[96] That was precisely the situation in *Saumur*, as Cotler remarked:

> The discussion centered around the distribution of legislative power. Four judges [Rand, Kellock, Estey and Locke JJ.] held that the legislation was in relation to religion and free speech and was therefore within federal competence. Four other judges [Rinfret C.J.C., and Taschereau, Fauteux and Cartwright JJ.] held that the Province could validly legislate regarding freedom of worship. Kerwin J. held that, in principle, freedom of religion was a s. 92.13 *B.N.A. Act* civil right within the province, but that the distribution of religious pamphlets was specifically protected by a pre-Confederation Freedom of Worship statute of Lower Canada continued under s. 129 of the *B.N.A. Act*.[97]

All of the judges thus accepted as valid the assumption advanced by Cartwright that freedom of assembly could be curtailed by application of either federal or provincial law. "No principle of freedom of assembly was established," said Cotler.

> The only limitation emerging from this case which may be imposed upon municipal permit systems, apart from legal federalism and the im-

---

93 Tarnopolsky and Beaudoin, *supra*, note 78 at 142.

94 Thomas Berger, "The Supreme Court and Fundamental Freedoms: The Renunciation of the Legacy of Mr. Justice Rand" (1980), 1 Sup. Ct. L. Rev. 460 at 466.

95 *Saumur, supra*, note 11 at 384.

96 *Ibid.*

97 Tarnopolsky and Beaudoin, *supra*, note 78 at 146.

plied bill of rights *dicta*, is that a by-law may be invalid if the discretion conferred upon non-elected officials is unduly broad. That is, the by-law should define the discretion of an officer and should prescribe standards for the exercise of that discretion. The only judicial supports for this limitation, however, are to be found in the judgments of Kellock and Rand JJ. in *Saumur*.[98]

It was precisely this view advanced by Justices Kellock and Rand that Mr. Justice Beetz abandoned in the *Dupond* decision when the Supreme Court "allowed a municipality to legislate in relation to the minds of citizens using streets under the guise of regulation of the streets themselves."[99]

Cotler regarded *Saumur* as being "an excellent case-study of legal federalism as the organizing frame of reference for the determination of 'religion,'" but he added that "unfortunately, it is almost impossible to determine the essential ratio of the decision, dramatizing the problem of the 'double-override.'"[100] Nonetheless Cotler tried to clarify the *ratio* with respect specifically to religion:

> Four judges held that the by-law was *ultra vires* as being in relation to freedom of religion and therefore beyond provincial jurisdiction, four judges held that it was *intra vires*, but only two held that freedom of religion was within provincial jurisdiction. The other two held that the by-law was not in relation to freedom of religion, but that it was *intra vires* since it was in relation to the use of streets, parks and sidewalks (s. 92.13). The swing vote was cast by Chief Justice Kerwin, who held that the by-law was *intra vires* but in breach of the Freedom of Worship Act of 1851 and therefore invalid. Accordingly, Jehovah's Witnesses, and for that matter any religious group, would not have to seek the permission of the Chief of Police for the distribution of their literature.[101]

Cotler emphasized that the influence of the *Saumur* cases transcended issues of applicability of by-laws or even jurisdiction over religion. Although *Robertson and Rosetanni* had held that the *Canadian Bill of Rights* did not repeal the *Lord's Day Act* since the issue before the court could be characterized as secular rather than religious, nonetheless the majority there had declared that "the position of religious freedom in the Canadian system was that outlined by Mr. Justice Rand in the *Saumur* case."[102] If this were so, then could not the *dicta* in *Saumur* be "relevant, if not

---

98 *Ibid.* at 146–47.

99 *Ibid.* at 148–49.

100 *Ibid.* at 196.

101 *Ibid.* at 196–97.

102 *Ibid.* at 197.

persuasive" for s. 2 of the *Charter* as a whole? Cotler proceeded to list various statements from the judgments of Rand and Locke to show just how broad-ranging the judgment was:[103]

> *On Freedom of Religion:* From 1760 . . . to the present . . . religious freedom has . . . been recognized as a principle of fundamental character; and although we have nothing in the nature of an established church, that the untrammelled affirmations of religious belief and its propagation, personal or institutional, remains as of the greatest constitutional significance thoughout the Dominion is unquestionable.[104]

> *On Freedom of Speech & Religion:* Freedom of speech, religion and the inviolability of the person, are original freedoms which are at once the necessary attributes and modes of self-expression of human beings and the primary conditions of their community life within a legal order.[105]

> *On Prior Restraint:* Their [original freedoms] significant relation to our law lies in this, that under its principles to which there are only minor exceptions, there is no prior or antecedent restraint placed upon them: the penalties, civil or criminal, attach to results which their exercise may bring about, and apply as consequential incidents.[106]

> *And again:* Government rest[s] ultimately on public opinion reached by discussion and the interplay of ideas. If that discussion is placed under license, its basic condition is destroyed: the government, as licensor, becomes disjoined from the citizenry.[107]

> *On Freedom of Expression:* What the practice under the by-law demonstrates is that the language comprehends the power of censorship. From its inception, printing has been recognized as an agency of tremendous possibilities.[108]

> *On Freedom of Assembly and Expression:* What is proposed before us is that a newspaper . . . can be placed under the uncontrolled discretion of a municipal officer. . . . [A] more objectionable interference, short of complete suppression, with that dissemination which is the 'breath of life' of the political institutions of this country than that made possible by the by-law can scarcely be imagined.[109]

---

103 *Ibid.* at 198–99.

104 *Saumur, supra,* note 11 at 327.

105 *Ibid.* at 329.

106 *Ibid.*

107 *Ibid.* at 330.

108 *Ibid.* at 326.

109 *Ibid.* at 332.

If these *dicta* from *Saumur* are joined with those in the *Alberta Press Case*, *Switzman*, *Roncarelli*, and other similar cases "there is a formidable jurisprudence that may be invoked as authoritative precedent under the Charter," said Cotler. Indeed the *Saumur dicta* have been cited even by the Quebec Court of Appeal, as by Judge Casey in *Chabot* v. *School Commissioners of Lamorandière*:[110]

> The denial of appellant's right of inviolability of conscience . . . is coupled with or effected by . . . active interference with his right to control the religious education of his children. . . . The rights of which we have been speaking, find their source in natural law. . . . If, as they do, they find their existence in the very nature of man, then they cannot be taken away and they must prevail should they conflict with the provisions of positive law.[111]

The *Education Act* could not legally be applied in such a way as to deny a parent control over the religious education of his children, and the school board was compelled to accept the Jehovah's Witness children without insisting that the children observe Roman Catholic instruction. Cotler commented,

> Freedom of conscience and religion under the Charter may not be "inalienable" in the sense in which Casey J. has spoken of them, but they are certainly more fundamental under the Charter than the ordinary positive law, which Casey J. felt "can be taken away." Admittedly, the new override of s. 33 coupled with the s. 1 limitations clause may yet create a new "double override"; and the "double override" of the past, while now contained, has not been removed. But a new order of fundamental freedoms has been entrenched. And it is to be hoped that these preferred freedoms will not be taken away, while freedom of conscience together with religion now has the distinguishable status of which Casey spoke.[112]

Cotler described *Roncarelli* v. *Duplessis*, "the 'cause celebre' of Canadian public law," as "perhaps the most compelling judgment repudiating the conditioning and denial of government benefits on the basis of associational ties." In reviewing the facts of the case, he noted that Roncarelli had "enjoyed an excellent and unblemished reputation," and that not only was his licence cancelled upon the order of Duplessis as punishment for Roncarelli's association with Jehovah's Witnesses, but a

---

110 (1957), 12 D.L.R. (2d) 796.

111 *Ibid.* at 807.

112 Tarnopolsky and Beaudoin, *supra*, note 78 at 199.

pending application for renewal was denied "with a further provision that it was cancelled 'forever'":

> It was, in effect, a classic example of an attempt by a government to condition a benefit on membership in a disfavoured association, or to deny a government benefit on grounds of associational ties. Moreover, not only were Roncarelli's ties with the Jehovah's Witnesses regarded as a provocative act, but the exercise of his citizen's rights to act as surety for bail for Jehovah's Witnesses was characterized as an interference with the administration of justice in the province, if not also seditious behavior.[113]

After reviewing the history of the case at trial and in the Quebec Court of Appeal, Cotler focused on the 6–3 judgment of the Supreme Court of Canada, in particular the decision of Mr. Justice Rand, who "in a series of memorable passages, not only articulated the protected nature of freedom of association as an incident of citizenship, but warned against, in an almost prophetic sense, the threat to the rule of law of unchecked and arbitrary governmental power."[114] Cotler quoted Rand's famous application of the rule of law:

> That an adminstration according to law is to be superseded by action dictated by and according to the arbitrary likes, dislikes and irrelevant purposes of public officers acting beyond their duty, would signalize the beginning of disintegration of the rule of law as a fundamental postulate of our constitutional structure.[115]

Cotler also cited selections from the Rand judgment to demonstrate the justice's position on freedom of association without retribution. Rand had remarked, "Beyond the giving of bail and being an adherent, the appellant is free from any relation that could be tortured into a badge of character pertinent to his fitness or unfitness to hold a liquor licence."[116] He added:

> To deny or revoke a permit because a citizen exercises an unchallengeable right totally irrelevant to the sale of liquor in a restaurant is equally beyond the scope of the discretion conferred . . . to which was added here the element of intentional punishment by what was virtually voca-

---

113 *Ibid*. at 178.

114 *Ibid*.

115 *Roncarelli* v. *Duplessis*, (1959), [1959] S.C.R. 121 at 142, 16 D.L.R. (2d) 689 [hereinafter cited to S.C.R.].

116 *Ibid*. at 132.

tion outlawry . . . arbitrarily and illegally attempting to divest a person of an incident of his civil status.[117]

Canadian law protects the rights and privileges of religious assoc-iations as well as the free exercise of religion, Cotler stated. Taschereau in *Chaput* v. *Romain* had held that "there is no state religion in Canada." Accordingly, every citizen can belong to the church of his choice or to no church at all. Religious beliefs and practices are not controlled by the law; in fact religious affiliation is protected by laws which make discrimina-tion based on religion illegal.[118] These laws include the various provin-cial Human Rights Acts and the *Criminal Code*, s. 176(1) of which provides that obstruction or prevention of or endeavoring to prevent a minister from conducting a service or from "performing any other function in con-nection with his calling" is an indictable offence. Subsections (2) and (3) are even broader:

(2) Every one who wilfully disturbs or interrupts an assemblage of persons met for religious worship or for a moral, social or benevolent purpose is guilty of an offence punishable on summary conviction.
(3) Every one who, at or near a meeting referred to in subsection (2) wilfully does anything that disturbs the order or solemnity of the meeting is guilty of an offence punishable on summary conviction.

In *Chaput* v. *Romain*, it was the policemen rather than Chaput who were in violation of the law, as the Supreme Court of Canada unanimously found:

Three of the justices decided that the conduct of the police was in clear violation of the *Criminal Code*, while the other five agreed that the acts were illegal, *inter alia* for contravention of the *Criminal Code*. Therefore, the Witness of Jehovah was entitled to succeed in his action for damages under the *Quebec Civil Code*. The ninth judge concurred as to the illegal-ity, but he did not refer specifically to the *Criminal Code*. In effect, then, the Supreme Court gave unanimous protection to the appellant's freedom of religious worship.[119]

The *Criminal Code* also figured prominently in the *Boucher* case, especially with respect to the definition of "sedition." Cotler wrote that "a network of limitations has grown up around the criminal law,"[120] and he pointed to *Saumur*, *Boucher* and *Switzman* as illustrations of the

---

117 *Ibid.* at 141–43.
118 Tarnopolsky and Beaudoin, *supra*, note 78 at 158.
119 *Ibid.* at 208–209.
120 *Ibid.* at 163.

ways in which one fundamental freedom dovetailed with another to curb
statutory restrictions such as freedom of assembly, association, religion,
speech—in short the "generic freedom of expression."[121] The *Criminal
Code* sections on sedition (ss. 59–61) were applied in the *Boucher* case, and
to this day *Martin's Criminal Code* lists *Boucher* as "the leading case" on
s. 59:[122]

> The Court was divided on whether a "seditious intention" required
> proof in all cases of an intention to incite acts of violence or public
> disorder. Kerwin, Rand, Kellock and Estey, JJ., were of the view that it
> did. Taschereau, Cartwright, Fauteau and (*semble*) Locke, JJ., were of the
> view that it did in all cases except those related to the administration of
> justice which required only proof of an intention to bring the administra-
> tion of justice into hatred or contempt or incite disaffection against it.
> Rinfret, C.J.C., did not come to a firm conclusion on the matter but mere-
> ly pointed out that the advocating of force was not the only instance in
> which there could be a "seditious intention."[123]

The Supreme Court held that strong, even virulent, criticism of the Province of Quebec and the Roman Catholic Church did not meet the test of
advocating force and therefore did not amount to sedition. Again Cotler
quoted Justice Rand, who in *Boucher* defined the scope of freedom of
religion in the context of strong disagreement:

> Freedom in thought and speech and disagreement in ideas and beliefs,
> on every conceivable subject, are the essence of our life. The clash of
> critical discussion on political, social and religious subjects has too
> deeply become the stuff of daily experience to suggest that mere ill-will
> as a product of controversy can strike down the latter with illegality.[124]

The courts have been reluctant to define "religion," said Cotler, but
have been quite open-minded about allowing individuals to define it for
themselves.[125] He gave as an example *Donald v. Hamilton Board of Education*,[126] in which Jehovah's Witnesses successfully argued before the
Ontario Court of Appeal that saluting the flag and singing *God Save the
King* were offensive to their religious beliefs. The Jehovah's Witness
children concerned therefore could not be compelled to engage in such

---

121 *Ibid.*

122 *Boucher* was decided on s. 133 of the 1927 *Code*, which was essentially the same as s. 59.

123 Edward Greenspan, ed., *Martin's Annual Criminal Code 1989* (Aurora: Canada Law Book
Inc., 1988) at 64.

124 [1951] S.C.R. 265 at 288.

125 Tarnopolsky and Beaudoin, *supra,* note 78 at 194.

126 *Supra,* note 51.

activities, just as the Jehovah's Witness children in *Chabot* v. *School Commissioners of Lamorandière*[127] could not be compelled to participate in specifically Roman Catholic religious exercises which they found to be offensive to their own religious beliefs, while being forced by the sheer constraints of geography to attend the only school in the area. Cotler also noted that in *Ruman* v. *Lethbridge School Board Trustees*,[128] on similar facts as those in *Donald*, "the court held that the children involved would have to comply or be expelled." Cotler lamented the fact that the court "did not employ any of the jurisprudential tests which had led the American courts to conclude that legislation requiring patriotic observances is an infringement of freedom of religion."[129] Cotler did not factor into the observation the fact that Jehovah's Witnesses had up to that time been under ban and that wartime policy may therefore have been a major consideration in the decision. But he alluded to the persecution of the Jehovah's Witnesses during the Second World War, comparing their experience in Canada with those in Australia: "Even more extensive measures were taken against the Jehovah's Witnesses in Canada under similar regulations passed pursuant to the War Measures Act," Cotler wrote. "But the constitutional argument never surfaced in the same fashion, and no disposition in terms of freedom of religion was made."[130]

Similarly no disposition has been made in the Supreme Court of Canada with respect to religious freedom to refuse blood transfusions for one's children, a major issue among Jehovah's Witnesses and one that has generated a great deal of controversy. Cotler cites *Pentland* v. *Pentland*[131] as authority for the proposition that "a country's health requirements may prevail over religious objections. Thus objections of Witnesses of Jehovah to blood transfusions for their children, even though based on religious grounds, will be overruled. Indeed, under s. 208 of the *Criminal Code*, such a parent may be liable to a criminal prosecution."[132]

Cotler's brief analysis of this issue is surely an oversimplification; there are greater policy issues involved here than "the country's health requirements." Jehovah's Witnesses have been urged in their official magazine *The Watchtower* to refuse blood transfusions ever since the end of the Second World War on the grounds that they were "morally wrong

---

127 *Supra*, note 56.

128 (1943), [1943] 3 W.W.R. 340, [1944] 1 D.L.R. 360 (Alta. T.D.).

129 Tarnopolsky and Beaudoin, *supra*, note 78 at 205.

130 *Ibid*. at 202.

131 (1978), 20 O.R. (2d) 27, 86 D.L.R. (3d) 585 (H.C.).

132 Tarnopolsky and Beaudoin, *supra*, note 78 at 204.

and medically dangerous."[133] The issue did not become pronounced in Canada until the mid–1950s, when several cases in succession received attention in the press. In some cases the patients pulled through without blood transfusions, in other cases they didn't. But the issue came to a head in November 1958 when Donald Holland, a Jehovah's Witness youth of 14, was accidentally shot in the thigh, severing his femoral artery. The Manitoba government was asked to intervene to force a blood transfusion upon the boy, but Attorney-General Sterling Lyon responded that under existing provincial legislation "the doctors were legally bound not to give him blood without parental consent."[134] In response to the overwhelming negative publicity and upon the recommendations of a coroner's jury, the Manitoba *Child Welfare Act* was amended[135] to allow physicians to give transfusions to minors without parental consent whenever they are deemed medically necessary.

On 8 December 1958, Lori Lynn Campbell, an Rh baby, was born at Newmarket, Ontario. When the parents indicated their desire to refuse their newborn daughter a blood transfusion, the baby was taken to Toronto, made a ward of the Toronto Children's Aid Society by order of a family court judge, was given a transfusion, and then was returned to the parents.[136] A similar case occurred the following spring in which the Rh baby died. A coroner's jury found that the death had occurred because the transfusion, given with the sanction of the Children's Aid Society, had not been given soon enough. Glen How attempted to have the jury's findings overruled at a higher court, taking the matter to the Ontario Supreme Court and the Supreme Court of Canada, both of which refused to reopen the case.[137]

The *Holland, Campbell* and *Wolfe* cases motivated Glen How to write "Religion, Medicine and the Law," which was published in the *Canadian Bar Review* in October 1960, and which formed the basis for the Watch Tower Society's *Blood, Medicine and the Law of God*, published the following year. In two other cases in 1962, the Children's Aid Society was

---

133 James Penton, *Jehovah's Witnesses in Canada* (Toronto: Macmillan, 1977) at 230; see also Gary and Heather Botting, *The Orwellian World of Jehovah's Witnesses* (Toronto: University of Toronto Press, 1984) at 29–30.

134 Penton, *ibid.* at 233.

135 S.M. 1959, c. 9.

136 Penton, *supra*, note 133 at 234–35. The eventual outcome of the case, including the eventual disfellowshiping of most of the family, is reported at length in Heather Botting, "The Power and the Glory: The Symbolic Vision and Social Dynamic of Jehovah's Witnesses" (Doctoral Dissertation, University of Alberta, 1982). Botting was a close personal friend of the Campbells.

137 *Wolfe* v. *Robinson* (1961), [1962] O.R. 132, 132 C.C.C. 78, 31 D.L.R. (2d) 233 (C.A.), aff'g (1961), [1961] O.R. 250, 27 D.L.R. (2d) 98, 129 C.C.C. 361 (H.C.).

refused legal custody of Jehovah's Witness children after the fact. In *Livingston* v. *Waterloo Children's Aid Society* (unreported), Mr. Justice Hughes of the Ontario Supreme Court held that the original order making the Livingston child a ward of the Children's Aid Society was invalid since it had been made on a Sunday.[138] In *Forsyth* v. *Children's Aid Society of Kingston*,[139] Hughes returned the custody of the Forsyth child to its parents, saying that he was unable to say that the "haphazard" initial hearing met the test of a fair judicial proceeding.

In the years that followed, Jehovah's Witnesses increasingly avoided hospitals where the threat of forced blood transfusions arose, and increasingly the medical community adapted to the situation, finding alternative therapy to blood tranfusions, including "bloodless surgery" and use of blood substitutes. The issue has yet to be resolved by the Supreme Court of Canada, however.

2. Peter W. Hogg, *Constitutional Law of Canada*

It can be seen that the Jehovah's Witnesses cases remained of central importance not only for the shaping of the *Charter* itself but also for the application of fundamental principles of civil liberties to the *Charter* once it was adopted. That this trend continued over the transitional period before and immediately after the adoption of the *Charter* can be demonstrated by examining almost any text on the Constitution, and specifically on the *Charter*, to be published during the transition years.

Yet many scholars have been guarded about relying on pre-*Charter* cases to support or illustrate *Charter* interpretation. Peter W. Hogg, for example, in his second and third editions of *Constitutional Law of Canada*,[140] focused on *Saumur* as being significant for constitutional interpretation generally, including classification and characterization of laws, but was far more reluctant about using the Jehovah's Witnesses cases of the 1950s in *Charter* analysis.

Statutes that are vague or ambiguous may be struck down as being invalid or *ultra vires* simply because of their vagueness, said Hogg. He quoted the "famous dictum" of Mr. Justice Rand in *Saumur*:

> Conceding, as in the Alberta Reference, that aspects of the activities of religion and free speech may be affected by provincial legislation, such legislation, as in all other fields, must be sufficiently definite and precise to indicate its subject matter. . . . The courts must be able from its language and its relevant circumstances, to attribute an enactment to a

---

138 Penton, *supra*, note 133 at 242.

139 (1962), [1963] 1 O.R. 49; 35 D.L.R. (2d) 690 (H.C.).

140 Toronto: Carswell, 1985; 1992.

matter *in relation to which* the legislature acting has been empowered to make laws. . . . To authorize action which may be related indifferently to a variety of incompatible matters by means of the device of a discretionary license cannot be brought within either of these mechanisms; and the Court is powerless, under general language that overlaps exclusive jurisdictions, to delineate and preserve valid power in a segregated form. If the purpose is street regulation, taxation, registration or other local object, the language must, with sufficient precision, define the matter and mode of administration; and by no expedient which ignores that requirement can constitutional limitations be circumvented.[141]

Although the principle of exhaustive distribution has been interpreted to mean that every law must be competent to either the federal or the provincial government, "a law that is excessively broad or vague will be incompetent to both levels of government," said Hogg. It must be sufficiently particular to be attributable to a specific and identifiable "matter" that falls under one head of power or the other.[142] In *Saumur* the vagueness and ambiguity of the legislation was a "fatal flaw." Did the by-law address littering? If so it would be valid. But if it addressed censorship of religious or political content of tracts, it would be invalid, either because it came under federal powers as a matter of religion,[143] or because it was altogether too vague to classify or categorize. "For Rand J., the absence of any standards in the by-law to guide the chief of police's discretion was, by itself, fatal to the validity of the by-law. Without more precision in the drafting of the by-law, it was impossible to classify it as in relation to any particular matter."[144]

Hogg noted that the *dicta* by Rand J. "seems to be the only suggestion in the Canadian cases that a sweeping delegation might run foul of the federal distribution powers."[145] He also noted that the court probably had the option in *Saumur* to "read down" the offensive legislation, as it later did in *N.S. Board of Censors* v. *McNeil*.[146] Thus in *Saumur*, "it could have been said that those exercises of the chief of police's discretion directed to the censorship of political or religious ideas were invalid, while preserving the by-law as a vehicle of street regulation."[147] However, as it stands *Saumur* is authority for the proposition that "a law that is excessively vague and broad so that it cannot be characterized as

---

141 [1953] 2 S.C.R. 299 at 333; cited in Hogg, *supra* note 140 at 346.

142 Hogg, *supra*, note 140 at 412.

143 *Ibid.* at 945.

144 *Ibid.* at 412.

145 *Ibid.* at 346.

146 (1978), [1978] 2 S.C.R. 662, 84 D.L.R. (3d) 1.

147 Hogg, *supra*, note 140 at 346.

in relation to a matter within a head of power will not be rehabilitated by a massive exercise in reading down."[148]

Characterization of laws in terms of their "matter" or "pith and substance" to determine whether a given law is constitutional is an important part of classification, particularly with respect to determining which of the heads of power is applicable. Again Hogg cited Rand's judgment in *Saumur* as authority for the proposition that the "matter" must be "sufficiently specific to come within a class of subject."[149] This process will always entail an examination of the effect of the statute, including in the case of *Saumur* an examination of the manner in which a statute is administered:

> Five judges—a majority—took note of the way in which the by-law was actually administered. They found that, on an application for permission to distribute literature, the chief of police would examine the contents of the material to be distributed, and would make his decision on the basis of whether he found the contents to be objectionable or not. In other words, the chief of police used the by-law as a vehicle of censorship, and the by-law constituted an effective bar to the dissemination of literature by an unpopular minority group such as the Jehovah's Witnesses, who had brought the action challenging the by-law. On the basis of these findings, the majority classified the by-law as in relation to speech or religion, and held that it was incompetent to the province. Of course, the reason for the by-law's invalidity was not its administration by the chief of police, but the fact that its language was apt to authorize a regime of political and religious censorship; and it is possible that the majority judges would have reached the same result solely on the basis of the language of the by-law. But it is obvious that the judges were influenced by the actual use of the by-law, and it is even more obvious that they regarded the facts as to the actual use of the by-law as relevant and admissible on the question of classification.[150]

Hogg also used the *Saumur* case as authority for the distinction between "civil rights" as that term is used in s. 92(13) of the *Constitution Act, 1982* and "civil liberties," noting that "the distinction between rights and liberties . . . has been emphasized by Rand J. in *Saumur* v. *Quebec*":

> Even civil liberties which are guaranteed by an effective bill of rights are juristically distinct from civil rights arising from the law of property, contract or torts. A bill of rights is addressed to legislative bodies, not individuals, and it will prevent the making of, or render invalid, any law

---

148 *Ibid.* at 394.

149 *Ibid.* at 377.

150 *Ibid.* at 386–7.

which purports to deny the guaranteed civil liberty. The bill of rights will not necessarily give any redress to an individual whose civil liberties are wrongly violated, although s. 24 of the Charter of Rights may well permit the granting of such redress.[151]

Hogg also noted that Rand, Kellock and Locke JJ. all "suggested the possibility of an implied bill of rights" consonant with the opinion of Chief Justice Duff in the *Alberta Press* case.[152]

It can be seen that Hogg relies on the Jehovah's Witnesses cases for non-*Charter* constitutional issues, but unlike Cotler he seems almost reluctant even to allude to Jehovah's Witnesses cases in relation to the *Charter* itself. In his chapter "A Comparison of the Canadian Charter of Rights and Freedoms with the Canadian Bill of Rights" in *Canadian Charter of Rights and Freedoms Commentary*, he does not allude once to the Witness cases. In the third edition of *Constitutional Law of Canada*, the only allusion to the Canadian Jehovah's Witnesses cases in the context of the *Charter* are two adjacent footnotes with respect to s. 2(*a*) summarizing *Donald* v. *Hamilton Bd. of Education* "(Jehovah's Witnesses held exempt from flag salute and national anthem)" and *Saumur* "(Jehovah's Witnesses held exempt from municipal street by-law)."[153] He also alludes to the American Jehovah's Witness case, *West Virginia State Bd. of Education* v. *Barnette*, implying that refusal to salute the flag is a form of freedom of expression under s. 2(*b*).[154]

Three other cases—*Roncarelli*, *Chaput* and *Lamb*—Hogg relegates to a treatment of common law civil liberties outside the *Charter*. "The Duplessis regime in Quebec offered the courts many . . . opportunities to protect civil liberties," he states, including

> *Chaput* v. *Romain* (1955), in which police broke up an assembly of Jehovah's Witnesses who were meeting peacefully in a private house, and *Lamb* v. *Benoit* (1959), in which police arrested a Jehovah's Witness who was distributing pamphlets on a street corner. In both those cases, the Supreme Court of Canada awarded damages against the responsible policemen on the ground that they had acted without legal authority.[155]

---

151 *Ibid.* at 540.

152 *Ibid.* at 775.

153 *Ibid.* at 950.

154 *Ibid.* at 962.

155 *Ibid.* at 769.

Hogg cites *Roncarelli* not as authority for the principle of "rule of law" but rather as authority for the "principle of validity—that every official act must be justified by law":

> One of the best-known modern cases is *Roncarelli* v. *Duplessis* (1959), in which Premier Duplessis of Quebec ordered the cancellation of restaurateur Roncarelli's liquor licence because Roncarelli was a Jehovah's Witness who had made a practice of acting as bondsman for the numerous Jehovah's Witnesses who were arrested for distributing their literature in breach of municipal by-laws. The Supreme Court of Canada awarded damages to Roncarelli. Duplessis could not rely on his high office, nor his judgment as to the demands of public interest, as justification for his act. Only a statute would suffice to authorize the cancellation of the licence, and the statute which did authorize licence cancellations gave the power to another official, not the Premier.[156]

3. Alan Borovoy's *When Freedoms Collide*

The tendency reflected in Hogg to move away from pre-*Charter* cases as a body of *Charter* law develops is reflected in less formal legal writing as well. Compare Thomas R. Berger's *Fragile Freedoms* published in 1982 at the time of the adoption of the *Charter* with A. Alan Borovoy's *When Freedoms Collide: The Case for Our Civil Liberties* (1988).[157] Berger devotes a complete chapter to the Jehovah's Witnesses cases. Armed with more recent *Charter* cases, Borovoy manages two scant references to Jehovah's Witnesses, both of them forward-looking in the sense that they ask, "What if?"

> There has been some indication also of an attempt to remove the safeguards for certain religious discussions. While this change might make it easier to take action against racist sermonizing that periodically occurs, it also creates a serious risk. How far, for example, would such a deletion increase the vulnerability of a group like Quebec's Jehovah's Witnesses for repeating today the nasty things they said about the Roman Catholic Church during the late 1940s and early 1950s? Believing as they did that the Church hierarchy was behind the persecution they suffered at the hands of the Duplessis regime, the Witnesses published a stream of anti-Catholic material. The response of the Duplessis government was to charge the group's leaders with seditious libel. The Supreme Court of Canada was widely praised for dismissing the charge on the grounds that, by itself, the creation of inter-group ill will was not an offence. Ironically, some of the very constituencies that hailed that judgment as

---

156 *Ibid.* at 768–9.

157 Toronto: Lester & Orpen Denys, 1988.

a landmark protection for civil liberties have been recently advocating amendments that could undo its effect.[158]

As counsel for the Canadian Civil Liberties Association, which was an intervener on the side of the defence in *R. v. Keegstra*, Borovoy presented an almost identical argument to the Supreme Court of Canada on 6 December 1989.

Borovoy also pointed out that Jehovah's Witnesses had been the target for prosecution for allegedly "spreading false news":

> While the false news section has not given rise to many prosecutions, it has nevertheless produced some questionable ones. After the sedition prosecution of the early 1950s failed to convict the Jehovah's Witnesses for their anti-Catholic material, the Quebec authorities attempted to nail them for spreading false news. Again, there was an acquittal. But what a message this must have conveyed to Quebec's Jehovah's Witnesses and other dissenting minorities. If you insist on attacking the Quebec and Catholic establishment, beware! This was another case in which the ultimate acquittal would not have been adequately consoling. The charge itself must have chilled the free speech of the aggrieved minorities. The very existence of the false news law contributed to the resulting oppression.[159]

Rather than charging and prosecuting alleged hatemongers under the anti-hate and false news laws, said Borovoy, alternative methods should be found at the political level for coping with bigots, "including their removal from relevant positions of influence," for "unlike prosecution, public censure in such situations can be both legitimate and effective":

> Once such people lose their positions of influence, they should be left to wallow in the obscurity which they so richly deserve. In such circumstances, prosecution becomes pointless. The important lesson of the Zundel and Keegstra trials is the need to develop a strategy that is at once less dangerous to freedom of speech and more effective against racism than criminal prosecution.[160]

Unfortunately, Borovoy is here advocating a system of lynch-mob justice not much better than that experienced by Jehovah's Witnesses in Quebec. The "influential" Roncarelli was very effectively taken out of circulation by the removal of his liquor licence simply because he supplied bail for an unpopular group. More recently, Duncan McKillop,

---

158 *Ibid.* at 46.

159 *Ibid.* at 52.

160 *Ibid.* at 53.

former president of his riding association for the Progressive Conservative Party and former president of the Alberta Chamber of Commerce, in which capacity he had made several important contributions to constitutional review in 1981,[161] agreed to represent James Keegstra at his preliminary hearing. Before long, he was removed from his positions of influence in just the manner that Borovoy has described.[162] Even neutral subpoenaed expert witnesses who testified in the *Keegstra* and *Zundel* trials regarding such matters as neutral surveys taken to determine the potential of bias in the community and hence among jurors, or neutral statements about crematoria, or the literary distinction between "fact" and "opinion" have subsequently "lost their positions of influence" or been threatened by pressure exerted upon their employers, despite unambiguous public statements that they do not support the opinions of Keegstra or Zundel.

For example, in 1985, I responded to a subpoena issued by a Justice of the Peace in Ontario to testify at Zundel's trial as an expert witness with respect to the recent history of censorship in Canada. At the time, Canada Customs had circulated to customs officers a list of about a thousand titles that were considered pornographic or politically tainted, including titles that were considered anti-Semitic, such as *The Protocols of Zion* and *The Hoax of the Twentieth Century*. At the second trial, for which I was also subpoenaed, I was asked by the trial judge to go through Zundel's tract sentence by sentence to determine whether each sentence constituted a representation of "fact" or "opinion." The Crown had already conceded that the author of the tract that Zundel had reprinted was entitled to his opinions but was not entitled to misrepresent the facts. I made it clear that I did not agree in the least with the position of Zundel. Upon returning to Alberta, the Chairman of the Board of Governors of Red Deer College, where I was employed as an instructor of English and creative writing, indicated that he had received a great deal of flak from the office of the Minister of Advanced Education and other members of the provincial cabinet, who took the position that I should not have testified at the trial at all.

Subsequent to his testifying for Zundel, Professor Robert Faurisson had his office picketed and was beaten unconscious by a mob in France,

---

161 See *Proceedings of the Special Joint Committee on the Constitution* (1980–81) at 27:37–44, 52–65, and 71–73.

162 In an interview with the press in February 1985, McKillop allegedly stated that it was possible that his client might be right in certain respects, such as in his thesis that Holocaust figures had been inflated. The Canada-Israel Chamber of Commerce protested his statement, and according to McKillop, drummed him out of office. *Edmonton Journal*, 4 March 1985, and personal interviews.

sustaining a fractured skull; eventually he lost his professorial position at the Sorbonne. Dittlieb Felderer, a former Jehovah's Witness who had researched the persecution of Witnesses at the hands of the Nazis and who testified at the first Zundel trial with respect to photographs he had taken at Auschwitz, was upon his return to Sweden beaten by a mob using iron bars. Ivan Legace of Leyden's Funeral Chapel in Calgary, a crematorium expert who testified at Zundel's second trial regarding the efficiency of modern crematoria, was warned by his employer not to speak publicly about his evidence, on pain of dismissal. John Ball, an experienced photographic analyst, was called as an expert to analyse aerial photographs of concentration camps, including Auschwitz. He was forced to resign as Social Credit candidate in the 1991 British Columbia provincial election when it was disclosed that he had testified at Zundel's trial. David Irving, author of more than twenty books on Germany and World War II, several of them exploring the role of Hitler, testified at the second Zundel trial that his research revealed no evidence of the existence of gas chambers at Auschwitz. When he returned to Canada in 1992, he was ordered deported in a manner reminiscent of Russell's summary deportation a century earlier.[163]

In 1990, the Supreme Court of Canada decided that although the "hate laws" did indeed violate the *Charter* principle of freedom of expression, nonetheless the laws were "saved" by application of s. 1 of the *Charter*:

> 1. The *Canadian Charter of Rights and Freedoms* guarantees the rights and freedoms set out in it subject only to such reasonable limits prescribed by law as can be demonstrably justified in a free and democratic society.

Nonetheless a strong minority opinion written by Madame Justice McLachlin indicated that the Supreme Court of Canada was far from unanimous on the issue of whether s. 1 applied.

Interestingly, two of the Supreme Court justices, Chief Justice Dickson, who wrote the majority judgment, and Madame Justice Wilson, who supported him, resigned shortly after the *Keegstra* decision came down. The *Zundel* case, which concerned the publication in Canada of a widely circulated booklet that questioned the extent of the Jewish Holocaust, went the other way, striking down the "spreading false news" law as being unconstitutional. Madame Justice McLachlin this time wrote the majority judgment in the 5–4 decision. *Zundel* had striking parallels

---

163 Personal interviews, supported by news accounts.

to the early Jehovah's Witnesses cases, particularly *R. v. Carrier*, which was concerned with the same law. Just as attempts were made to silence Carrier, Boucher, and Saumur and to keep them from distributing *Quebec's Burning Hate* and other Watch Tower literature that attacked the Roman Catholic Church, so in the 1980s and 1990s attempts have been made to silence Zundel, Keegstra, Malcolm Ross and others for distributing or holding ideas that question the "Holocaust," which has become a central icon of the contemporary Jewish faith.

The recent affirmation of the validity of the "hate laws" by a slim margin and the later ruling in *Zundel* that the "spreading false news" provision of the *Criminal Code* is unconstitutional is indicative of the fact that the Supreme Court of Canada is taking a balanced view. Madame Justice McLachlin in particular has become as influential as was Rand J. in protecting the fundamental freedoms of unpopular voices. As long as she continues to uphold minority rights and the principles of freedom of expression, there is little likelihood of a return to the relatively dark ages of the 1940s and 1950s or of unravelling all the circumspection of the Supreme Court of Canada in the Jehovah's Witnesses cases under the tutelage and wisdom of Justices Rand and Locke. Informal social sanctions more appropriate to the notion of a "free marketplace of ideas" would seem to be preferable to the relatively rigid and easily abused sanctions implied by Borovoy's recommendations, or to the even more rigid controls effected by criminal prosecution.

4. William Kaplan's *State and Salvation*

In 1989, University of Toronto Press published the third of a series of books on Jehovah's Witnesses, this time by Professor William Kaplan of the Faculty of Law, University of Ottawa. *State and Salvation: The Jehovah's Witnesses and Their Fight for Civil Rights* focused in detail on the persecution of the Witnesses during World War II, examining thoroughly the background of Justice Minister Ernest Lapointe, whose decision to outlaw the group came in the wake of a long and controversial debate in the House of Commons over the *Defence of Canada Regulations*.[164] Kaplan's study fills in some important gaps in the record in terms of the attitudes and psychological state of the principal perpetrators of the persecution. Despite the ban on Jehovah's Witnesses, the *Regulations* under which they were banned could not be used to ban their literature, the Office of Press

---

164 William Kaplan, *State and Salvation: The Jehovah's Witnesses and Their Fight for Civil Rights* (Toronto: University of Toronto Press, 1989) at 52.

Censors decided;[165] yet paradoxically the literature contained the very essence of Witness attitudes that caused them to be designated "a disturbing, possibly dangerous, and definitely unpatriotic group" in the first place.[166] Another dimension of this paradox is that despite the fact that the literature itself was not banned, possession of the literature was taken as prima facie evidence of an offence under Regulation 39A, which forbade the circulation of "literature likely to cause disaffection to His Majesty."[167]

Kaplan notes that Lapointe's actions in banning the Witnesses were endorsed half-heartedly by Prime Minister William Lyon Mackenzie King and enthusiastically by Cardinal Jean-Marie-Rodrigue Villeneuve and his assistant Monseigneur Paul Bernier;[168] but within a week of the announcement of the ban, while officials at the Watch Tower headquarters in Toronto scrambled to destroy membership lists and other incriminating evidence, Lapointe visited Prime Minister King and "announced that he was afraid that he was suffering a complete nervous breakdown."[169] As if to prove his point to the Prime Minister, the Justice Minister repeatedly burst into tears.[170]

Kaplan outlines the practice that was used in Ontario to curb the Witnesses:

> No attorney general was more zealous than Ontario's, G.D. Conant, and scores of Jehovah's Witnesses in the province were soon arrested. . . . The practice in Ontario was generally as follows. Local crown attorneys would write the attorney general in Toronto and request permission to lay charges. Sometimes a summary of the case would be included with the request; whether it was or not, all requests, according to available records, were granted.[171]

The Ontario Provincial Police and the Royal Canadian Mounted Police were equally ineffectual in curbing Witness activities, Kaplan's research reveals. "Overall," he observes, "the investigation and prosecution of the Jehovah's Witnesses during the first part of the ban is a tale of incompetence and stupidity."[172]

---

165 *Ibid.* at 63.

166 *Ibid.* at 52.

167 *Ibid.* at 70.

168 *Ibid.* at 65–66.

169 *Ibid.* at 66.

170 *Ibid.*

171 *Ibid.* at 70.

172 *Ibid.* at 78–80.

Kaplan examines in detail the relationship between the American and Canadian flag-debate cases such as *Gobitis*,[173] *Barnette*,[174] *Ruman*,[175] and the *Donald* case;[176] in *Donald*, the application of the Hamilton Board of Education was dismissed out of hand.[177]

If Kaplan's treatment of the flag salute controversy is the high point of his book, his treatment of the alternative service issue is flawed by a major oversight. "There was nothing wrong with directing Witness men called up for national duty to alternative-service camps," Kaplan states, "and if they refused to accept the conditions established for alternative-service work outside the camps, that was their decision."[178] But he fails to note that during the war, Jehovah's Witnesses were incarcerated in alternative service camps simply as a punishment for being Jehovah's Witnesses. Once they declared that they were conscientious objectors on religious grounds, incarceration was almost inevitable—despite the fact that many Jehovah's Witnesses had other grounds for refusing alternative service, grounds which, although clearly expressed, were ignored by authorities once the applicant's religious affiliation was known. Whereas virtually any Canadian farmer could escape conscription and alternative service, for example, farmers who also happened to be Jehovah's Witnesses invariably found themselves shunted off to camps in the wilderness, where their frustration at their unfair treatment found vent in letter after letter to the government authorities.

As James Penton has made clear, the method of establishing who was destined to be transported to the camps was suspect to say the least. Most conscientious objectors were given the option to pay a "forced contribution" to the Red Cross of about $15.[179] But Jehovah's Witnesses regarded the Red Cross as merely an extension of Christendom and yet another tool of war, and therefore they invariably refused to contribute:

> Why, they asked, should a man who was a bona fide farmer or farm labourer be required to pay a forced contribution to the Red Cross because he belonged to a faith which regarded war as wrong, when no such regulation applied to other men who were exempted for agricultural purposes? Why, also, should a man be subject to alternative-service regulations simply because of his belief, if he was in no way liable to

---

173 *Minersville School District* v. *Gobitis*, 310 U.S. 586, 60 S. Ct. 1010, 87 L. Ed. 1375 (1940).

174 *Barnette* v. *West Virginia State Board of Education*, 47 F. Supp. 251 (Dist. Ct., 1942).

175 *Ruman* v. *Lethbridge School Board Trustees*, *supra*, note 128.

176 *Donald* v. *Hamilton Board of Education* (1944), [1944] O.R. 475,, [1944] 4 D.L.R. 227 (H.C.), rev'd (1945), [1945] O.R. 518, [1945] 3 D.L.R. 424 (C.A.).

177 Kaplan, *supra*, note 164 at 164.

178 *Ibid.* at 213.

179 James Penton, *Jehovah's Witnesses in Canada* (Toronto: Macmillan, 1976) at 169.

military service? Evidently there was nothing "alternative" about alternative service. In such cases conscientious objectors were being penalized simply because of their beliefs.[180]

This sense of injustice, more than an inborn obstreperousness or strident air, motivated Jehovah's Witnesses in the camps to be less cooperative than other conscientious objectors such as the Mennonites.

In his "Epilogue," Kaplan refers to the *Boucher*, *Saumur* and *Roncarelli* decisions as reaffirming "the principle that all Canadians are subject to the rule of law"; but he follows this observation with this curious conclusion:

> However, there was nothing inevitable about the decision in any of these cases, and each of them could have been decided differently. In the *Boucher* case a majority of the Supreme Court came close to saying that all Canadians enjoyed certain fundamental rights that no legislature could infringe, but the *Saumur* case demonstrated that this principle was not yet part of Canadian Law.[181]

Clearly, however, these cases demonstrated that the fundamental freedoms (including freedom of religion) *were* already a part of Canadian law, a point made even in those cases that did not uphold the *Canadian Bill of Rights* such as *Robertson and Rosetanni* v. *R.* Indeed, Kaplan ignores the essence of the arguments in these cases that there was such a thing as an implied bill of rights, and that civil liberties are not the same thing in Canada as "civil rights." Kaplan's use of the American expression "civil rights" in the title of his book to refer to civil liberties demonstrates a failure to come to terms with the central arguments in the Jehovah's Witness cases, particularly *Saumur*, perhaps because these cases were beyond the scope of his study.

Kaplan goes on to state, correctly, that the *Canadian Bill of Rights* would be of little help to minority groups like Jehovah's Witnesses:

> As far as the Jehovah's Witnesses were concerned, the Diefenbaker bill of rights did not do them much good. The bill applied to federal law only, and by and large, it was in the provinces, like Quebec, where their rights were most frequently attacked.[182]

But this too is misleading, for at the time of the passage of the *Canadian Bill of Rights*, Jehovah's Witnesses were full of optimism that the Bill

---

180 *Ibid.* at 169–70.

181 Kaplan, *supra*, note 164 at 254.

182 *Ibid.* at 270.

would meet their needs, especially given the "copycat" bills of rights in the various provinces. Yet clearly such spokesmen for the Witnesses as Glen How and F.R. Scott believed that an entrenched bill of rights would be infinitely superior to a federal statute.

Although Kaplan does not explore the role of the Jehovah's Witnesses cases in indirectly developing the *Charter of Rights*, he nonetheless concludes his book by avowing the importance of Jehovah's Witnesses as reluctant players on the stage that was set eventually to accommodate the *Charter* and the fundamental freedoms it guarantees:

> The Charter of Rights is the culmination of a long process that began before the Second World War, accelerated during the war, and bore fruit after the war. In this process, the Jehovah's Witnesses played an important part, although they did not volunteer for the role. They pushed Canadians' rights to their existing limits, and those rights were found lacking. They then made their cause every Canadian's cause, and one of the results was the long process of discussion and debate that led to the Charter of Rights.[183]

Yet the *Charter* is by no means a perfect instrument; nor does it protect everbody's rights at all times. It is only as strong as the Supreme Court of Canada, Parliament and the legislatures of the various provinces allow it to be. The Supreme Court has shown its power to limit freedom of expression by applying s. 1 of the *Charter* with seemingly little regard for the long-term consequences of legislation designed to muzzle unpopular people who hold or seek to broadcast or publish unpopular views. Similarly, the "notwithstanding" clause of s. 33(1), as F.R. Scott anticipated, effectively vitiates all rights at the whim of a single legislature, as in Bill 178, Quebec's law restricting non-French signs on stores and in store windows. Quebec invoked s. 33(1) of the *Charter* despite the fact that such signs could hardly be characterized as a national emergency requiring "an express declaration," as is the clear intention of the constitution.

Once again, Quebec, this time under Robert Bourassa rather than Maurice Duplessis, has been heavy-handed in suspending the fundamental freedoms of any who wish to use a language other than French on signs designed to draw customers into their stores. The need for further constitutional reform to remove the "notwithstanding" clause to further protect the fundamental freedoms of all Canadians could not be more obvious.

---

183 *Ibid.* at 270.

8

Full Circle, or Reinventing the Wheel?

Jehovah's Witnesses were persecuted in both world wars because, as conscientious objectors, they refused to fight and instead advocated pacifism. Their publications, radio stations, and even their moving picture shows were censored or curbed by authorities, often by injudicious use of licensing powers. For several years during the Second World War, they and their umbrella publishing organizations were banned in Canada as seditious. After the war, persecution of Jehovah's Witnesses continued in Quebec.

The Witnesses were persecuted and prosecuted mercilessly, and after losing several declaratory writs in *Greenlees and Saumur* v. *Attorney-General of Quebec*,[1] they succeeded in overturning unconstitutional legislation in *Saumur* v. *City of Quebec*,[2] and in actively suing officials for overstepping their bounds in defiance of the rule of law in *Chaput, Roncareli*, and *Lamb*. These cases are widely considered to be landmarks on the way to the establishment of civil liberties in Canada, leading directly to the establishment of a *Canadian Bill of Rights* and less directly to the *Canadian Charter of Rights and Freedoms*. In this sense, Jehovah's Witnesses have left a truly indelible impression on Canada's civil liberties.

The role of the Jehovah's Witnesses cases over three decades—from the *Boucher* decision of 1951 to the adoption of the *Charter* in 1982—establishes them as of more than passing interest. Jehovah's Witnesses, through their very persecution during and after two world wars, drew attention to the need in Canada of legislation that would protect the rights of minority groups. From 1946 on, Jehovah's Witnesses argued for a Bill of Rights, seeking from the outset to have such a document

---

1 (1945), [1945] O.R. 411, [1945] 2 D.L.R. 641 (H.C.); aff'd (1946), [1946] O.R. 90, [1946] 1 D.L.R. 550 (C.A.); leave to appeal to S.C.C. refused (1946), [1946] S.C.R. 462.

2 (1953), [1953] 2 S.C.R. 299, [1953] 4 D.L.R. 641, 106 C.C.C. 289.

entrenched in the Constitution of Canada. Enduring widespread opposition and, in Quebec, persecution, they pushed for a Bill of Rights in resolution after resolution, garnering hundreds of thousands of signatures on petitions.

John Diefenbaker rewarded their persistence in 1960 with the *Canadian Bill of Rights*. But that document was not entrenched in the Constitution, and the courts virtually ignored it for 20 years after its passage. Ivan Bernier and Andree Lajoie succinctly explained why in *The Supreme Court of Canada as an Instrument of Political Change*:

> . . . In the absence of objective and easily applicable standards, the Court was very reluctant to substitute its opinion for that of democratic institutions, and it developed the concept of "valid federal objective," giving these institutions an almost uncontrollable margin within which to manoeuvre. Consequently, the mandate given to the courts—to declare inoperative legislation that was contrary to the *Bill of Rights*—was challenged indirectly, with the result that the Supreme Court no longer found an opportunity to exercise it.

Finally, with the assistance of such men of vision and determination as F.R. Scott, Pierre Trudeau and Walter Tarnopolsky, the dream of Jehovah's Witnesses for an entrenched "Bill of Rights" crystallized into reality as the *Canadian Charter of Rights and Freedoms*. Yet even this important constitutional enactment allows for almost arbitrary limitations on fundamental freedoms, specifically ss 1 and 33, that leave Canada far behind the United States when it comes to safeguards to civil liberties.

Sad to say, since 1982 Canada has taken some major steps backward rather than forward with respect to the central issue of the importance of civil liberties. The notion of "politically correct" language and behavior has sought to elevate collective rights over individual freedoms to such a degree that it is no longer safe to hold a minority opinion on such controversial subjects as, for example, racial aptitude, feminist bias, or Jewish influence in business or the media. Any genuine questions one might have with respect to the extent of the enormity of modern history known as the "Holocaust" are muted by the insistence of Jewish lobby groups that they have a monopoly on this particular subject. Those who have the temerity to persist in expressing opinions that diverge from the establishment view have been subjected to censure and arrest, sometimes spending years in the courts to fight for the right to hold their unpopular opinions. Such are the recent cases of James Keegstra, convicted in 1985 for promoting hatred against an identifiable group, and Ernst Zundel, convicted in the same year for allegedly "spreading false news" about the Holocaust but finally acquitted by the Supreme Court of Canada after the "spreading false news" provision of the *Criminal Code* (s. 181) was found to violate the *Charter*.[3] Ironically, their martyrdom has led to an upsurge in bitter anti-Semitic feeling in Canada, and a determination on the part of their supporters to organize and expand their ranks.

Undoubtedly Keegstra believed as a matter of faith that much of history, including the world today, has been controlled by Zionist Jews. Keegstra was fired from his high school job for teaching these opinions to his students, and the Attorney–General of Alberta followed through with criminal proceedings. Keegstra asked pointed rhetorical questions about the influence of Jews on the media and political establishment in precisely the same manner that Jehovah's Witnesses asked pointed questions about the influence of Roman Catholics in Quebec. Jehovah's Witnesses stated that organized religion, epitomized by the Roman Catholic Church, was the "Whore of Babylon" and the "Seed of the Serpent," operating under the influence of Satan the Devil. Keegstra made similar rhetorical statements about the Jews. For this he was charged under s. 319(2) of the *Criminal Code*:

> 319(2) Every one who, by communicating statements, other than in private conversation, wilfully promotes hatred against any identifiable group is guilty of (*a*) an indictable offence and is liable to imprisonment for a term not exceeding two years; or (*b*) an offence punishable on summary conviction.

Obviously, on its face, this law could apply just as easily to Jehovah's Witnesses when they impugn rival religious groups as evil and urge their members to "hate that which is evil." However, the section is carefully qualified by subsection (3):

> (3) No person shall be convicted of an offence under subsection (2)
>   (*a*) if he establishes that the statements communicated were true;
>   (*b*) if, in good faith, he expressed or attempted to establish by argument an opinion upon a religious subject;
>   (*c*) if the statements were relevant to any subject of public interest, the discussion of which was for the public benefit, and if on reasonable grounds he believed them to be true; or
>   (*d*) if, in good faith, he intended to point out, for the purpose of removal, matters producing or tending to produce feelings of hatred towards an identifiable group in Canada.

Jehovah's Witnesses would in all likelihood argue that their literature over the years has conformed to subsection (3) (*a*), (*b*) and (*c*) of the new hate law. Keegstra argued precisely the same way that his Protestant,

---

3 *Zundel* v. *The Queen* (1992), [1992] 2 S.C.R. 731.

specifically Dutch Reformed Church, beliefs had led him to adopt some of the conclusions he had reached. To the extent that Keegstra regarded his remarks to his students to be relevant to a subject of public interest and public benefit, and believed his statements to be true, and to the extent that he was motivated by religious belief rather than by hatred, Keegstra committed no crime. In fact, his supporters regard him as being a scapegoat for a provincial Department of Education that had virtually no guidelines as to what could or could not be taught to high school students beyond broad subject headings such as "The French Revolution," "The American Revolution" or "The Second World War." Keegstra, who had been hired to teach auto mechanics, had precisely one university course in history, in which he obtained a marginal 63%, yet the Alberta public school system assigned him to teach in the very area of his weakness.[4]

The Alberta Court of Appeal overturned his initial conviction, holding that s. 319(2) contravened s. 2(b) of the *Charter* by making imprudent speech a crime.[5] The Supreme Court of Canada was unanimous in finding that the section contravened s. 2(b) of the *Charter*, but a bare majority found that the legislation was "saved" by section 1.[6] The Supreme Court sent the matter back to the Court of Appeal for resolution of residual issues, and the case bounced back and forth between the Supreme Court of Canada and the Court of Appeal of Alberta twice before the Court of Appeal finally ordered a new trial, at which Keegstra, representing himself, was again convicted.

In light of the Jehovah's Witnesses cases, the *Zundel* case seemed even more to be a reinvention of the wheel of freedom of expression than *Keegstra*. Zundel published a booklet that was little more than a glorified book review, a precis of the suspect opinions of Paul Rassinier that the Holocaust had been greatly exaggerated. It asked the rhetorical question, "Did Six Million Really Die?" Its answer was unambiguous: in the opinion of the author, the casualty rate of Jews in the concentration camps may have been as low as 10,000.

This central thesis of the tract seems on its face to be ludicrous. There is little doubt that millions of Jews disappeared during the Second World War, and ample evidence to show that most of the missing died in abominable conditions in concentration camps such as Auschwitz, Treblinka, Sobibor and Maidjenak as part of the Nazi "Final solution to the Jewish Problem." Nonetheless the legal question, all too familiar from the Jehovah's Witness cases of the 1950s, remained: In Canada, does a pub-

---

4 Personal interview with James Keegstra, 15 May 1985.

5 *R. v. Keegstra* (1988), 65 C.R. (3d) 289, 43 C.C.C. (3d) 150 (Alta. C.A.).

6 *R. v. Keegstra* (1990), [1990] 3 S.C.R. 697, 61 C.C.C. (3d) 1.

lisher have the right to print and circulate a tract offering an unpopular, even a ludicrous, opinion without fear of reprisal in the criminal courts?[7]

In *Zundel*, the Court of Appeal for Ontario found that s. 181 did not violate s. 2(*b*) the *Charter*, although in the wake of the *Keegstra* decision, in which all seven justices found that the "hate laws" violated s. 2(*b*), it was obvious that neither *Zundel* appeal at the Court of Appeal level was correctly decided. Section 181 reads:

Spreading False News

181. Every one who wilfully publishes a statement, tale or news that he knows is false and that causes or is likely to cause injury or mischief to a public interest is guilty of an indictable offence and liable to imprisonment for a term not exceeding two years.

The crime of "Spreading False News" is ancient; it was designed initially to protect the reputation of the King and his noblemen, and later designed to prevent mischief from being perpetrated by rumor-mongers in time of war. The section was used once in Alberta to muzzle a disenchanted farmer, George Hoaglin, who printed a poster to warn Americans to stay away from what he regarded as an inhospitable socio-political climate at a time when the government was promoting immigration.[8] Hoaglin was found to have usurped the public interest, which was defined by the judge in terms of "public policy."

The second case of spreading false news in Canada, *R. v. Carrier*,[9] reached the courts 45 years later, in 1951. Not too surprisingly, Wellie Carrier was a Jehovah's Witness, and the "false news" he was alleged to have been spreading was in the form of a booklet called *Quebec's Burning Hate*. Carrier was ably represented by W. Glen How, who pled *autrefois acquit* on the basis that Carrier had already been charged with seditious libel along with Aime Boucher and others, and had been acquitted. Furthermore the Supreme Court of Canada had found in *Boucher* that the booklet *Quebec's Burning Hate* had been published in good faith as to its truth. Mr. Justice Drouin of the Quebec Court of King's Bench cited Justice Rand's famous lines at length (". . . The clash of critical discussion of political, social and religious subjects has too deeply become the stuff

---

7 The Ontario Court of Appeal held that "spreading false news" covers only statements of fact known to be false, not statements of opinion, and those statements of fact known to be false must have been likely to cause injury to a public interest. *R. v. Zundel (No. 1)* (1987), 56 C.R. (3d) 1, 31 C.C.C. (3d) 97 (Ont. C.A.); *R. v. Zundel (No. 2)* (1990), 53 C.C.C. (3d) 161 (Ont. C.A.); rev'd (1992), [1992] 2 S.C.R. 731.

8 *R. v. Hoaglin* (1907), 12 C.C.C. 226 (Alta. T.D.).

9 (1951), 104 C.C.C. 75 (Que. K.B.).

of daily experience to suggest that mere ill-will as a product of controversy can strike down the latter with illegality. . ."), and added:

> I have cited this long extract in order to show the idea that seems to have prevailed in the mind of the majority Judges of the Supreme Court on the subject of these offenses and on the subject of the attitude that one should adopt as to the definitions of the authors as to what constitutes seditious libel.
>
> Further on Rand J. speaking of the same pamphlet as that in the present case says at p. 80: "No one would suggest that the document is intended to arouse French speaking Roman Catholics to disorderly conduct against their own Government, and to treat it as directed, with the same purpose, towards the Witnesses themselves in the Province, would be quite absurd."[10]

In Drouin's opinion, drawn from the definitions given by Rand and the other justices in *Boucher*, "sedition" or "seditious offence" must "refer to the intention to create disorder, to disobedience or defiance in the English sense of the word, that is to say, open disobedience with regard to the established authority or violence with regard to said authority." He added:

> Is it not in this sense that the words of s. 136 (now 181) must be interpreted: "False news or tale whereby injury or mischief is or is likely to be occasioned to any public interest?" How otherwise define these words? And, if in order to define what the legislator understood by the words "whereby injury or mischief is or is likely to be occasioned to any public interest" one falls into the definition of sedition, it would certainly be necessary to take into account this plea of *autrefois acquit*.

In *Boucher*, Justice Locke had defined the offence of publishing false news as "the first definite instance of . . . a quasi-seditious offence," and therefore a precursor to seditious libel. From Locke's observations, Drouin concluded that "spreading false news" must incorporate an element of sedition, and that the target of the false news must be the state.[11]

The Supreme Court judges in *Boucher* did not find *Quebec's Burning Hate* in the least laudable. In fact, said Drouin, "I believe that all the Judges who examined this pamphlet agree in saying that it could create discontent, hostility, and the four dissenting Judges as well as the five Judges of the Court of Appeal for Quebec and the trial Judge, in fact,

---

10 *Ibid.* at 80.

11 *Ibid.* at 82.

seem to have seen much more than that."[12] Nonetheless, the Supreme Court had concluded that the pamphlet was not of a nature to cause any injury or mischief to the public interest that could be construed as criminal.

Drouin drew from this that "spreading false news" must aim at the suppression of seditious offences. In the case of the Alberta farmer, *R. v. Hoaglin*, said Drouin, either "the facts under which Hoaglin was charged involve the definition of sedition or . . . Hoaglin ought to have been acquitted."[13] Applying this argument, Zundel was correctly acquitted, although in *Zundel* the deciding factor was the unconstitutionality of the law itself.

Within a few months of the *Carrier* decision, F.R. Scott published an article called "Publishing False News" in *The Canadian Bar Review*.[14] Interestingly, he was inspired to write the article not by the *Carrier* case, of which he indicated no knowledge, but by the "new dangers" of "anti-semitic and other forms of propaganda fomenting racial and religious discord." He regarded this discord as "a continuing menace."[15] In the article, one of the few on the subject until comparatively recently, he reviewed the history of the "spreading false news" section in detail and concluded that the Canadian law was in some ways unique:

> Canadian law, based on statute, is more clearly formulated and goes farther than the actual holding in any English decision. Its roots are nevertheless to be found in what is an operative principle of the common law. It is wrong for anyone knowingly to cause a public mischief by publishing or telling lies. Lying itself does not constitute the crime. Injuring the public interest does.[16]

This begs the question as to what is "public interest." Citing Odgers, who listed "seven such types of matter, including all affairs of state, the administration of justice, public institutions and local authorities, and ecclesiastical affairs," Scott concluded that "public interest" was of far greater consequence than mere "public mischief," which "scarcely seem[s] of the magnitude and generality that seem implied in the crime of spreading false news."[17] He gave as an example of a borderline case the fictional situation of a man who published a false report of an impending riot which induced a mayor of a town to call out the militia.

---

12 *Ibid.* at 83.

13 *Ibid.* at 86.

14 (1952), 30 Can. Bar Rev. 37.

15 *Ibid.* at 37–38.

16 *Ibid.* at 42.

17 *Ibid.* at 45.

Scott found the *Hoaglin* case, which he described as the *only* Canadian case, "to verge on harshness." But he quite perspicaciously saw the potential of the law:

> Laws do not become obsolete by non-usage, however, and section 136 could at any moment be resurrected from its very shallow grave were the law enforcement agencies to change their policy. Any strict application would cut large holes in the accepted area of freedom of communication. . . . But there seems little doubt that good sense and preference for the risks of freedom over the restrictions of harsh rules would counsel a very infrequent and moderate use of this ancient prohibition.[18]

In 1992, the Supreme Court of Canada went one step further by killing the "ancient prohibition" altogether. "The only lesson to be gleaned from the history of s. 181," said Madam Justice Beverley McLachlin, citing the *Carrier* case in her majority decision in *Zundel*, "is that the offence was aimed at protecting the rule of law and the security of the state, in the guise of the head of power, whether that be the monarchy or later the government."[19]

Assuming continued common-sense application of the *Charter* in the Supreme Court of Canada, Jehovah's Witnesses and every other religious minority in Canada should henceforth be protected from arbitrary government action. Yet this can be so only if individual rights are asserted as being preeminent over group rights. If the majority, or even minority groups, are able to sway governments and the courts against unpopular opinions and those who hold them, we shall return to the dark days of persecution by prosecution once visited upon Jehovah's Witnesses.

Canada has developed enough maturity to put faith in itself as a nation of individuals with diverse opinions, rather than as a cultural mosaic in which the appearance of harmony is legislated and enforced by threat of criminal sanction. As Pierre Elliott Trudeau said of the editorial staff of the newly resurrected federalist magazine, *Cité libre*, "People here do not disagree with the notion of collective rights, they disagree with the notion that the collectivity is supreme, they believe individual rights are supreme." Individual rights must take precedence over collective rights if Canada is to succeed as a nation. Otherwise we shall become a nation of factions at war with one another, one group seeking to outvie each of the others for power and influence. Suppression of individualism is appallingly myopic. It constitutes a form of censure that will lead those

---

18 *Ibid.* at 46-47.

19 *Zundel* (1992), *supra*, note 7 at 746.

who hold unpopular opinions to do what Jehovah's Witnesses did during the war years: to go underground, where a new movement will grow and eventually emerge with volcanic force. Far better be it to allow anomalous thought to be expressed openly, where it can be dealt with by application of logic and ridicule in the free marketplace of ideas.

Fundamental freedoms are only as strong as the weakest link in the chain. The greatest justices of the Supreme Court of Canada recognized that fact in protecting the rights of Jehovah's Witnesses to speak out against the establishment. But as Thomas Berger has said so succinctly, the freedoms that Mr. Justice Rand established for all Canadians with his monumental judgements are *fragile* freedoms. Only with careful jurisprudence carefully applied will the Supreme Court of Canada and the other courts of the land continue to protect the fundamental freedoms of all Canadians.

Bibliography

Abel, A.S. *Towards a Constitutional Charter for Canada.* Toronto: University of Toronto Press, 1982.

Anisman, Philip and Allen M. Linden, eds. *The Media the Courts and the Charter.* Toronto: Carswell, 1986.

Berger, Thomas R. *Fragile Freedoms: Human Rights and Dissent in Canada.* Toronto: Clarke Irwin, 1982.

Borovoy, A. Alan. *When Freedoms Collide: The Case for Our Civil Liberties.* Toronto: Lester & Orpen Dennys, 1988.

Botting, Gary and Heather. *The Orwellian World of Jehovah's Witnesses.* Toronto: University of Toronto Press, 1984.

Botting, Heather. "The Power and the Glory: The Symbolic Vision and Social Dynamic of Jehovah's Witnesses." Doctoral dissertation, University of Alberta, 1982.

Chafee, Zechariah. *Free Speech in the United States.* Boston: Harvard University Press, 1941.

Conklin, W.E. *In Defence of Fundamental Rights.* Amsterdam: Sijthoff and Noordhoff, 1979.

Covington, Hayden C. "The Dynamic American Bill of Rights." (1948) 26 Can. Bar Rev. 638.

Djwa, Sandra. *The Politics of the Imagination: A Life of F.R. Scott.* Vancouver: Douglas & McIntryre, 1989.

Djwa, Sandra and R. St J. Macdonald. *On F.R. Scott Essays of His Contribution to Law, Literature and Politics.* Kingston: McGill-Queen's University Press, 1983.

Finkelstein, Neil. "The Relevance of Pre-Charter Case Law for Post-Charter Adjudication." (1982) Sup. Ct. L. Rev. 267.

Forsey, E.A. *Freedom and Order.* Toronto: McLelland and Stewart, 1974.

Greenspan, Edward L., ed. *Martin's Annual Criminal Code 1993.* Aurora, Ont.: Canada Law Books, 1992.

Hogg, Peter W. *Constitutional Law of Canada,* 3rd edn, Toronto: Carswell, 1992.

How, W. Glen. "The Case for a Canadian Bill of Rights." (1948) 26 Can. Bar Rev. 758.

How, W. Glen. "The Too Limited Jurisdiction of the Supreme Court." (1947) 25 Can. Bar Rev. 573.

Kaplan, William. *State and Salvation: The Jehovah's Witnesses and Their Fight for Civil Rights*. Toronto: University of Toronto Press, 1989.

Laskin, Bora. *Canadian Constitutional Law*. Toronto: Carswell, 1975.

Laskin, Bora. "An Inquiry into the Diefenbaker Bill of Rights." (1959) 37 Can. Bar Rev. 77.

Laskin, Bora. "Note on Civil Liberties and Legislative Power," *Canadian Constitutional Law*, 2d ed. Toronto: Carswell, 1960.

Macdonald, R. St. J. and J.P. Humphrey, eds. *The Practice of Freedom*. Toronto: Butterworths, 1979.

Manning, M. *Rights, Freedoms and the Courts*. Toronto: Emond- Montgomery, 1983.

Magnet, Joseph Eliot. *Constitutional Law of Canada: Cases, Notes, Materials*. 3d ed. Toronto: Carswell, 1987.

Mahoney, Kathleen and Sheilah Martin. *Broadcasting and the Canadian Charter of Human Rights and Freedoms [sic]: Justification for Restricting Freedom of Expression*. Calgary: self-published, 1985.

McDonald, D.C. *Legal Rights in the Canadian Charter of Rights and Freedoms*. Toronto: Carswell, 1982.

Penton, James. *Apocalypse Delayed: The Story of Jehovah's Witnesses*. Toronto: University of Toronto Press, 1985.

Penton, James. *Jehovah's Witnesses in Canada: Champions of Freedom of Speech and Worship*. Toronto: Macmillan, 1976.

Radwanski, George. *Trudeau*. Toronto: Macmillan of Canada, 1978.

Rand, I.C. *The Role of an Independent Judiciary in Preserving Freedom*. Toronto: University of Toronto Law Journal (reprint), 1951.

Schmeiser, D.A. *Civil Liberties in Canada*. London: Oxford, 1964.

Scott, F.R. *The Canadian Constitution and Human Rights: Four Talks for CBC Radio*. Toronto: Canadian Broadcasting Corporation, 1959.

Scott, F.R. *Civil Liberties and Canadian Federalism*. Toronto: University of Toronto Press, 1959.

Scott, F.R. *Essays on the Constitution: Aspects of Canadian Law and Politics*. Toronto: University of Toronto Press, 1977.

Scott, F.R. *A New Endeavor: Selected Political Essays, Letters and Addresses*. Toronto: University of Toronto Press, 1986.

Special Joint Committee on the Constitution of Canada. *Final Report*. Ottawa: Queen's Printer, 1972.

Special Joint Committee on the Constitution of Canada. *Proceedings*. Ottawa: Queen's Printer, 1970-71; 1980-81.

Tarnopolsky, W. S. *The Canadian Bill of Rights*. Toronto: McClelland and Stewart, 1975.

Tarnopolsky, W. S. and Gerald-A. Beaudoin, eds. *Canadian Charter of Rights and Freedoms: Commentary*. Toronto: Carswell, 1982.

Trudeau, Pierre. *Federalism and the French Canadians*. Toronto: Macmillan, 1968.

University of Toronto Press. *Canadian Annual Review for 1960*. Toronto: University of Toronto Press, 1961.

Watch Tower Bible and Tract Society. *Yearbook of Jehovah's Witnesses*. New York: Watch Tower Bible and Tract Society, 1933-1979.

Winnipeg Free Press. *Constitutional Freedom in Peril: The Jehovah's Witnesses' Case*. Winnipeg: Winnipeg Free Press, 1954.

Index